The Emptiness of Oedipus

Lacan's seminar on identification marks a turning point from the early to the later years of his work. In this book Raul Moncayo builds on many of the concepts that Lacan developed in his seminar, focusing on the relationship between the unary trait and narcissism that occurs via ruling ideas, master signifiers, and the *objet a* as a part object and a partial form of identification. Moncayo advances Lacanian psychoanalysis not only for its scholarly value, but also for its bearing on the clinical practice of psychoanalysis today.

The question of Oedipus as a myth of Freud is the touchstone from which Lacan proposed to go beyond Freud and beyond the rock of castration. The Emptiness of Oedipus examines how the interpretation of Oedipus as a myth or dream, rather than a complex, provides a new way of understanding the end of analysis as the end of the identification with the analyst. The concept is proposed as Lacan's postmodern or poststructuralist turn and as a fourth moment of Oedipus that is organized around the lack or emptiness of the Other.

The Emptiness of Oedipus offers a fresh approach to Lacanian psychoanalysis and will appeal to analysts and psychotherapists as well as academics and post-graduates with an interest in Lacan.

Raul Moncayo is training director for Mission Mental Health, San Francisco and a supervising analyst at the Lacanian School of Psychoanalysis of the San Francisco Bay Area, California. He also has a private practice in which he provides psychoanalysis, psychotherapy, consultation, and supervision.

The Emptiness of Oedipus

Identification and non-identification in Lacanian psychoanalysis

Raul Moncayo

Routledge
Taylor & Francis Group

LONDON AND NEW YORK

First published 2012
by Routledge
27 Church Road, Hove, East Sussex BN3 2FA

Simultaneously published in the USA and Canada
by Routledge
711 Third Avenue, New York NY 10017

Routledge is an imprint of the Taylor & Francis Group, an Informa business

British Library Cataloguing in Publication Data
A catalogue record for this book is available from the British Library

Library of Congress Cataloging in Publication Data
Moncayo, Raul.
  The emptiness of Oedipus: identification and non-identification in
  lacanian psychoanalysis / Raul Moncayo.
    p. cm.
  Includes bibliographical references and index.
  ISBN 978–0–415–60828–2 (hardback) — ISBN 978–0–415–60829–9
  (paperback) 1. Oedipus complex. 2. Identity (Psychology)
  3. Lacan, Jacques, 1901–1981. I. Title.
  BF175.5.O33M66 2012
  150.19'5—dc23   2011018178

ISBN: 978–0–415–60829–9 (hbk)
ISBN: 978–0–415–60828–2 (pbk)

Typeset in Times
by RefineCatch Limited, Bungay, Suffolk
Paperback cover design by Andrew Ward
Cover image: René Magritte, *The Therapist II*, 1962.
© 2011 C. Herscovici, London/Artists Rights Society (ARS),
New York
Printed and bound in Great Britain
by TJ International Ltd, Padstow, Cornwall

Contents

Practice

Culture

Acknowledgements

This book is dedicated to the memory of Roberto Harari (1943–2009) who was my first teacher and mentor in psychoanalysis. In addition to his exegesis of Freud's texts, Roberto's exemplary introductory texts to Lacan's work bridged the gap between my understanding and the vast continent of "unknown-knowing" represented by Lacan's work. A bridge reterritorializes and links a land mass but leaves open the space of *jouissance* that travels through the surfaces and holes of the signifying body.

I also want to take this opportunity to thank two of my students and colleagues for their help in the writing of two chapters of this book. Dr. Ayelet Hirshfeld sparked my interest in the topic and was my co-author in the writing of the chapter on "Brief Analysis." Dr. Roberto Lazcano directed my attention to Magritte's work and did the research in art history that laid the foundation for the ideas I developed in the chapter on "Magritte, the Void, and the Imagination." This chapter had a prior history in *The Psychoanalytic Review* 96(5) under the title "Magritte, the Object of Art, and Lacan's Three Dimensions of Experience." Finally, my student and colleague Dr. Fernando Castrillon read chapter 5 and provided me with helpful editorial suggestions.

I also need to mention my friend from youth and Latin American social theorist Martin Hopenhayn. It was through Martin's writings that I was first exposed to the work of Lyotard and postmodern thought. Martin did his dissertation with Gilles Deleuze in Paris and introduced me to him and his work. Via the international network of alternatives to psychiatry, I also had the pleasure to meet and invite Felix Guattari to speak to the Wright Institute in Berkeley back in the early eighties. I distinctly remember asking Guattari about the difference between mechanical and *machinic*. He looked at me and answered with an action by successively pressing the buttons in my shirt with his index finger. Alas, for that moment, my body–mind had become a creative machine!

I wish to thank Cormac Gallagher for his permission to reprint extracts from his unofficial translation of Lacan's seminar "On Identification" (distributed by Karnac Books).

Finally, I want to thank my sister Roxane Moncayo Eikhof for studying psychology before I did, and my partner Deborah Rifkin for her support during the endless hours of writing this book.

Introduction

This book grew out of the seminar that I teach for the candidates of the Lacanian School of Psychoanalysis (LSP) in the San Francisco Bay Area. Founded by Andre Patsalides and a group of founding members in 1993, LSP was the first school to formally transmit the *practice* of Lacanian psychoanalysis in the United States. The book is organized around two seminars: the 2008–2009 seminar on Lacan's Seminar IX "On Identification" and the 2009–2010 seminar on "The Ends of Analyses." These two seminars resulted in the writing of chapters 1 and 3 respectively.

Seminar IX marks a turning point in Lacan's thought from the early Lacan to the later years of Lacan's work. The many themes that Lacan develops in this seminar include the notion of the unary trace or the One (*il y a de l'un*), the topological figure of the double torus, the differentiation between the letter and the signifier, and the notion of Oedipus as a myth or dream (of Freud) rather than as a complex. Many of these themes are continued in Lacan's later seminars on "A Discourse That Might Not Be a Semblance," "Love and the Unknown That Knows about the One-mistake," "The *Sinthome*," and others.

Just as Lacan's seminar "On Identification" laid the foundation for much of Lacan's later work, chapter 1 on identification lays down the theoretical foundation for much of this book. This chapter examines the difference between identity and identification, and between the unary trait and the unary trace. The concept of the unary trait was Lacan's way of approaching the Freudian concept of identification, particularly from the point of view of the third type of identification described by Freud.

Freud invented the concept of identification to explain how identity develops by incorporating aspects of the parents into their children's own mind. This outside–in movement regulates both social actions and sexual activity. In the process, society, culture, and the species transmit their values and structure from one generation to the next. Following Freud, Erikson emphasized that children need to scrutinize and often reject societal and parental identities in order to make them their own.

Identity is ambivalent because identification is as important as the rejection of identification. However, both are only apparent or a semblance. Within Lacanian theory identification and its rejection contain their opposites. It is often missed how much an identification can hide the refusal of identification, as well as how much the refusal of identification can hide the existence of identification. The opposite is not behind identification but in the identification or the refusal itself. Refusal is a form of identification and identification is a form of refusal or negation of identification. The identity of opposite identifications also speaks to the plurality of identifications. The plurality of identifications represents the plurality of objects and others that populate an individual's life, especially in childhood. It also speaks of the different agencies and aspects of character and personality, pretty much like the different characters of a play.

Lacanian theory highlights the import of the third type of identification described by Freud as the unary trait. The concept of the unary trait points to the fact that identifications are mostly partial traits, and combinations of traits, rather than reified apparatus, things, or rooms within subjectivity. This view is consistent with a postmodern or poststructuralist view of subjectivity that regards the ego or personality as an illusory construction. Reifying subjective agencies may make them more difficult to change as well as strengthen the illusions of individuality.

Erikson distinguished between identification and identity by emphasizing the need to scrutinize parental identifications in the direction of ego identity. However, Erikson's studies on identity did not emphasize the relationship among identity and the three types of identification outlined by Freud, and the fact that the ego, despite ego identity and autonomy, remains unconsciously identified with rejected or ego-dystonic identifications.

Lacanian theory can be used to examine these questions in a new light. Lacan's "*matheme*" for the ego-ideal (I [O]), points to the ideals and ideas that populate the Other of society as the source of identifications. These ideal ideas are unary traits. In an age characterized by the death of the ego, the notion of a unary trait has the advantage of providing a lighter, more fluid and molecular, if not a micro basis for understanding identity.

Lacan takes the concept of the unary trait in three directions: narcissism, the question of the letter and nomination within language, and the import of the partial object and identification within Freud and psychoanalysis. I distinguish between the unary trait and the unary trace – a distinction (without distinction) found implicit in Lacan's work. The unary trait is a relative difference whereas the unary trace is an absolute difference.

The unary trace, as an absolute difference, constitutes a groundless ground for identity beyond the trappings of primary and secondary narcissism and the master's discourse. The unary trace as a form of emptiness is linked to the zero that makes the One, as distinct from the imaginary oneness of the trait.

The unary trace that is both zero and One, or the emptiness and form linked to the Sanskrit "cipher," is rooted in a logic of contradiction that is both something and not-something and neither of them at the same time. I apply this distinction between trait and trace to what is unary about the Name (of the Father) and the specular image of the body. The logic of contradiction and negative dialectics are the methods necessary to understand the profound paradoxes located at the heart of the problem of the ego and identification within Freudian theory. Moreover, the problem of identification goes not only to the heart of Freud's second theory of the psyche (id, ego, and super-ego), but also to the problem with the metapsychology that led to the development of the so-called structural theory to begin with. When we understand that identification is used as a formation of what I call the repressive unconscious, then it becomes possible to understand that negation is also present within the unconscious and that the relationship between consciousness and the unconscious takes place within the Möbius strip or what Bion called reversible perspectives.

I also define the unary trace and zero as infinite time and as the vanishing point of a single instant. Once they have co-produced an event, the Symbolic structure and the unconscious disappear at the same time that they function as an experience of emptiness or lack for the subject. It is the unary trace or the emptiness of consciousness (and the unconscious) that stimulates the psyche to be continually re-written or to "not stop from being written" (as Lacan would have it) as well as to have the opposite characteristic of being under permanent erasure.

The unary trace explains how identity can be single and multiple as well as constant and non-substantial at the same time. The first has important implications for cross-cultural identity in a postcolonial world, whereas the second explains how I can be the same and not the same person at any given time as a necessary condition for the healthy functioning of the subject.

Finally, I follow Lacan in exploring the relationship between the unary trace and the partial *objet a*. Like trait and trace, the *objet a* has imaginary and real dimensions. In what Lacan calls the traversing of the phantasm, the *a* no longer provides support for imaginary identity, only for real desire. It is here that the subject is most himself/herself in the form of an unrepresentable *jouissance*. I distinguish between the subject in the Real of the drive, and the subject of the Real which functions as a place of permutation of the symbolic structure. In addition, I distinguish two types of primary signifiers (S_1) and two related forms of primary repression. The first type of S_1 is related to the *objet a* and to what I call infinite Life, whereas the second represents the child as the mother's imaginary phallus.

The analyst's task is to occupy the place of the Real *a* that appears in Lacan's formula for the discourse of the analyst. In the discourse of the analyst the *a* becomes a representative of infinite Life and signifies unknown-knowing, and the emptiness of both the Other and the desire of the analyst.

Chapter 2 follows the analysis of the relationship between the letter and the signifier from the seminar on identification to the seminar on the semblance (Seminar XVIII). In the latter seminar, Lacan connects these two notions to the question of *jouissance*. I also read Lacan retroactively, by elucidating the question of identification from the point of view of the different types of *jouissance* that he later began to outline in *La Trosieme*. I examine the notion of the Semblance in relationship not only to the signifier but also to the question of the mask and the face particularly as manifesting in the transference relationship.

In chapter 1 I begin to examine the question of what Lacan calls the identification with the *sinthome*. With the concept of the *sinthome*, Lacan focuses on the aspect of the symptom that is in the Real (of a drive) as a form of *jouissance* (pleasure/pain). However, since both a symptom and a *sinthome* have an aspect of the Real in them, I distinguish between a symptom in the Real and a *sinthome* of the Real. In the latter, pain is not masochistic and serves the subject rather than the other way around. In addition, the *sinthome*, as a unary trace, although a rogue element that transforms the symbolic order, the *sinthome* does not represent a semiotic challenge of the mother to the Name of the Father as found in the work of Kristeva. The *sinthome* represents an opening to new signifiers and significations.

In the chapter on the semblance (chapter 2) I link the analysis of the letter to the question of the *sinthome*, the Name of the Father, and to the relationship between the face and the mask. At the end of this chapter I begin to consider the work of the semblance within the transference relationship in the direction of the end of analysis that will be the topic of chapter 3.

One of the criteria used to distinguish between a trait and a trace is that the trait has a narcissistic component whereas the trace does not or is tied to a narcissism degree zero, to a differentiation within narcissism beyond narcissism (Moncayo, 2008). The trait is a form of insignia or medal of the ego-ideal linked to the inscription of the Name of the Father within the Imaginary register. The Name of the Father as a unary trace functions as a senseless letter between the Symbolic and the Real. I distinguish between the formal semblance of the signifier and the semblance of unbeing or the *jouissance* of the letter, and between the imaginary identification with the analyst that sutures the gap of being and the lack in the Other, and the identification with the *sinthome* as a permutation of the Name of the Father that opens the subject towards empty being.

Following Lacan, my analysis and development of Lacan's thought is not only scholarly or introductory (to his work) but is meant to have a direct bearing and elucidation of the clinical practice of psychoanalysis. To this effect, I am careful to ground Lacanian theory not only in the clinic but also on the basis of Freud's work. Chapter 3, on the aims and ends of analysis in the Lacanian school, is an example of this. In this chapter, I unfold three main themes: the connection between identification and the end of analyses, the question of the analysis of resistance, not only from the point of view of the well-known Lacanian concept of the resistance of the analyst, but also from the development of the concept of the analysis of the repressive unconscious that I derive from the work of both Freud and Lacan.

The question regarding the end of analysis implies an articulation between the aim and the end of analysis. I contrast the definition of the end of analysis within Lacanian analysis and the rest of the analytic field. In contrast to other perspectives, within Lacanian psychoanalysis, the aim of the analysis of identifications is the end of the identification with the analyst. Identifications have to be first recognized/deconstructed and then relinquished, or taken away. When identifications are abandoned, the subject finds his or her identity (which is no-identity) in the larger symbolic structure and the wondrous emptiness of unbeing (*desetre*).

This chapter considers the differences between what is terminable and interminable in analysis in terms of the differences between the symptom and the *sinthome*. Within this context I examine whether the aim of analysis is to strengthen the ego defenses and weaken the drives, or to weaken the ego and produce transformations within *jouissance*. Strengthening ego defenses also reinforces unconscious defenses. This perspective is consistent with Lacan's focus on the resistance of the analyst rather than the analysis of ego resistances. The problem with the analysis of ego resistances is that this is usually done with the aim of strengthening the ego and the "mastery of the drives." In the same way the resistance of the analyst has to do with the wish to be recognized by the analysand as a master or a "subject supposed to know(ing)." This keeps the treatment in the Imaginary dimension of the ego-ideal rather than carrying the analysis further in the direction of the subject and subjective destitution. The subject is a metaphor rather than an egoic type of identification. In a Lacanian analysis the support given to the ego defenses in the early phase of the treatment is only a strategy within the transference.

I argue that the ego is not what unifies the psyche/subject. The opposite is true: the ego divides the subject. What unify the subject as a unit, and as a unary trace, are the symbolic order and the One of the Real.

From a Lacanian perspective defenses are not opposed to desire since repression produces desire as much as it represses desire and desire invokes repression as much as it opposes repression. Again, the logic of contradiction is required to understand this. In addition, I argue that what represses is not the ego but the laws of the Code and of language. Defenses are generated within discourse, and the latter reveals as much as conceals desire. I propose the concept of the analysis of the repress<u>ive</u> unconscious as an alternative to the analysis of ego resistances. In this I agree with both Lacan and Freud: with Freud because the analysis of defenses is important, but with Lacan because the analysis of defenses is not ego analysis. The analysis of the ego is to deconstruct rather than strengthen the ego. In the process, the unity of the ego is not lost but is rather replaced by the One of the Real and the symbolic order. In contrast to Lacan, I argue that the pleasure principle is both a principle of wish fulfillment and of defense. Lacan only considers the latter. The laws of the unconscious serve both the purposes of wish fulfillment and object seeking, and the defensive motives of anxiety and pain avoidance.

I argue that the affirmation and negation that take place in judgment are similar in form to the affirmation and negation that takes place in language and in the dream-work. The latter represent the interplay of the primary forces of being and non-being, life and death, from which the conscious intellectual functions of judgment originate.

Finally, the question of Oedipus as a myth of Freud becomes the touchstone from which Lacan proposed to go beyond Freud and beyond the rock of castration. I deploy this concept in three different directions: as a new way of understanding the end of analysis as the end/aim of identification, as Lacan's postmodern or poststructuralist turn and a Lacanian response to Deleuze and Guattari's Anti-Oedipus (1972), and to formulate a fourth phase/face of Oedipus that could help differentiate analysis proper from the notion of brief analysis that I propose in the chapter by the same name (chapter 4).

I clarify that when Lacan says that Oedipus is a dream of Freud he is saying that oedipal desire is not only repressed but is also a form of repression. However, this repressive production of sexuality is not the same as the historical analysis of sexuality and of Oedipus championed by three key figures of poststructuralism: Foucault, Deleuze, and Guattari. Oedipal desire is a defense not of Catholicism (the confession of sin) or Capitalism. Desire is not inscribed as oedipal in order to enslave it to a cruel Big Other. Oedipal desire is mobilized against the lack in the Other rather than against the repressive strength of the Other.

Lacan proposes to go beyond the rock of castration and Freudian oedipal theory. Unconscious fantasy is traversed and the shore of the unconscious is reached when fantasy can be realized as a defense or constructed in the void of the desire of the analyst. The figure of the analyst as a formidable forbidding paternal figure needs to be recognized as a fantasy of the subject. The analysand wants what he/she can't have due to the prohibition of a strong figure that has "it." This fantasy is erected as a defense against the realization that the analyst or a parental figure does not have it. The Other is empty: the emperor, the revolutionary liberator, and the gods have clay feet.

Subjective destitution, or ego and object loss, at the end of analyses, differ from the idea of a strong or unified ego, just as identifying with the *sinthome* differs from identification with the analyst. The recognition of an inevitable lack also means letting go of the recriminations against the Other who did not give this or that recognition or this or that object.

In phase IV of Oedipus a boy/man needs to get past the sense of having the imaginary phallus in order to have access to the symbolic phallus and the emptiness of the symbolic order. In turn a girl/woman needs to get past the envy for an imaginary phallus that does not exist, and realize her own place in the Symbolic as a woman.

Both sexes will have to make do with a limited phallic *jouissance* (not precisely a genital ideal), whereas women, in relationship to the phallus, also experience a supplementary form of feminine sexual *jouissance* that both sexes may also experience in the form an *a*sexual Other *jouissance* similar, if not identical, to the Freudian principle of sublimation.

Chapter 4, on variable-length analysis and the question of brief analysis, addresses current realities in the analytic and mental health fields. Freud had criticized Rank for trying to adapt psychoanalysis to the fast pace of the "American way of life" by shortening the length of the treatment. However, this was at a time when Freud's analyses were one year long as opposed to the ten- and twenty-year-long analyses that became a common occurrence under the post-Freudian classical standard frame. In addition, nowadays there are an array of alternative treatments and psychotherapies that were not available during Freud's time. In addition, the legitimacy and efficacy of psychoanalysis has been questioned by both *scientistic*/empiricist discourse and the ideology of cost effectiveness under managed care. Not many patients are willing – and not many patients or analysts, for that matter, are able – to follow an analysis to its logical conclusion.

Despite his criticism of Rank, Freud (1919) already observed that in making psychoanalysis available to the wider population the pure gold of psychoanalysis may have to be combined with the copper of psychotherapy widely defined.

The problem with not making psychoanalysis available to the general public, and restricting it to the upper classes that can pay for it, is that eventually even the latter will stop using psychoanalysis. This is precisely the current predicament of psychoanalysis. In order for those with means to continue using psychoanalysis, psychoanalysis has to remain influential in the larger culture.

Finally, the model proposed distinguishes brief analysis from short-term psychotherapy and regards the former as preparation for rather than a replacement or a watering down of analysis proper. In considering the possibility of a brief analysis, the study of the different phase or moments of analysis led to the formulation of a fourth phase of Oedipus that also helped me differentiate between analysis and brief analysis. Only analysis is capable of reaching a fourth phase of Oedipus.

Analysts or therapists who have themselves undergone an analysis of long duration are considered qualified to conduct variable-length Lacanian analyses. Brief analysis is also differentiated from brief therapy because of the focus on unconscious fantasy. It is anticipated that by identifying and incorporating the distinct phases of Oedipus into the treatment, effectiveness will be enhanced and maximized.

Following Freud and Lacan I distinguish between ending and termination. Ending indicates the end of an activity, whereas termination is also linked to an aim or the end as aim. In analysis, termination indicates a phase or logical moment of treatment. I use the logic behind the scansion or cutting/shortening of the session as hastening a moment of separation between analyst and analysand that brings the future termination of the analysis to the analytic experience of both parties. This is true for both analysis and brief analysis, but in the case of brief analysis the end is much closer, and therefore much more impacting.

Understanding time as the fourth dimension of space imbues time with some of the properties of space. Just like in space one can turn right or left, in time-space one can move from future to present and past. The fact that the end is near for a brief analysis intensifies the experience of the scansion of the session.

The following variable-length Lacanian analysis model suggests 30 to 40 sessions as a second-best practice to an entire course of Lacanian analysis when constraints such as lack of financial resources, time, or desire to engage in long-term treatment are operative. It is intended as preparation for or as an introduction to analysis proper.

In fact this was the most common outcome of the cases that have been treated thus far with a brief Lacanian analysis format. Initially the clients themselves were not interested in long-term treatment and wanted resolution of their symptoms and behavioral outcomes rather than more in-depth understanding/ transformation of themselves or of their history. This presentation coincides with prevailing views of psychotherapy available within North American culture at large (professional and otherwise). However, after a brief analysis the clients consistently became more interested and more open to self-exploration and to redefining their views of themselves and their families. As a result of the treatment, their productive capacity and income increased to the point that towards the end of their brief analysis they developed the desire to pay for a regular course of sliding-scale analysis with a frequency of two to three sessions per week and a commitment of two to three years in length.

In general the Lacanian approach to the frame of analysis is a response to ineffective analyses and long-term treatment courses that stay trapped within the first, second, or third phases of oedipal structure. A careful analysis of the phases of psychoanalysis and their correlation to the phases of oedipal structure and transference yielded some interesting results. The intent of the investigation of the phases of psychoanalysis was to determine what could be accomplished by a short analysis in contrast to psychoanalysis proper. The result was the clarification of the goals of psychoanalysis and the elaborations of a fourth phase of oedipal structure that can only be reached by psychoanalysis, not by brief analysis. The chapter carries out a discreet differentiation of the various components of analytic treatment and of the phases of the transference relationship in the four phases of treatment (pre-treatment, beginning, middle, and end).

The notion of the phases or what Lacan calls the moments of Oedipus was developed out of Lacan's ideas in Seminar V. There he spoke of only three moments of Oedipus, and this formulation did not include his later ideas on Oedipus. The notion of a fourth moment of Oedipus is a retroactive reading of the early Lacan via the lens of his later work. Paradoxically, and via the method of a logic of contradiction, the examination of the phases of long-term analysis yielded a form of short-term analysis, and the study of short-term analysis yielded a new aim/end for long-term analysis.

When speaking of phases I speak also of "faces" and include both diachronic and synchronic dimensions of time. Lacan appeals to the notion of a moment in time to emphasize the synchronic dimension of a period or phase in contrast to a developmental perspective associated with an ideal of progress or maturation. Phases are also dimensions in synchronic time and the synchronic reading of a structure. At the same time, the structure is built in diachronic phases over time. But once evolved, phases are never abandoned or completely superseded.

Phase IV of Oedipus goes beyond the rock of castration and overcomes the impasses of Freudian theory and postmodern culture. In phase III of Oedipus the boy/man stays fixated to having the phallus and his mother and the girl/woman is fixated to not having it and having penis envy instead. Instead her only alternative project is to have children and complete herself in relationship to a man. Instead of facing the rock of castration, postmodern culture and object relations, psychoanalysis went into denial and regressed to earlier phases of Oedipus by privileging the so-called pre-oedipal phase of development.

Chapter 5 argues that Lacanian psychoanalysis is a postmodern form of Freudian psychoanalysis needed to address, understand, and transform the postmodern condition. Freudian psychoanalysis, as a product of modernity, contains positivistic and hermeneutic strands that have been divested of its traditional uses for biblical exegesis and textual analysis. Freud agreed with the belief that modern science aims at the discovery of objective truths and natural laws that describe the facts and regularities found in nature. At the same time, Freud studied human psychical phenomena that could only be understood and transformed through the medium of language and the practice of interpretation. This is the hermeneutic side of his theory.

Freud linked heterogeneous human phenomena such as dreams, slips of the tongue and pen, mistaken actions, as well as jokes, to sexuality, aggressiveness, and the formation of clinical symptomatology. Freud also used the method of interpretation to examine cultural forms such as myth, art, and religion that he considered parallel symbolic forms to dreams and wit. Freud's materialistic hermeneutics went from the spiritual to the material, inverting thereby the traditional direction of interpretation (from the material to the spiritual). The Freudian use of hermeneutics is consistent with the modern project of secularizing traditional principles and perspectives.

Modern structuralism (in Anthropology and Linguistics), as distinct from empiricism, established a specific logic for the social sciences parallel to that of hermeneutics. Structuralism also differed from both hermeneutics and natural science. According to Gadamer, hermeneutics constitutes an on-going re-interpretation of tradition where the historical story or narrative becomes inseparable from the so-called "facts" of history. From this perspective empiricism and hermeneutics (whether modern or traditional) are in perfect opposition to one another.

Structuralism finds regularities within symbolic/cultural forms that are independent from natural laws (for example, the prohibition of incest, language rules, and the difference between the sexes). Symbolic laws organize the narratives and ideologies about personal or historical events. The facts don't speak for themselves, nor are they the simple reflection of the stated intentions of speaking beings. The facts speak for themselves as signifiers organized by symbolic principles of signification. Most of us know that Lacan's early work was influenced by structuralism.

However, according to Lacan's later work, or what I will call here Lacanian poststructuralism, objective reality is a function of the Other and the Other has a necessary and irreducible lack built into it. The chaos or emptiness/impermanence built into a conceptual structure is more than simply a form of anti-structure (the anti-Oedipus in the case of Deleuze and Guattari). Emptiness is what facilitates the transformations and evolutions of the structure. For example, language contains a relationship to *jouissance* and to a Real beyond signification.

According to Lacanian theory, lower-case social reality is defined along the Imaginary and Symbolic dimensions of a structural text rather than by an objective reality existing independently from them. On the other hand, for Lacanian theory the register/dimension of the Real and of *jouissance* is in fact outside of the text although it is also defined in reference to a text. The concepts of the Borromean knot and the Real makes Lacanian theory postmodern yet beyond hermeneutics because it retains a dimension of intensity within *jouissance* that remains distinct from the signifier. The intensity of *jouissance*, although manifest within experience, is also beyond empirical measurement and instrumental rationality.

Psychologically speaking or in reference to a text, language has the structure of fiction or continually conceals as well as reveals truths about desire. The lack in the Other is the place in language, and in the Borromean knot, where human beings construct an Imaginary fantasy about reality, or objective reality as a form of "objectality." The lack in the Other is also the place in the knot where the Symbolic meets a senseless Real beyond fiction/meaning and signification.

Structuralism finds regularities in symbolic forms, but Lacanian psychoanalysis, as a form of poststructuralism, and as a properly psychoanalytic form of discourse, discovers the interrelationships between fantasy and reality, between the symbolic forms that organize fantasy or fiction, and the Real of the void of space/time and the unknown life (matter and energy that lives within biological life and outlives it) that lives in it (*das Ding* or the no-thing).

Non-Lacanian poststructuralism – or what I would call anti-structuralism, to distinguish it from Lacanian poststructuralism – represents a critique of modernity, and yet in many ways it takes modern ideas to their ultimate consequences. The critique of modernity is still identified with modernity. In this chapter I use the same logic of contradiction and identification developed in the first chapter to consider whether oppressed groups still remain unconsciously identified with the oppressor. By the same token the oppressor remains identified with traits of the oppressed. The fight against oppression produces unintended consequences that can be understood by the logic of the excluded Third (the Freudian unconscious).

In addition, emancipation or liberation is not only a modern value. I submit that with modernity only the purpose/object of emancipation changes from the id to the super-ego. Traditional culture uses the super-ego to achieve emancipation from passion and from nature (id), whereas modernity uses the ego to seek emancipation from the same super-ego that was the agent of emancipation for traditional culture. In the same way that in traditional culture the id creeps up into the super-ego despite repression, the same thing happens to the modern ego: the super-ego creeps up into the ego, and dogmatism transforms into scientism.

Postmodern theory critiques the dominance of the master narrative of the modern rational ego; yet without any glue to hold it together, postmodern theory and culture succumbs to the id or to identification with the object of the fantasy and the drive. Within the postmodern condition, the id creeps up into the ego. In fact this follows the distinction that Lacan made between polymorphous perversion of childhood and perversion proper as a meta-level diagnostic structure. In perversion, the id-object is occupying the function of the imaginary ego. Postmodern theory is a reflection of the postmodern condition. Lacanian postmodern theory, however, can be used to critique postmodernism within the culture.

Both majority and minority groups suffer from being unable to turn the psyche towards non-identity or non-identification. **Non** is a dialectical prefix that can be differentiated from **not** as an adverb that represents a formal rather than a dialectical negation. Non-identity and non-identification represent the potential *unariness* of the One within multiplicity, as distinct from the imaginary unity or narcissistic trait of the oneness of national identity, and as distinct from a multiplicity without the function of the zero in each of its parts or numerical components. Multiculturalism represents a dispersion or migration without any glue or Third to hold it together.

Lacanian psychoanalysis can be viewed as a postmodern form of Freudian psychoanalysis that can be used to critique postmodern culture and non-Lacanian poststructuralism or ultramodernism. Postmodern culture is also associated with negative qualities: fragmentation, the breakdown of the (bourgeois) nuclear family and the social-familial order, and the unleashing of imaginary drives and impulses.

Postmodern culture becomes intrinsically associated with the borderline and narcissistic character disorders and an inability to postpone gratification and tolerate frustration. Lasch (1979) had already indirectly recognized the negative characteristic of the postmodern in his book on the culture of narcissism. However, Lasch, or the object-relations approach to the borderline condition, did not associate the borderline condition with a decline in the paternal function. If anything, it was the mother and the lack of secure attachment or good-enough mothering that was responsible for the condition.

According to Lacanian theory, the rejection and disavowal of the necessary function of the father, due to blurring the difference between the imaginary and symbolic fathers, between oppression and repression, led to a problem with recognizing lack, limits, and boundaries widely spread across postmodern culture and the baby-boom generation. Just as early modernity and the Protestant ethic suffered from neurotic forms of inhibition and avowals of the law of the imaginary father, and rejections of the feminine and homosexuality, the postmodern condition of the consumer society of late capitalism suffers from the disavowal of the symbolic father and avowals of the desires of the imaginary mother. For poststructuralist or anti-structuralist Gilles Deleuze, the masochist is rendered free for a new life in which the father and the signifier play no role. The masochist is bent on empowering the Venus in furs or the phallic mother.

Capitalism is driven by the master's discourse, not by the discourse of the analyst or psychoanalysis. The symbolic function of castration undermines the master's discourse, because symbolization requires the scansion of the imaginary phallus as a master signifier. Within psychoanalysis, the phallus is a lack, not a victorious emblem or flag of masculine supremacy. Psychoanalysis as an ethics of desire is a basis for a critique of conformity, hypocrisy, and traditional morality while at the same time understanding and theorizing the fundamental ethical structures that organize both society and desire: the differences between the sexes and the prohibition of incest.

The dimension of the father needs to be correctly understood as a symbolic function that supports desire and organization while not being intrinsically hierarchical. Although the imaginary ego, associated with modern individualism, is cancelled by symbolic/metaphoric representation, the symbolic function is a negative dialectic that also cancels itself in support of symbolic organization. Masculinity wins in the Imaginary only to lose or lack in the Symbolic, and the reverse is true for femininity (loses in the Imaginary and wins in the Symbolic). The Imaginary looks like a gain but it's a loss, and the Symbolic looks like a loss but is an overall gain that remains unrepresented or represented as the signifier of a lack or emptiness of self-identity.

Finally, many of the dichotomies and contradictions/differences between the modern and the postmodern, between words and images, between meaning and sensation and no-meaning, between language and asignifying intensities, the verbal and the pre-verbal, are contained within Lacan's multidimensional theory of the Borromean knot (Real, Imaginary, Symbolic). At the same time, the latter is never fully totalized because the Name of the Father (as the fourth ring that ties the other three together) is a no-name, or a One that is a zero, and the All requires the not-all as its necessary foundation.

The final chapter, on Magritte, the void, and the imagination, explores the work of art from the perspective of the unary trace. Artifacts, like fantasies, both fill the void and reveal it at the same time. In the example of Magritte, the work of art represents a unary trace of the void and the One of a mystery at the core of being.

Magritte represents a non-dual or postmodern alternative to both modern and classical art. Classical art represented the subject of painting and the painting subject with idealized images. Classical art elevated nature to the dignity of culture. Modern art instead represents the subject of painting and the painting subject as lacking and as an object of waste in identification with the fantasy object, cause of desire. Following Lyotard, the object of art is represented not via idealization or devaluation, but as a form of sublimation without the repressive interest of classical or baroque art.

In Magritte, S_1 is not elevated to S_2, nor is S_2 regressed to S_1. S_1 does not mean a form of identification with the object of unconscious fantasy. In Magritte, S_1 is revealed as S_0 or as what sustains the (Real empty) form of S_2 or of the laws of form, whether visual or linguistic. The painting in-itself is not the object of fantasy, or the Id as an object, but the unary traces and infinite lines of wondrous being. In chapter 1 on identification I differentiated between imaginary similarity, symbolic resemblance, and real similitude. Similitude is Real and points to unbeing. I also pointed out that similitude is related to Benjamin's (1936) concept of aura as the quality of a modern painting or "its unique existence at the place where it happens to be." A painting's place is represented by the evocation of non-identity.

In addition to the concept of the lack and its application, the chapter builds on another characteristic of Magritte's painting: its value to evoke the experience of a mystery beyond representation (the Real). The concepts of the void and of emptiness serve as transitional terms between the concept of the lack in Lacan and the notion of the mystery in Magritte. In a first approximation the concept of the void is similar if not identical to that of the lack. Zizek (2000) has argued that it is as important for the artist to cover the void as it is to unveil it. For example, he explains contemporary painting as representing what is missing or the pain of existence rather than the idealized images of classical painting. However, this concept of the void as an unveiled lack or limitation is not identical to the notion of the mystery in Magritte. To reach the mystery requires a different conception of the void. What paintings reveal is not only the void as a traumatic experience of childhood or of human existence but also the void of the mystery itself. This latter sense of the void diverges somewhat (although not entirely) from the usual interpretation of Lacanian ideas and comes closer to Zen Buddhist conceptions of emptiness and the void. The latter is already contained in Heidegger's notion of *das Ding* that Lacan closely followed. This more positive dimension of the void and the mystery in Magritte's painting builds on prior work where I have distinguished among the void representing traumatic experiences, repressed desires, and the absence/presence of the object and the meaning of a positive emptiness or the presence of the Real or of the Sublime as an emptiness beyond symbolization. These distinctions do justice to both a psychoanalytic interpretation of Magritte work and to his sense that the mystery cannot be reduced to psychological explanations.

Chapter 6 also agrees with Lyotard (1994) when he conceives the aesthetic of the Sublime as the mediating link between modernism and postmodernism. In fact this chapter further proposes that the aesthetic of the Sublime is precisely what differentiates modernism (not modernity) and postmodern theory. Modernism antedates postmodern culture and the chaos of late capitalism.

Magritte is a better reflection of a postmodern theory that may antedate a culture yet to come. Placing the philosophical and postmodern concept of the Sublime next to Freud's concept of sublimation helps resolve and understand the problems that Freud had in formulating the concept and differentiating it from idealization and other defense mechanisms. Postmodernism contains the possibility of a realization of the Sublime that may be deeply satisfying to the subject yet equally disturbing to the conventional ego of classicism or bourgeois modernity.

This chapter develops criteria to differentiate idealization from sublimation. Idealization supports or is a function of the relationship between the ego-ideal and the ideal ego that has the defensive function of closing a gap within the ego. The change of object in sublimation goes beyond the notion of a social or conventional object accepted by society. The aim of sublimation reveals a positive form of the death drive and the return of the drive to a radical form of emptiness. Becoming reconciled to the emptiness within the desire and the subject requires a benevolent form of depersonalization, as a movement that includes a painful tear to the fabric of narcissism that proves to be ultimately rewarding.

Lacan argues that since the drive is not an instinct, the nature of the drive bears an intrinsic relationship to what he calls *das Ding*. From a Lacanian perspective, the change in aim of the drive that characterizes sublimation according to Freud involves a change from sexual pleasure to *das Ding*. I explore the meaning of the drive from the perspective of *das Ding* since Lacan implies that *das Ding* is more fundamental than the pleasure principle.

The world as Id, as instinctual nature, is not "It." This It is the no-thing or the presence of emptiness rather than "<u>The</u> Thing." Here the "The" needs to be barred or crossed out in the same way that in Lacan's formulas of sexuation "The" woman is barred. Thus I distinguish between two notions of *das Ding* found in Lacan: the thing and the no-thing or the *a-chose*. The It is the absolute difference of how things-are-in-themselves.

Lacanian theory is a form of dialectical rationality that establishes a structural relation between two apparently contradictory notions: appearance and reality, or fantasy and reality. The Imaginary includes the deception of fantasy, or the perception of a subject without an external object, and the deception of the senses or of formal analytical reason in the form of the appearance of a perception of an object/objective reality without a subject. However, up to this point Lacanian theory has still left untheorized the further question of an Imagination or an imaginative faculty that reveals new images within the field of vision that, despite being subjective, gives an accurate depiction of reality.

I contrast what I call the imaginary dual Oneness of dreams with the Oneness of duality at work not in the Imaginary but in the forms of the Imagination.

The Oneness of dreams conceals the divisions, dualities, and contradictions contained within the oneness of the image and therefore preempts the possibility of a correct apprehension of the relations between the elements and terms in question. The distinction between the duality of Oneness and the One contained within the duality corresponds to the distinction that Lacan makes between the unifying unity, the *Einheit*, and the distinctive unity or *Einzigkeit* (Seminar XI: 10) discussed in chapter 1. I propose that the Oneness of duality, the unary trace, or the function of the "One," as Lacan called it, within dreams and daydreaming, far from being irrational, is a function of negative dialectics and critical reason. The One or the Oneness of duality reveals the non-duality, or the S_1–S_0 relation contained within duality (S_1–S_2). In the creative imagination, both One and Other are simultaneously revealed. One does not hide two or three, nor do two and three conceal One or how the three of a chain are connected.

I conclude that classical art was a form that concealed the absence of the object and therefore laid the ground for modern art as the return of the repressed. Modern art in turn reveals the absence of the object, which lays the ground not only for a possible return of repressed classicism but also for the evolution of what may be postmodern about modernism. What is postmodern about Magritte is how he uses similitude to make symbolic uses of the Imaginary/Imagination. Symbolic uses of the Imaginary/Imagination represent the Real of what things are not only within but also beyond the Imaginary, as the presence of a mystery of plenitude beyond symbolization.

References

Benjamin, W. (1936). The work of art in the age of mechanical reproduction. In P. Du Gay et al. (1997). *Doing Cultural Studies*. London: Sage Publications.

Deleuze, G. and Guattari, F. (1972). *Anti-Oedipus: Capitalism and Schizophrenia*. (Robert Hurley, Mark Seem, and Helen R. Lane trans.). New York: Continuum, 2004.

Freud, S. (1919). Lines of advance in psycho-analytic therapy. *SE*, 17: 159–68.

Lasch, C. (1979). *The Culture of Narcissism: American Life in an Age of Diminishing Expectations*. New York: W.W. Norton

Lyotard, J.F. (1994). *Lessons on the Analytic of the Sublime: Kant's Critique of Judgement*. Stanford: Stanford University Press.

Moncayo, R. (2008). *Evolving Lacanian Perspectives for Clinical Psychoanalysis: On Narcissism, Sexuation, and the Phases of Analysis in Contemporary Culture*. London: Karnac.

Zizek, S. (2000). *The Fragile Absolute, or Why the Christian Legacy Is Worth Fighting For*. New York: Verso.

Chapter 1

Trace and trait

Non-identification as the aim of identification in psychoanalysis

In his well-known studies on identity, Erikson (1968) defined identity as the individual's "link" with the unique values of his/her people. Erikson's definition of individual identity is consistent with the Freudian concept of the ego-ideal that Lacan (1961) has written as: I(O). It is also well known within psychoanalysis that parents transmit cultural values to their children in the form of the psychical agency that Freud called the ego-ideal. What connects the individual to social values is a social trait or link that has been implanted or transplanted into the heart of subjectivity. The relationship between the unary trait, the ego-ideal, and what Lacan calls the Name of the Father will be explored further on in this chapter.

Upper-case I, as the capital of identification, represents social ideals that are the source of ego identifications. O represents the social Other of society but as a complete and consistent whole with nothing lacking. This complete Other produces an incomplete or lacking subject ($) that can then be completed via identification with the Ideal. Social ideals are always linked to the individual via the ego-ideal. The individual can become an ideal ego via identification with social ideals. Within the ego-ideal, ruling ideas reflect the uniqueness of either/or and both/and the ego and the group or nation. The ego is to the individual what the nation concept is to the society, or the group.

The ruling idea or trait that points to the special quality or peculiarity of a nation, whether it be the Americans, the Russians, the Japanese, the Chinese, the Germans, the French, the English, the Muslims, or the Jews, always refers to some special or unique trait that Lacan also wrote as I(O). It is with this S_1 or master signifier that the individual identifies. In this instance, one finds identity or similarity between the core of being of the individual and group values or between desire and the desire of the Other. What Lacan (1961) calls the unary trait represents both the individual and the totality of the group: I(O).

In Lacan's *matheme*, in my opinion, the "I" represents the individual or the ideal, the ideal of the individual and the individual ideal, whereas the "O" repre-sents the group/society or the structure. Former British Prime Minister Margaret Thatcher (1987) has been quoted as once stating: "there is no such a thing as society." For individualistic capitalism, the big Other does not exist. In some limited way this statement coincides with the barred Other (Ø) of the later Lacan.

A "Thatcherian" interpretation of the lack in the Other would argue that the bracket surrounding the O represents the absence of a society, despite the supposition of one, and that only individuals or ideals exist. However, the lack in the Other [Ø], points to the fact that although it is true that the Other does not exist, the subject does not either. The lack in the Other is the same as the absence of the subject within the Other. Although institutions don't exist without subjects, there is no subject that can ultimately represent the institution.

In addition, this unary trait or I(O) also represents two forms of alienation: one symbolic and necessary, and another imaginary that needs to be surpassed and overcome. In imaginary alienation the desire of the subject is alienated in the desire of the Other often while thinking that desire is their own autonomous desire. In life, as in psychoanalytic treatment, the individual or the subject has to recuperate a singular relationship to desire or to what desire is independently from the Other. In addition, imaginary and symbolic alienation are often confused. Humanistic perspectives often believe that what I call symbolic alienation or the production of a divided or split subject is the product of a bad environment, a bad mother, or bad object relations. Lacanian theory would consider this an imaginary apprehension of a structural fact.

Moreover, not only is a structural feature misunderstood as a correctable environmental deficit but the ego or the individual is construed as naturally undivided. When the ego is construed as unified and as an independent center of initiative, what is overlooked is that what the individual refers to as his or her own initiative represents a conscious or unconscious identification with the desire of the Other. Since symbolic alienation in cultural or symbolic laws (incest prohibition, sexual difference, rules of grammar, murder prohibition) is inevitable and constitutive of subjectivity, humanism offers the false promise of a life or a culture without frustration. The emancipation from imaginary alienation or the beyond frustration proceeds from the possibility of recognizing the alienation of desire and the appropriation of desire out of the desire of the Other.

Erikson's interest in identity can be considered an integral part of the "New World" ideal of independence from traditional Europe. At the same time, New World values are an outgrowth of modern European enlightenment values and the meaning of the individual emerging from the Renaissance. For example, both the value of reason and value of the individual are embedded within Freud's modern theory of the ego. For Freud, the ego was the site or locus of modern reason within the individual. In the language of Habermas' (1968) critical theory, the ego is the site of emancipatory cognitive interests and the possibility of social and personal change.

Thus, it is to ego identity that Erikson appealed in his study of youth and the rebellions of the 1960s that led to the hippie movement, feminism, the sexual revolution, and gay rights, to name only a few. The culture of the avant-garde and the beatniks that pre-dated the sixties also implied a rebellion against a conservative establishment. However, when social change is linked to a specific phase of development, such as adolescent rebellion, the question of ego identity acquires a different meaning. In the search for autonomy and independence the ego rejects the values of tradition or the previous generation, yet these oppositions/repudiations/contradictions hide unconscious identifications with the perceived establishment. The ego rejects the traditional master, or the imaginary father, but only to become himself/herself the new face of the old master. Conventional parents produced unconventional children and unconventional children reproduce conventional children in the next generation (yuppies, for example). Capitalists bred socialists and socialists bred capitalists. Theists bred atheists, and atheists bred religious or spiritual children, "masculinists" became feminists, feminists became masculinists, and so on and so forth.

Lacan criticized the theme of ego autonomy because the ego only appears to emancipate itself from the unconscious. In actuality, the ego itself is an unconscious and ideological mental formation. In the United States, for example, there is more liberty and protection of individual rights, while at the same time the United States became the new face of the master or a new form of imperialism.

The illusions of the ego, similar to those of adolescence, include the dream of a society without frustration, renunciation, law, or repression (an unbarred Other or O). The defenses of the ego live in ignorance of unconscious desire and unconscious repression or the mutual interpenetration of both.

Ego autonomy cannot be realized without subjective heteronomy. Neither the ego nor the Other are complete by themselves. Lacan proposes embracing the subjection of the subject without sugar coating it with humanistic dreams of happiness, liberty, or autonomy. On the other hand, psychoanalysis, as a project of modernity, also represents an alternative to traditional or pre-modern religious culture that propounds a subjection of the subject to the Law or the Other at the expense of desire, the drives, and the possibility of change and transformation of cultural or religious laws.

While rejecting the theme of ego autonomy, Lacan also rejects the subjection of desire to the desire of the Other. Under this subjection the subject wants to become or have the signifier of the Other's lack/desire. In addition, the subject wants to give or take this signifier from the Other. Instead, the subject has to scrutinize his/her own identifications and the signifiers of his/her unconscious desire in order to make desire truly the subject's own. The subject has to speak with his/her own words/voice rather than those of the Other. This appropriation of the Other is consistent with the tradition of *Diegesis*: the Platonic virtue of speaking in one's own name.

The subject asks is this what I really want or was this what I wanted? Do I agree or disagree with the Other? If I agree then the question is one of choice and responsibility and no longer one of obedience or subjection. If I disagree then the subject has to take responsibility for authorship and aggressiveness. Finally, while affirming or denying/negating the Other, the subject has to take great care to not reproduce the conditions of unconscious repression that only perpetuate his/her neurosis or division. What we vehemently reject may be precisely what we are identified with, and in time the subject may come to manifest the very characteristics that he/she rejected in the Other. When rejecting the master signifier of the Other, this denial represents an affirmation of the mastery of the ego that, in the end, represents the same ideal or identification.

Within the context of his study of youth and adolescence, Erikson drew a sharp distinction between identity and identification. For most adults the two terms of identity and identification would seem to be naturally related and interchangeable. Erikson observed, however, that for true identity development, the identifications of childhood and with parents had to be challenged and scrutinized. Erikson did his studies during the 1960s when the great social projects of modernity (of revolutionizing society via social theory, drug experimentation, changes in family structure and child-rearing practices, civil rights, feminism, etc.) still held sway over the minds of the new generations.

Today we are in the midst of a postmodern period characterized by, among other things, a loss of modern ideals and an experience of social anomie wherein youth are either lost in a vacuum of values and criminal behavior, teen pregnancy, failing in school and dropping out or are taken by the technocratic consumer society of late capitalism. The lack of economic access to consumer goods, which are otherwise fervently desired, leads to an increase in crime as a means to procure unnecessary objects of consumption. Crime can no longer be explained as a simple means of survival or as a means to satisfy basic needs for shelter, food, and clothing. The current late phase of capitalism has absorbed the ideals of modernity within the context of consumer society. Any modern or traditional cultural feature can be used to sell goods. Furthermore, the postmodern period is also characterized by a return of pre-modern traditional values in basically two ways: fundamentalism unaffected by or in complete rejection of modernity, or traditional values that are combined with modern values in various ways. Both Lacanian psychoanalysis and Zen Buddhism are examples of the latter.

Erikson makes a sharp distinction between identification and identity because identity requires that identifications be challenged in some way. But identity cannot be acquired without some form of identification with ideas, ideals, and signifiers. What Erikson considers to be a dichotomy between identity and identification may simply be a conflict between identifications or ideals, or between the ego and the super-ego, or between the ego-dystonic super-ego and the ego-syntonic ego-ideal. What is true, however, is that identification with parents in the formation of what Freud called the super-ego and the ego-ideal is not exactly the same as identification with social educational values, although the two are also related. As Freud acutely observed, the super-ego is rooted in the id and is fueled by the ego's own aggressiveness towards the parents. This is another way of saying that identification includes contradicted experience and needs to be understood via the logic of contradiction.

Erikson observed that identifications with parents do not lead to functioning personalities. However, he did not have at his disposal the concepts of linguistics for his formulations. What Lacan will call the unary trait does not amount to a character trait as it is known in the field of psychology. As we shall see, Lacan's unary trait is more of a trace or a stroke than a trait in the psychological or genetic sense of the term. A trace is a singularity, a state or an instance in time, in this moment and in the next, whereas a trait endures across time and constitutes a chain or a series. The question remains, however, how traces or traits, in the Lacanian sense, organize into traits as the functions of character or personality. How a character, in the sense of a letter, leads to character in the sense of personality. Perhaps the process is similar to how things transform into letters, letters into words, and words into sentences and rules of grammar. The rules of grammar would be the equivalent of a functioning personality structure. In this way, identifications with parents and with the law are mediated by language, desire, love, etc. Lacan observed that the paternal/parental metaphor is intrinsically bound up and intertwined with the acquisition and structure of language as well as vice versa.

It is impossible to have individual identity, in the modern sense of the word, without identification. Among other things, the concept of identification explains how social values are acquired by the individual and do not merely constitute an external locus of control that was more typical of the societies of the Middle Ages that fundamentalists want to return to. Social ideas are not simply norms that regulate the actions of individuals in the public sectors of society. Although the protection of privacy and private property is a modern ideal, the values of society reach deeply into the private recesses of the home and of the mind. This is what Freud had in mind with his concepts of the super-ego and the ego-ideal.

But what do we gain by following Lacan and thinking of identity in terms of language and the signifier, other than simply introducing a new theory, however elegant this may be? The signifier "values" refers to qualities and quantities of a system or group of ideas and representations – for example, the idea and value of education. Just like language, the latter begins at home and with the parents. A subject cannot emerge as a social individual without a name pointing to a time of birth and to a spatial location within a specific temporal dimension of language and culture. In other words, naming or nomination lies at the intersection of family life and language. Naming is the beginning of the acquisition of language.

For example, my name is Raul Moncayo and this name is a basic signifier of identity. If I am asked: "Who are you," then this is one of the basic possible answers. I could also give a more complex answer: my name is Raul Leon Moncayo de Bremont. The second answer says even more about my background and the paternal and matrilineal lines of descent. Now, how did I get this name? The answer cannot be simplistically given in terms of genetic inheritance. A name is a cultural inheritance mediated by language. Moncayo is the name of my father and Raul was my father's second name that was given to me by my father but not before my mother had accepted and recognized it and managed to give me her own brother's and father's name for a middle name.

The proper name is a unary trait for an individual that makes him/her different from the rest of the family and at the same time it is a same difference that is shared with the rest of the family and all the other Moncayos in Latino-American and Spanish culture. I can feel unique by being the only Raul in my family, but at the same time it is a signifier of my status as a subject to my father and mother. They chose my name for me and I was named after my father, and therefore it is a cultural and linguistic trait that I inherited from him. For many years and particularly during my childhood, my name did not seem to me to be a signifier of my uniqueness; rather I experienced it as a signifier of my subjection to and (imaginary) castration by my father. I did not like either one of them (the subjection or the name).

Identity begins by being different. It is only with identification that identity can become identity. I needed to appropriate the name, find its meaning/signification, for it to become identity. In this sense one can say that there are degrees of identification. One can identify with the name in the sense that one answers to the name, but it is not identity in the sense of coinciding with desire or with the core of being. Identity can only be identity via identification, but identification is not yet identity. Identification can be voluntary or involuntary, chosen or compelled.

Before identification is chosen, or when the signifier chooses the subject, the subject exists within a battery of signifiers or a group of subjects (family) with similar characteristics. But the subject experiences this sameness or similarity as a difference or as a form of alienation. The uniqueness of the group or of the individual subject, as defined by the group, is experienced as a form of alienation rather than as what makes the subject different from all the others. The uniqueness of the subject's wants and values that stand in contrast to those of the group, as Erikson puts it, represents a difference from the group that may have also pre-existed the subject. For example, very conservative parents may have suppressed a bohemian streak (or a freak uncle/aunt in the family) that then is covertly and unconsciously passed on to the children, despite the fact that it may represent an opposition to the overt and stated parental wishes for their children.

What differentiates me from my father is that his second name becomes my first name and that my second name is my maternal uncle's name. It is this difference that makes me who I am at a certain level. As Lacan (1961) has pointed out, it is this "difference that makes character just as it makes value and the unit" (III: 10). The One is the Other in the sense that the one is one of the possible values available within the system/structure.

The proper name represents the unary trait as Other, whereas the patronymic (last name) is what is shared by all the values/subjects belonging to a particular class.

Finally, to name is to negate or to say that this name is not the other possible names that it could potentially be. The name also supplants the primacy of the relationship to things and images. The mind takes primacy over the body, the Name of the Father over the desire of the mother. The name circulates within society to a much greater degree than the images of the body. The former is the subject of the law, whereas the latter its object.

Lacan on identification: from *Einheit* to *Einzigkeit*, from one to zero, and from zero to One

In his seminar "On Identification" (Seminar IX, 1960–1), Lacan examined the question of identification from the point of view of the relationship between the subject and the signifier.

> Let us say it right away, in a formula that all our future development will subsequently clarify: what I mean is that, for us analysts what we understand by identification – because that is what we encounter in identification – is a signifier-identification or signifying identification.
>
> (Seminar IX, Session II: 1)

It is through identification that subjects can separate from loved parents and authorities, become independent, and arrive at their own decisions. The Greek word *autonomy* means "same law" and came to designate the capacity for self-government or independence under the law. Identity is equivalent to self, to identical, and to sameness.

> I will begin by putting the accent on that which in identification, poses itself immediately as identical, as founded on the notion of the same, and even of the same to the same, with all the difficulties that this gives rise to.
>
> (Session I: 3)

The signifier is the word that reproduces the law of the Other and of the Code. Subjects both separate and identify via speech. The signifier or the Other of language, which contains our identifications or our social identities, is not another subject but, rather, is, as Lacan argues following Aristotle,

> A locus to which one strives . . . to transfer the knowledge of the subject . . . The Other is the refuse dump of the representative representations of this supposition of knowledge, and this is what we call the unconscious in so far as the subject has lost himself in this supposition of knowledge.
>
> (I: 10)

The Unconscious as a locus of unconscious knowledge is equivalent to Freud's preconscious or unconscious in a descriptive sense. This concept is equivalent to that of a storehouse consciousness of humanity or to Jung's collective unconscious except that archetypes are not primarily visual representations.

All the contents of the storehouse consciousness are marked by a unary trait that makes them different.

> This is to introduce you to what constitutes the essence of the signifier and which it is not for nothing that I will illustrate best in its simplest form which

we have been designating for some time as the *einziger Zug* . . . Unary is not
a neologism. It is used in set theory: the word unary instead of the word single
(unique) . . . The letter is the support of the signifier.

(IV: 7)

The fact is that signifiers only manifest at first the presence of difference as
such and nothing else. The first thing therefore that it implies is that the relationship of the sign to the things should be effaced . . . This is One as such, in
so far as it marks pure difference.

(IV: 11)

The notion of pure difference is rooted in a distinction between relative and
absolute differences. An example of relative difference is a unique letter in a
group of letters. All letters share the same quality of being letters, yet they are all
distinguished by a singular characteristic. In contrast to this, absolute difference is
the absolute value that each unary element has in-itself independently from its
relative value. This absolute value, or unary **trace**, is empty of signifying value
and yet this emptiness of signifying value is also revealed in its uniqueness as a
relative value.

What makes letters One is what makes them Other. But One has more than one
meaning. "By reversing, as I might say, the polarity of this function of unity, by
abandoning the unifying unity, the *Einheit*, for the distinctive unity, the *Einzigkeit*"
(XI: 10). One represents a unit and every unit also represents the possibility that a
unit could be zero since zero is the first unit. Letters as a unit or members of a class
are all identical, and as a specific unit they are similar yet relatively different.
They are one or a whole as Other in the sense of a totality of interdependent and
differentiated elements. Letters are one in the sense of their relative particularity,
but they are One in the sense of being empty in their own being without the value
given by the structure. The fact that each One is empty without the structure is
what allows each One to take their relative place within the structure. The Other
of the Real or of emptiness is what undergirds the Other of the Symbolic interdependent structure.

Letters and language also represent the effacing of the relationship to things via
verbalization of things that are not present. This is the beginning of symbolization
but also the beginning of a difference between words and images. Before the
human distinction between presence or absence, images and words, reality was
not known as either images or words. Things were just what they were, and as
such they were known in pre-conceptual and instinctual actions or activity. Once
images and words are known, words evoke images and images words, words are
revealed as written images, and visual images become discreet signifying sounds.

I demonstrated, designated it for you the last time in the unary trait, in this
function of the stroke as figure of the one in so far as it is only the distinctive
trait, the trait precisely all the more distinctive in so far as there is effaced

from it almost everything which distinguishes it, except the fact of being a trait.

(V: 8)

The unary stroke or trace of a letter effaces from the letter the distinguishing characteristic of the thing and of what linked the letter to the thing. Letters transition from iconic signs that represented certain animals, for example, to letters where the iconic aspect has been effaced. The letter becomes a distinctive mark or a remarkable mark without distinction. What is remarkable about a distinctive mark is that it is a distinctive mark without distinction. The letter as a unary trace or as a single stroke is what unites letters by virtue of being empty of differentiating marks.

When Lacan speaks of the ideal of what I will call similarity (as distinguished from similitude), he refers to the effacing/eliminating of distinctive marks that differentiates things from one another. In contrast to similarity, a unary trace does not eliminate distinctions because it is a distinction albeit without distinction. This refers to what Lacan calls the paradox of radical otherness designated by the trace: it is a paradox because the relative value of uniqueness of a being other or different from b is sustained on the basis of a more radical difference that allows a to function as a in relationship to b. In my opinion, this radical difference is the function of a being not a and therefore being able to be a. A not being a does not mean that a should be effaced but, rather, that not a is the foundation of a or what is unary or One about a trace.

If $a = a$ represents identity, $a = -a$ (not-a) points to the fact that the signifier is different to itself. When Lacan defines a signifier as what represents a subject to another signifier, in this definition the subject is excluded/represented by the signifier. At the same time when the signifier is understood as different to itself, then the signifier is also excluded in the process of representation. Lacan says that the signified/meaning of a signifier is another signifier. In other words, a signifier S_1 is defined by another signifier S_2 and in this signifying process S_1 becomes excluded by S_2. By representing a signifier with another signifier, the first signifier is excluded. The principle of identity ($a = a$) is the same as the principle of non-contradiction, whereas the principle of contradiction is the same as the principle of non-identity ($a = $ not-a).

The not-a that allows a to function as a different value from b, or as *differance*, to use a term coined by Derrida (1982), is what the unary trace is built upon. "Not-a" points to what about an object or a subject is beyond imaginary resemblance or symbolic difference. In modern art, "not-a" is represented as similitude in contrast to resemblance (for example, Magritte's painting "This is not a pipe" discussed in chapter 5). In the seminar "On Identification," Lacan equates similitude and resemblance, but the two can also be differentiated. Similitude is Real and points to unbeing, whereas resemblance is symbolic and similarity is imaginary. Similitude is also related to Benjamin's (1936) concept of aura as the quality of a modern painting or "its unique existence at the place where it happens to be." A painting's place is represented by the evocation of non-identity.

Similarity and resemblance point to the figurative relationship between letters and the objects that they originally represented. At the same time, letters represent an erasure of the original relationship to the object. The letter is the death of the object. This is the negative function of the letter that then is preserved as pure erasure without an object. The negativity of the letter points to emptiness and senselessness as an absolute value.

The negativity of the letter erases the resemblance/relationship to the object and converts it into the similitude not between letters but between the letter and the paper or parchment on which the letter is written. It is the paper or the space between letters that makes a letter be a One in the Real. What Lacan (1971) calls *Lituraterre* can be understood as the erasure of the letter on the ground upon which the letter is written. On the ground/sand, the letter is a One (landmark) that is erased by a littoral or river of *jouissance*.

The unary trace sustains the relation between *a* and *b*, but also makes both completely independent as not-*a* and not-*b*, or zero.

According to Lacan, a **trace** is surrounded by a ring that then erases the trace, and gives birth to the signifier as a repetition of the same but different. There is a step or an action marked by the trace, then the vocalization/reading of the trace negates/erases the step/trace; this vocalization leads to writing on condition that one forgets that the vocalization originally referred to a step or action, and thus it gives rise to a new beginning of numbers and letters. So then we have 1 and 2, or *a* and *b*, instead of trace and ring. An echo or an acoustic image is a ring or a round figure of sound.

> The first proper name for Mr. Russell – I already alluded to it in my preceding seminars – is the "this," *celui-ci* (this is the question). Here the demonstrative has passed to the rank of proper names. It is no less paradoxical that Mr. Russell coolly envisages the possibility of calling this same point John.
>
> (VI: 6)

Drawing a circle in the air would be an example of a traceless trace or of how a trace is erased by a circle, which then is itself erased or negated by being simply "this." Then "this" may become a proper name or Jack and Jill.

I → ① → ○ ------------ → **Signifier**

Trace Ring Vocalization/this Name

> Having said this, **if the trace is effaced** the subject surrounds its place with a ring, something which thenceforward concerns him; the mapping out of the place where he found the trace, well then, here you have the birth of the signifier. This implies a whole process involving the return of the last phase onto the first, that there cannot be any articulation of a signifier without these three phases. Once the signifier is constituted, there are necessarily two others

before. A signifier is a mark, a trace, a writing, but it cannot be read alone. Two signifiers is a bloomer, a cock and bull story. Three signifiers is the return of what is involved, namely of the first. It is when the *pas* (step) marked in the trace is transformed in the vocalization of whoever is reading it into *pas* (not) that this *pas*, on condition that one forgets that it means the step, can serve at first in what is called the phonetics of writing, to represent *pas*, and at the same time to transform the trace of *pas* eventually into the *pas* of the trace.

(IX: 4)

Lacan puns on the French *pas* of step and *pas* of negation. The vocalization of the step erases the step (trace of *pas* is transformed into *pas* of the trace) and transforms the step or the action into made-up stories. The vocalization/writing of the step or S_1 cannot be read alone, it needs S_2 but S_2 transforms S_1 into a made-up story or narrative.

The letter represents a form of erasure that does not preserve a link to the object that was erased. The letter or S_1 now represents the void rather than an erased or effaced act/trace. Instead of the erased object of an iconic sign, or of a step or action, the blank paper or the sand on which the letter is written represents the void. The act or object now is transformed into writing with erasure and the act of erasure is not only preserved in the writing but also in the void represented by the blank slate of the paper. The pleasure/pain or *jouissance* that accompanied the erased act or object are now in the ink as the very substance of expression. It is the paper as void or the ink that makes letters be a symbolic One of the Real. It is ink and paper that links letters, the same way that letters link words.

The letter represents the void as form, form in lieu of the void, but the letter itself is also void or under erasure on the grounds of the material with which it is written. The ink erases the letter on the paper, just like water erases the letter written on sand.

The unary trace is a signifier without a signified, is an S_1 without an S_2, a pure signifier without a story: the unary signifier is a signifier of the void, rather than of a master, or is the signifier of a master of nothing. Here one can also differentiate between **trait** and **trace**. Lacan, or the translator, inadvertently switches from the unary **trait** to the unary **trace**.

Lacan speaks of unary traits and not simply of genetic or character traits, although unary traits may also be helpful in understanding character as a letter. But by linking the unary trait to I(O), and to the ego-ideal, therefore, the unary trait represents identification to a ruling imaginary master signifier. Hitler's mustache could be an example of this. When Lacan begins speaking of a mark without distinction, he also begins to speak of a trace instead of a trait. Kristeva derived the term semiotic from the Greek word for trace or mark. However, for Lacan, the letter, as a trace, for example, supports the signifier and not simply represents a maternal challenge to the symbolic order of the father. Like identification, the concept of a unary trace both supports and challenges the symbolic order. It challenges the imaginary uses of the father and the master signifier, but at the same time represents the groundless foundation of the name and the Symbolic in the empty void (Real).

S_1 can also be thought as a thought, whereas S_1–S_2 is thinking or a story looking for a thinker (to use Bion's words) to help the story be naught once more. The story that keeps everyone busy, or that does not stop from being spoken, is being passed on in search of a thinker that could decipher it back into being much to do about nothing. Thought is a naught that can be taught.

This phenomenon is equivalent to how the imaginary aspect of the Name of the Father in Lacan functions as a stop-gap of the lack within the symbolic order. The gap in the order appears to be closed by the worthiness of a name. But the symbolic aspect of the Name of the Father emerges out of the Real of the unary trace. In this I disagree with Lacan that the unary trace is the same as the I(O) that represents the ego-ideal. I argue that the unary **trait** may be the same as I(O), or the imaginary aspect of the Name of the Father, but the unary trace refers to a link between the Symbolic and the Real or to how Lacan views the name as emerging from "This." The latter is what the name surrounds, for example in the paradigmatic Biblical name: "I am Who (This) this I am."

The narcissism of small differences, associated with the unary trait (rather than the unary trace), is used to engage in hair splitting or disagreeing for disagreement sake in order to make small distinctions (**with** distinction) and establish territorial allegiances and claim ownerships of various kinds. The unary trait may be used to oppose for the sake of opposition, or for purposes of sectarianism, on the basis of a very small margin of difference. For example, each theorist may build a new theory out of a small group of ideas, instead of illuminating aspects of great ideas and using this as a platform from which to generate beneficent and generous transformations of the symbolic structure.

This is the difference between making a name for oneself, or building the imaginary aspect of the Name of the Father, and using the absolute difference of the name to manifest permutations and evolutions within the symbolic/psychic structure.

These differences allude to the difference between unary trait and trace. The insignia of the ego-ideal, and the medals of honor of the Other are traits, while the unary trace represents subjective destitution, the headless subject, and the void itself.

The distinction without distinction is the nameless name or the unary trace as the signifier of the void. A trait that can be taught is not the naught of thought. The naught of thought is a unary trace. Lacan's *matheme* I(O) is a unary **trait** or S_1–S_2, whereas a unary **trace** is better represented by an S_1–S_0 relationship.

Lacan says that the totality of a circle can be reduced to any point of the circle. Any point along the line of the circumference of a circle represents a vanishing point, a micro-circle, or the place where the circle can be folded back on itself. This folding or vanishing point for a totality or a whole structure is the unary trace. This is the point where the subject becomes a no subject and the no subject becomes a subject.

Russell's paradox

In his seminar "On Identification," Lacan (1960–1) takes a great detour from the topic of identification in psychoanalysis to examine Russell's paradox in philosophy and mathematics. I believe that the logic of this detour, rather than being circumstantial and purely "intellectualoid" in nature, represents Lacan's attempt to account for the structure of oppositions and contradictions ingrained or built into the structure of identification and development.

Negation or difference is built into the structure of identification, and identification is built into the structure of self–other oppositions, at the same time that negation/opposition and identification as sameness can be differentiated from each other. Far from being solely pathological or breeding psychopathology, negation and opposition constitute an integral part of a normal process of identification. Identity is a form of non-identity, and non-identity is a form of identity. The clinical and social problem remains, however, of how to differentiate the healthy from the pathological versions of both identity and non-identity. In the postmodern world it has become abundantly clear that identity does not simply correspond to health and non-identity to pathology. Under modernity, assimilation to a single form of national, cultural, and linguistic identity was considered necessary for health, but in a postcolonial world, biculturalism or cultural diversity has become the normative ideal.

Erikson differentiated identity from identification by arguing that identity requires that identification with others be more than a simple reproduction or imitation of the other. Identification has to become the subject's own identity. Identification requires that the subject both affirm and negate the Other and the subject in very precise and distinct ways.

Freud (1937), for example, wrote that generosity and kind-heartedness were qualities associated with the alleged harmony of the ego, whereas miserliness and hostility were quantities of the id. In the developed character, the strength of the ego prevails over the strength of the id, or quantitative factors become qualitative. This refers to the question of identification involved in the formation of the ego-ideal. According to Freud, the ideal qualities of generosity and kindness are formed by identification with what is opposite to the tendencies/quantities of miserliness and hostility that have been abandoned. A child identifies with the generosity and kindness he/she is shown by his/her parents. However, such generosity and kindness may have been there all along since Freud grants that at the beginning the ego and the id evolve out of a single matrix. The actions of parents strengthen certain traits and weaken others.

The duality between self and Other also exists within the self and within the Other. If the child represents the id or desire and the parent represents the law, the law also exists within the child and so does desire within the parent or Other. It is as if the opposite qualities within the child required the relative reinforcement from the same qualities in the parent via the process of identification. At the same time, however, opposite qualities are also preserved in the Other or the Unconscious of both self and other.

Independence is achieved via identification with a parent, but the identification is the affirmation of a contrary wish or desire to that which is being negated/ repressed via the identification. The identification resolves the opposition between parent and child but also the opposition between contrary feelings held by the child towards the parent. Instead of homosexual love, or hate, for example, there will be a love for ideals or ideas. In the case of homosexuality, the same could be said for heterosexual love. The ideals substitute for the parent, but also for the censored love and hate felt towards the parent of the same or opposite sex. In fact, identification is a way in which the opposite tendencies and opinions are repressed. Sameness evokes difference at the same time that difference is preserved in sameness.

A common example of this is how imitation can be used for purposes of rebellion and ridicule rather than conformity. The hostility or defiance that is opposite to identification love can be safely revealed through mimicry and imitation. What is usually concealed via identification is revealed via a performance of the same identification.

In this instance, identification fails since imitation remains other-centered whereas the autonomy of the ego is revealed in performing identification in the form of an imitation. True autonomy is revealed via heteronomy, whereas heteronomy, or the will/desire of the Other, is transmitted by the subject advancing or positing identification as his/her own choice/principle or transcendent presupposition. When the subject deliberates or thinks, in that space where subjects believe they are exercising their freedom as subjects (of association and expression), it is precisely the place where the efficiency of the heteronomous structure is being transmitted and reproduced.

In the case of an ego-identification, the ego is represented by identification as if the identity provided by the identification was of his/her own making. In contrast to this, when the question of identification is examined from the point of view of the relationship between the subject and the signifier, the subject becomes replaced by the agency of the letter and the signifier rather than by the figure of the ego or of a social master. Although in speech words may be those of the subject or the Other, the subject does not own the signifier any more than the signifier owns the subject qua nothing.

Lacan points out that Russell's paradox begins with a question:

> This set of all the sets which do not include themselves, does it include itself or does it not include itself? In one case or another it's going to collapse into contradiction. Because if, as it might appear, it includes itself, we find ourselves in contradiction with the start which said that it was a question of sets that did not include themselves. On the other hand, if it does not include itself, how can we except it precisely from what is given by this definition, namely that it does not include itself.
>
> (IX: 9)

According to Cantor's set theory, a set is simply a collection of elements of some kind. Set theory is related to the concept of identification because the latter involves the activity of recognizing and identifying an object as belonging to a specific group, class, or set.

The elements contained in a group, class, or set may be other sets, and a set may even contain itself. For example, the set of mathematical ideas is itself a mathematical idea, so it contains itself. A set of non-mathematical ideas would not contain itself. The set would be a mathematical idea but not its content. Here there is no apparent contradiction: A is A or a set is a mathematical idea and B is B or the content of a set is not a mathematical idea. For example, individual human beings, plants, things, etc., would not be mathematical ideas. Contradiction for formal logic only appears at the next meta-level of the set of all sets.

Russell considered a set X defined by the fact that X does not contain itself, and the set Y of all sets X that do not contain themselves. Russell then asked if Y contains itself? If it does, then since all sets contained in Y are sets that by definition do not contain themselves, Y cannot contain itself. If, on the other hand, Y does not contain itself, then it satisfies the definition for inclusion in Y, and so it does contain itself. Either way we arrive at a contradiction. No matter how we approach the question, the result is self-contradictory.

For psychoanalytic purposes, Russell's paradox can be applied to the division of the subject. An example of this would be North American comedian Groucho Marx's famous statement that "I don't care to belong to a club that accepts people like me as members." But what if hypothetically he joined every club that wouldn't have him? If he joined then he wouldn't be a member, and if he wouldn't be a member then he would join: if yes, then no; if no, then yes.

Exclusive clubs are supposed to convey upon its members a trait of distinction or uniqueness. Marx's statement is absurd unless we have an understanding of the division of the subject into conscious and unconscious dimensions, or at least where the division or the defense itself is unconscious. The division itself is predicated on contradiction. You can only be on one side or the other, so long as the other side is temporarily excluded.

On the one hand, Groucho Marx sees himself as superior or unique (in reference to the group); on the other hand, he sees himself as inferior or as lacking the trait of distinction or uniqueness represented by the group or that represents the group. On one side of the fence of defense, he is superior to the other or the group, while on the Other he is inferior, or at least an ordinary commoner. The contradictory statement rests on a supposed distinction between the superior and inferior status of self and other, the individual and the group. But as soon as the comparison between self and other, individual and group, is reduced or self-referenced to a division within/between a conscious and a temporal or temporarily unconscious subject, then the contradiction and the appearance of absurdity disappears.

The set X could be composed of individuals with self-consciousness who are bothered or are unhappy with a characteristic or trait of their personality. At the same time, the set X does not include itself, because those same individual members of the set are not bothered by the same characteristic that they reported being bothered by. Those individuals, who have self-consciousness at the same time, in the same place, and in the same respect, do not have self-consciousness.

An analysand complained that productive use of her time at work was compromised by what she called random walks around her office. When the analyst focused on her difficulty with focused attention and asked whether she was bothered by hearing back from the analyst that she had a problem with attention, she denied being bothered by the question but then shifted to saying that she did not regard random walks as a problem and that staying in one task is a linear non-creative use of time. In contrast to this, random walks around the office are indeed a very positive and creative deed.

This analysand could report her own shortcoming or problem, but if she heard her own message about her flaw back from the analyst or the figure that represents the law (in her mind and the social laws that regulate the profession), then her response was to deny it. The defensive shifting between these two sides of her self is something that is unconscious, although the two sides of her division are not.

In the case of my patient, the paradox amounts to the wish or to the saying that things exist that do not exist. By the same token the denial that something does not exist implies the possibility that it could. In this example, the force of both desire and a defense against desire mediates the attribute or judgment of existence or inexistence.

Russell's own response to the paradox was his *theory of types*. Recognizing that self-reference lies at the heart of the paradox, Russell's basic idea was that paradox and self-contradiction can be avoided by arranging all statements into a hierarchy. The lowest level refers to the individual case. The next level refers to sets of individuals or groups that, psychoanalytically speaking, can also be considered the other of the self. The next level is the set of groups that is equivalent to the other of society. Finally, the group and the society are self-referenced back into the self via the Lacanian concept of the Other as the unconscious or the law within the self. In the formal logic proposed by Russell, you avoid contradiction by splitting/dividing the two sides of the contradiction into the different levels, types, or dimensions. A particular statement applies only to the same level or type.

However, by following the continental European and Asian tradition of dialectical logic, psychoanalysis can arrive at a different articulation of the principle of identity and non-identity, affirmation and denial, contradiction and non-contradiction.

Russell's work, and those of others that followed, can be considered attempts to rescue formal logic and the empiricist principle of non-contradiction or non-self-contradiction from the paradoxes posed by contradiction. According to the principle of non-contradiction, scientific disciplines should be both consistent (free of contradiction), and complete (powerful enough to prove the truth, or falsity, of all relevant statements). However, these attempts suffered severe blows when Kurt Gödel proved the incompleteness of all formal systems, and when Paul Cohen showed that in formal systems, the truth or falsity of some important mathematical theorems was simply undecidable. According to Gödel, undecidable propositions could only be possibly proven by appealing to arguments outside the particular system or perspective in question (Irvine, 2009).

Negative dialectics

Contrary to formal logic, the law of dialectical logic is that everything is mediated and therefore everything is itself and at the same times not itself. A is non-A because A is B. A is B and B is A because both exist only as difference. A is A or not B and at the same time A is B because the meaning of both terms depends on the differences between them. To claim for two different things that they are the same, at the same moment, is contradiction.

The law of dialectical logic is contradiction. This, however, is not destructive; on the contrary, opposites are interdependent and constitute relationships among distinct terms within a structure. The structure is not only different from its contradictory moments, but also more than them. The structure is a Third in which opposites are in a systematic relation with each other.

But the whole is not unity but *unicity* or *unariness* in the form of emptiness. The Other is lacking, holy or of the nature of a hole, empty or conspicuously absent. The Other is lacking because for the Other, the Other of the Other is simply the self. The self is the Other negated. But the true self is the Self that includes the Other and its own negation or the negation of the ego by the Other. To include the Other, the self has to get past the reified ego and the reified or imaginary Other.

Conversely, the same thing could be revealed by saying that the self is lacking and that everything is Other. In this case the Other is a One that includes self and other. To include the self the Other has to get past the reification of both self and other. The same principle or One can be revealed as either self or other. The One is either completely self or completely other. The same principle can be revealed in either side of the contradiction and in contradiction or non-contradiction.

The Law of Non-Contradiction forms a standard part of traditional, formal, Aristotelian logic. It states that a proposition and its negation cannot both be true of the same thing, at the same time, in the same respect. For many scientists this is a fundamental law of logic and a necessary principle of rational thought. If this is correct, dialectical thought must be rejected on purely logical grounds, for it quite explicitly violates this law.

According to dialectical thought, propositions need not be either true or false because other values are possible. In them, therefore, the traditional Law of the Excluded Middle does not hold. It is possible to develop systems in which the Law of Non-Contradiction is not valid.

It is logically possible to make valid statements that are contradictory in form. However, dialectical reason goes much further than this. It claims that not only are such statements possible but, for certain purposes, they are essential. For concrete things are necessarily in relation to other things, which are essentially changeable; and, according to dialectic, for a correct understanding of these features of things, it is ultimately necessary to recognize their contradictory nature and use contradictory forms of expression to describe them.

For purposes of the reader's convenience, and for the sake of my argument, I will review the identity principle in logic, although this can be easily found in any logic textbook. In the classical example, I will replace Socrates with Jesus, not because of any imagined hierarchy or preference for one over the other, but simply because the mortality or death of Jesus lends itself better to the dialectic of the presumed non-mortality or immortality of the imaginary body.

The Law of the Excluded Middle goes as follows,

If *P* is the proposition:

> *Jesus is mortal or dead*

then the Law of the Excluded Middle holds that the logical disjunction:

> *Either Jesus is mortal/dead or Jesus is not mortal and is alive or immortal*

is true by virtue of its form alone. The "middle" position, that Jesus is neither mortal nor immortal, is excluded by formal logic, and therefore either the first possibility (*Jesus is mortal*) or its negation (*Jesus is not mortal*) must be true.

The law is also known as the law (or principle) of the excluded third. Another name for this law is "there is no third (possibility)".

From a psychoanalytic perspective the unconscious is the third (consciousness and its object, or self and other, being the first and second) that is excluded from the conscious, thereby dividing the psyche and the subject. Instrumental techno-cratic reason that establishes criteria of objective validity and performance by its very definition represses aspects of experience that are essential for human activity and well-being. Either this or that, true or false, excludes the possibility of a struc-tural relation between true and false, reality and illusion or fiction. In the formal either/or logic, the either does not include the or (even if it is not mentioned), nor vice versa.

The Lacanian Symbolic is the third: Jesus is both dead and alive, and so are human beings. Jesus' body is mortal, yet his body can be seen or perceived in images and visions, and his mind is immortal or at least will live for a long period of time or for as long as the text of the Gospels survives. Alternatively, he is neither mortal nor immortal. Not mortal because his body/mind lives, and not immortal because he died. Mind and body, life and death, are neither one nor two: from this perspective, and as applied to the theory of drives, both monism and dualism would be incorrect or at least partial perspectives.

Human beings are alive, yet their consistency and completeness is imaginary or dream-like. Life processes are completely permeated by death processes, at both the physical and mental levels: birth and death cannot be separated and in fact could be re-named with the neologism *birdeath*. At the bodily level, cells are dying and new cells are being born on an on-going basis. At the mental level, although brain cells or neurons don't die, in one form or another, death is always present as an event horizon.

In the case of another analysand, who experienced the death of the father at an early age, her life became permeated by an imminent sense of doom. Although she reports not being that affected by the father's death at the time of his passing, her relationship to her father became transformed into a life-and-death struggle within herself. At some point she no longer knew whether she was alive or dead: although she was alive, she felt dead inside.

Knowledge and types of rationality

Turning to the law of contradiction proper, it is important to note that in Europe there are two "types" of logic, one founded on the law of contradiction, the other founded on the neglect of the law of contradiction. One is a dual form of knowledge, the other non-dual. Usually a distinction is made between an empiricist tradition and a hermeneutic or at least non-empiricist tradition, and between a logic for the natural sciences and a logic for the social sciences, but at this time I will consider the more narrow distinction between a law of contradiction and a law of non-contradiction.

Hegel inherited from Kant a distinction between Understanding and Reason. Understanding is definite and holds firmly to the differences between objects and phenomena, but Reason is negative and dialectical. According to Reason there are no differences between affirmation and negation, but for Understanding this difference is all-important. All objects, or concepts, are viewed by Understanding non-dialectically and by Reason dialectically.

But which one is the law of contradiction? The law of non-contradiction is the law that forbids different things to be one thing. It creates distinction and opposition and at the same time singles out one thing in the form of an analytical judgment. For formal logic, non-contradiction is the ultimate test of reality and truth.

In contrast to this, the law of contradiction allows opposite or distinct things to be one thing or One. By allowing contradiction or duality, the law of contradiction paradoxically eliminates contradiction. There is no contradiction between saying that there is no object, and that only the subject exists, and saying the opposite: that there is no subject, and that only the object exists. Therefore, the law of contradiction can be seen as the law of non-contradiction or non-duality, and the law of non-contradiction is the law of contradiction and duality.

In Kant's system, Reality (the Thing-in-Itself) is divorced not only from Logic but also from experience. In Hegel's system they become confounded. As Zizek (1989) has pointed out, in Kant the thing-in-itself remains as a positive entity albeit outside the bounds of time and space, and of the categories of logic and language. However, that which exceeds the grasp of thought and perception makes genuine or new Real experience possible. The Real points to the double meaning of the term experience. Experience can refer to the already known and to the past and the future (defined by the past), or it can refer to something in the here and now that exceeds the already known and formulated.

In the Hegelian and Lacanian interpretation, the Symbolic (logic and language) and the Real (the thing-in-itself) mutually determine each other. Language generates the conditions for the indefinable or a beyond language, at the same time that the Real, as a pure negativity, circumscribes what is possible or impossible within language. The thing-in-itself is a no-thing rather than a thing. "It" indicates a void within the Symbolic that is a plenum within the Real but that lies beyond (not without) any definition or formulation. This interpretation of Lacanian ideas is consistent with the philosophy of science of Gaston Bachelard (1940).

> The truly scientific philosophy is for Bachelard a "philosophy of no" (1940) which refuses to be confirmed within any given doctrine and which therefore promotes an openness that is in keeping with the open and unfinished quality of scientific progress itself.
>
> (Macey, 2000: 26)

The Real manifesting as a void within the Symbolic generates a perpetual movement and transformation within the Symbolic, but without ever becoming a final idea or synthesis as seen in the common interpretation of the Hegelian system. In this sense, the Real or the thing-in-itself functions within the power of negation at work within the Symbolic. In addition, the power of negation can also be redoubled as seen in the negation of the negation characteristic of dialectical logic.

I propose that the negation of the negation can have at least three different meanings. In formal logic the antithesis or the null hypothesis, as the negation of the thesis, could lead to a vindication of the original thesis. The antithesis, or the fallibility of the thesis, results in either the thesis or the antithesis being proven wrong. Negation is used as a tool for proving/probing the truth or falseness of a proposition. In dialectical logic negation is used as a process or as existing at different levels of logical organization.

At the first level of negation, A is not B and B is not A, and neither term includes one another. At the second level of a dialectical negation of the negation, A is B or not not B and B is A or not not A. Finally, at the third and final level of negative dialectics, the negation of the negation leads to non-identity or emptiness between and within both thesis and antithesis. A is neither A nor B and B is neither B nor A.

According to Adorno (1966) the aim of negative dialectics is to rid dialectics of the intention of achieving, gaining, or accumulating a positive idea by way of negation. Positivism, empiricism, and materialism attempt to achieve something positive by negating the subject but end up turning the object into a fetish, nonetheless. Conversely, idealism attempts the opposite objective by negating the object and turning the subject into an object instead. When emptiness is considered the final fruit of the dialectical process, since emptiness itself is devoid of idea or concept, it precisely accords with the task proposed by Adorno's negative dialectics.

Contradiction is inherent to thought or reason. Concepts and ideas never match up with the object or the subject because as soon as identification takes place, whether at the level of the object or of the subject, an opposite idea also arises along with it. As a Zen saying goes, "If you set up a target, you invite an arrow." Identity as an idea is necessarily untrue or different. Thus, with the negative dialectics of emptiness you always end up empty handed and without a fixed standpoint or target. Every concept or idea, or identification, brings with it a compulsive identification. To halt such a compulsion, in negative dialectics, the direction of conceptuality is turned towards non-identity or non-identification.

Non-identity and non-identification are not an essence in the traditional Western sense. In the West essence constitutes the first principles, the idea behind the thing. In dialectical materialism and critical theory, the essence constitutes the critical reason that debunks and articulates the reality behind the appearances. Within existentialism, Sartre argued that existence precedes the essence for two reasons: first, because he reduced the essence to an idea or a definition of existence which takes place after the fact. Second, because he does not conceive of the possibility that nothingness could be the essence, which nonetheless it is not. The idea does not occur to him, because the existentialist void is a dualistic and non-symbolic void of sheer absence without presence.

A different and almost Mahayana Buddhist notion of the void can be found in Lacan's concept of ex-sistence. When we appear on the scene, when we are born, when we turn up, we are outside of or no longer *sistence. Sistence* is the unborn and unrealized aspect of being or of the subject that disappears with manifest being or with birth. *Sistence* does in fact refer to the essence of existence except that the word essence does not capture it. *Sistence* came before existence and yet at the same time constitutes what being or existence means beyond itself. The subject is born and manifests with the word or the signifier. Yet the unborn aspect of the subject or what the subject is within the Real disappears when the signifier represents the birth of the subject. The unborn subject of the Real goes under the signifier and remains non-identical with it. Better even, the unborn is revealed with the fact of the signifier not being identical to itself. The unborn immortal life manifests as the aspect of the signifier that is not identical to itself.

The unborn Being/unbeing and/or the subject of the Real are neither comprehensible in concepts nor demonstrable through sensory experience. As Adorno (1966) writes, "In lieu of any critical authority for Being we get a reiteration of the mere name" (p. 71).

Emptiness as the final fruit of the dialectical process, the something beyond contradiction, is not an idea or a concept but simply a word used for heuristic purposes. Emptiness, like Derrida's *differance*, is permanently under erasure. Reason corrects itself in its logical and critical course and progression. Critical reason is finally the critique of reason itself whether formal, dialectical, instrumental, or critical. The foundation of logic and truth in emptiness is what establishes both in the first place and what prevents that any idea or ideology becomes fixed and totalitarian. Potential emptiness cannot be formalized. As Adorno put it, nonidentity is the secret telos of identification.

Within psychoanalysis, halting the compulsion of ego-identifications and using negative dialectics to turn the psyche towards nonidentity or nonidentification is equivalent to a critique of ego-ideals and identifications.

If someone says I am English, then this connotes both a national identity and a linguistic identity. In addition, a race may also be implied in this identity. From this it follows that if you live in England and you are from India and speak Hindi, then certainly the first group may not consider you to be English. This would also be confirmed by skin color. The facts that you live in England and are from India and speak Hindi signify that you are not English and that you lack the trait that defines the English. In this example, and in England, Indian signifies not English or the negation of English. This is particularly the case if large groups of Hindus are living in England.

According to formal logic, and the principle of non-contradiction, the propositions English and not English, or identity (unary trait) and the negation of identity, have very particular psycho-social-political ramifications. On the other hand, if the principle of contradiction is allowed and appreciated, then not-English does not necessarily contradict the principle of being English. In fact, it may make someone even more English because not-English may be consistent, for example, with core English values of gentleness/civilization and a cosmopolitan or universal education. So if English identity can over-include not-being English, in a narrow sense, then the principle of non-identity allows a subject to be English and Indian, or not-English, and, therefore, English in its true sense. Non-identity, or the emptiness of Englishness, allows for true identity and not-identity at the same time but without synthesizing either one of them.

Dialectical negation of the negation is not some grand positive idea, synthesis, or project, but is contained within or is immanent to the negative or to emptiness itself. Zizek's reading of negative dialectics follows Adorno's interpretation of Hegel. However, I also disagree with Zizek with respect to the idea of the negative or of emptiness. For Zizek, as for Western thought in general, emptiness or nothingness is a form of absence or lack. The Eastern Buddhist notion of emptiness coincides with the notion of a lack when it defines emptiness in terms of the impermanence of all things. The notion of loss, and therefore of lack, presupposes the basic idea and reality of change. But emptiness is a presence that is not an idea or a thing, although it can also appear as *das Ding* (the thing as seen from the perspective of no-thing).

Primarily, emptiness is a form of *jouissance* or a level of experience that Lacan (1972–3) said we know nothing of. Emptiness of the thing-in-itself is a third form of *jouissance* that is constructive rather than inconvenient or destructive. Please refer to my prior work for the definition of *jouissance* (Moncayo, 2008).

Ultimately, the logic of contradiction leads to the negation of the negation and to the experience of emptiness. But as aforementioned, emptiness cannot be separated from *das Ding* or the unary trace as the zero included within the One and the One included within the zero. I will return to this further on.

The Real as the symbolic effectiveness of a vanishing point instant

In reference to a knowing of *das Ding*, we must consider whether the possibility exists of knowing through the senses without the senses, understanding, or reason. Is the pure form of the negative, or the experience of *das Ding* as the no-thing, the same as what could be called *sensibilia* prior to the capture of the senses and their objects via perceptual understanding? Is this what the no-thing or A not being either A or B refers to? I am differentiating between the senses before and after perception (language, cognition, logic, etc.).

In animals and non-human species, there is an instinctual knowing prior to language, understanding, and reason. An example of this would be the auspicious rooster that, in the dark of the night, interacts with light and time, without confusion, and knows when to crow to announce the coming of the dawn and the sun. This knowing is manifested in the form of energetic intensities and preconceptual actions and sounds that involve the senses but not perception, language, understanding, or reason. The object does not exist as a presupposition for a linguistic subject.

Is emptiness or the quality of A not being A or B the same as what Magritte called the mystery and that is represented in the famous painting of a pipe that he called "This is not a pipe"? Is the object anything beyond its designation and negation within language?

In Magritte's painting rather than simply being a pipe, the pipe is not a pipe, but the pipe is also the not not pipe. This is not a pipe means everything else it could be other than a pipe, in other words the quality of being not-pipe. The pipe includes the non-pipe or everything else. At the same time, the pipe is the non-pipe negated or the not non-pipe, or, in other words, the pipe is absolutely "this" and only "this." The pipe as an affirmation is the negation negated. Everything that went into the production of the pipe or the not-pipe is negated in order to give birth to the pipe as a single event. "This" is also related to Benjamin's (1936) concept of "aura" as the quality of a modern painting in terms of "its unique existence at the place where it happens to be" (p. 125).

But what is the difference between the first and last or third pipe? The first is the naïve reality assumed and imagined to be a pipe, and this corresponds to the identity principle of formal logic. The pipe is A and not B, or C, etc. The second pipe is the non-pipe, meaning all the causes that went into the production of the event pipe as such. The pipe or A is not A, and it is B, C, etc. But the third pipe is the negation of the negation or the absolute difference of the things-in-themselves where the Real appears as the efficiency of a point instant. With the excluded or empty third, the efficiency of the whole or totality appears as evanescence, wherein the totality of causes or the structure disappears and only the event remains as a flashing into the phenomenal world. The universal whole is a fiction that both exists and does not exist. The whole is a fiction because it is emptied out by an event. In relationship to an event, the whole becomes a hole. At the same time, the whole exists both within the hole and within the event.

The event has no inherent nature, because it is produced by a series of causes that have now disappeared, and only appear as "this," or as the One that includes the third as emptiness. Only "this One is," *sensibilia*, the unary trace, or the aesthetic moment, takes place in a single moment or a single point of reality and not via perception or representation. It is the knowing of the non-definable. It is a moment of non-understanding and beyond reason. At the same time it is simply an object or a subject as *das Ding* or the no-thing, the Spirit as a bone, as Hegel and Bodhidharma would have it.

In a famous story of transmission of the Zen teaching, Bodhidharma, the Indian ancestor who brought the Zen teaching to China, asked his four disciples to say something to demonstrate their understanding. When the fourth disciple remained silent, Bodhidharma responded: "You have my marrow."

Das Ding, or the unary trace as it refers to identity, represents the absolute difference of the things-in-themselves, or their lack of inherent nature. The pipe, or any event, being what it is, also lacks the third, or the series of causes that produced it. But rather than as cause, the third now appears as emptiness, as the absent unconscious that is grounding this particular consciousness of an event or event-consciousness. Something is perceived from the perspective of infinity or of the unconscious, both as the unknown in the sense of the unknowable or inde-finable, and the unknown in the sense of the totality of causes that remain invisible or that have now disappeared. The event does not simply appear out of nowhere, although it does appear this way, nor does the totality totally disappear, since the totality is also present in the event. An event neither appears nor disappears. The event is not only arising just now and at the same time has never happened before. It is therefore neither before nor after anything, or it includes its own before and after.

The unary trace is composed of a piece of *sensibilia*, has links to the Real of the body (the marrow, for example), and is organized by dialectical logic: it is some-thing and not something, or Symbolic and Real, at the same time. In addition, the One of a trace in the Real can be differentiated from synthetic unity or judgments constructed by dialectical logic. The structure of dialectical polarities in language (signifier and signified) is a universal, whereas speech or the speaking being, including silence, is always something unary, the concrete abstract, an S_1 or unary trace.

The unary trace is a traceless trace that manifests in a real present moment and not as a conceived chain of moments or representations in time. Unary trace is a representation of a single subject/object in this moment.

By the same token, the Real can be defined as the effectiveness of a point instant: the point of reality where existence becomes the same as non-existence and the subject as metaphor in speech becomes the same as the subject qua nothing.

Each thing is present in one place and is completely unrelated not only to another similar thing but also to the same thing in the next moment, let alone in another place. But the difference between A is A (A=A) or A is not B (meaning that A has a unique set of causes and conditions that are different from B's), and A is not A (A≠A) or not B, etc., is the same difference than between imaginary oneness and the unary One that includes zero. Imaginary oneness is self-created and has a unique set of constructed causes (the ego representations or whatever the ego thinks is special about him/her), whereas in the unary One the cause as such is absent or lacking and this marks the thing with the mark of the no-thing, the markless mark, or the distinction of no-distinction. Zero as the place-holder for the excluded third makes each thing independent from one another.

This distinction between Imaginary and Real independence of things/phenomena can also be applied to thought. Discrimination on the basis of non-discrimination, or thinking on the basis of not thinking, signifies that the constructed conceptual world can be built upon a Real foundation not of objects but of the things in themselves, which is the same as saying nothing or emptiness. A form of thought built on no-thought or thoughts in search of a non-thinker.

The law of identity, which is the same as the law of non-contradiction (the law that forbids contradiction), is the law of a constructed separation or duality between this against that, self versus other, and truth over falseness. The law (of non-contradiction) erects a wall of separation that excludes the middle third between extremes. This wall is similar (although not identical) to what separates conscious and allowed experience from the repressed unconscious. The wall dictates or prescribes how and the way people are supposed to think about what is permissible and acceptable in reality. But the difference with the Freudian model and what comes closer to Lacan's notion of the Möbius strip, and to Bion's notion of reversible perspectives, is that either side of the extremes can be repressed. Consciousness can be repressed as much as the unconscious, and consciousness can be unconscious and the unconscious conscious.

The law of non-identity or of contradiction allows for multiple identities and contradictions, for middle areas between extremes, and for extremes to mutually determine each other. In the case of natural phenomena, such as light and dark, the extremes never exist without the middle areas between light and dark. Therefore, it is possible to argue that the law of contradiction is the real law, whereas the law of non-contradiction (either light or dark with the middle excluded) is the constructed or artificial one. At the same time, although the presence or absence of light conditions the presence or absence of darkness, and there are middle areas between the two, in emptiness, darkness and light are entirely independent from each other. In the presence of darkness, the absence/presence of the sun is erased and replaced by emptiness. In the presence of light, the absence/presence of darkness is erased and replaced by emptiness. The effectiveness of darkness has cancelled itself out in the phenomenon known as light. The night has become light and the light night. The light does not repress darkness since in the light there is also darkness, and in the darkness light. But we don't call light darkness, and in darkness light does not interfere.

The instance of the subject: the continuity and evanescence of the unary trace

Today it has become trendy to speak of the death of the ego or of the subject. This theme became a key feature of postmodernism and of poststructuralism. In a similar way, Lacan became the standard bearer of a critique of ego psychology and of a battle cry to return to Freud, although the trend towards ego psychology had begun with Freud himself. In addition, the influence of the Buddhist doctrine of no-self on postmodern culture has been significant and pervasive.

But without the ego, what gives unity and stability to the experience of the subject? Freud (1919) regarded the ego as the agency that unified the various agencies and experiences of the subject.

> In actual fact, indeed, the neurotic patient presents us with a torn mind divided by resistances. As we analyze it and remove the resistances, it grows together; the greater unity which we call his ego fits into itself all the instinctual impulses which before had been split off and held apart from it.
>
> (p. 161)

In the quote above, Freud conceived of the ego as a principle of unity within the psyche. Because of defenses, and the division of the psyche, the drives have become partial, and developed competing interests and desires. In *Beyond the Pleasure Principle*, and Freud's second theory of drives, it is the Life drive or Eros that strives towards greater unities, not the ego: "It grows together" (1919, p. 161). Lacan's definition of the aim of analysis follows the same idea: "Where It was the subject must come into existence" (p. 45). The ego "fitting in" the drives is the principle of mastery and of taming the animal or the Id instead of converging with its nature or "It nature." Ego unity is imaginary and represents the unity of Fascism and what Lacan (1969) calls the master's discourse. Symbolic unity is the unity of the Symbolic order and the signifier, not of the ego.

For Lacan, the signifier/subject, as a signifier of desire, helps regulate *jouissance* and is itself regulated by transformations within *jouissance*. There is the One of the signifier and then there is the One of *jouissance* or of the Real as a plenum. They both converge under the letter that Lacan calls S_1. S_1–S_0 would be another way of writing the relationship between an ordering symbolic element and the experience of the Real.

Roland Barthes (1984) and Lacan spoke of the subject and Saussure's signifier in similar terms. The subject of the sentence holds together both language and subject alike. The subject is a metaphor (not an entity) that is constantly changing (through metonymy) while remaining stable at the same time. Because the subject is the subject of a sentence, the signifying subject is under perpetual flux, while the name of the subject functions as an anchoring point for this perpetual motion within language. The Name stands still as a unary trace within language.

It is the quality or modality of *jouissance* that also helps bind the subject together. The subject of *jouissance* is the Lacanian subject of the Real, which is empty of definitions within language. As soon as one tries to define the agency of a Real subject within language, an empirical ego becomes reified or falsely constructed. Freud (1919) points to this when he refers to "the greater unity which we call his ego . . ." (p. 161).

Strictly speaking, the ego is simply a name ("which we call") within language that points to something (the greater unity) beyond language. What Lacan calls the One in the Real beyond language incorporates "into itself all the drives which before had been split off and held apart from it."

The subject as a Real and Symbolic *unary* traceless trace is not susceptible to reification. The unary trace is simply an *instance*, not in the sense of agency, but in the sense of a vanishing point instant. There are two important unary traces for the subject: the specular image of the body, and the name or names of the subject; one is linked to the ideal ego and the other to the ego-ideal. Both of these unary traces locate the subject within imaginary and cultural-linguistic-symbolic coordinates and provide continuity across time and space. A name has the distinctive function of pointing to identity, and language has the function of providing speaking beings with an individual and group identity. Through language, John Smith or Juan Perez can identify themselves as belonging to a particular cultural group. John and Juan identify with language to the same extent that language represents them or the signifier represents the subject (John) for another signifier (Spanish Juan).

The law of identity (of non-contradiction) is the law of the constancy of our cognitions that functions on the basis of naming and nomination within language. The name or the signifier gives the subject duration in time and location. But the signifier or a name of the subject does not require the reification of an ego agency in order to explain the order of the subject or subjective experience. It is only in the Imaginary or the imagined nature that the ego becomes reified as an agency. The ego becomes the cause of his/her own experience instead of the subject being caused by language and various forms of *jouissance* or energetic intensities.

It is the image of the body, or the body as object, and the name of the body, or the body as subject, that actually provide the continuity in experience that is usually attributed to the ego. Both allow me to say today that I am the same person I was yesterday. **Strictly speaking, the ideal ego and the ego-ideal are unary traces or instances and moments rather than substantial entities.** They are unary traces, rather than permanent entities, because the image disappears once the body is no longer in front of the clear mirror or the mirror of the mind, and the name, like speech, vanishes once it has been uttered. Both causes, although they persist throughout the person's life, and stand in for the subject, are themselves constantly being replaced by the void of inherent or substantial identity.

Without the constancy provided by the unary trace, neither cognition nor intelligible speech or purposive action becomes possible. Re-cognition with regards to identity requires formal uncontradicted experience: I am me, not you, I am John, not Juan, and I am this (Anglo-American) not that (Latino-American). But when the unary trace of the subject becomes covered over by the project of becoming someone or something in the Imaginary, then the actual subject becomes an entity known as the ego. The ego becomes an object of the drive and of the desire of the Other. In this sense, one can speak of the imaginary unity of the ego being the same as the unity of the (sexual) drive.

In the project of becoming the object cause of the Other's desire, the past becomes the future and the future the past or future anterior. Yet the "I" of yesterday is not the same as the "me" of today. Both are instances of instantaneous and evanescent being in the present moment that is not wholly determined by past experience.

In this instance, instantaneous being falls on the side of contradicted experience. The I of yesterday can be in contradiction with the me of today. I am the same person, still Raul, but I am a changed man, and therefore not the same person. The me of today or now is a different Raul.

I am both the same person (a) and not the same person (b). The ego is *a* minus *b*, the same person without the "not being the same person." The subject is "not being the same person" and because of this the subject is able to inhabit the same name or constant metaphor (*b* plus *a*).

The reason I have constancy and identity, and yet can be a changed person at the same time, is because there is no trace of constancy and identity. The law of identity is really a law of constructed identity because the law only exists in our head and not in the things themselves.

Today I am a changed person, not the same person that I was to others in the past, but it still feels like me. This is because the not I is still me in an absolute sense. I am me instead of those others that defined me in the past because I am "naught", the one that was not those others in the past (how I defined myself in contrast to others). The past one that I was and the past others are naught. I am still the one that was no one then and still is no one today.

Because I am still no one today, I can be the One and the name that I am but in a new way in this moment at this time and place. I allow myself, and reality allows me to contradict myself, to be constant in time, yet also different. The not me, or the *naught* that is me, allows me to contradict myself while remaining same in the void of absolute difference. Identity is the constructed relative identity, the cock and bull story, over time and in terms of S_1–S_2 (signifier/signified). *Das Ding* is absolute difference (the no-thing) whereas the Real is the efficiency of the vanishing point of the structure. To conclude this section, I offer a diagram representing the theory advanced thus far.

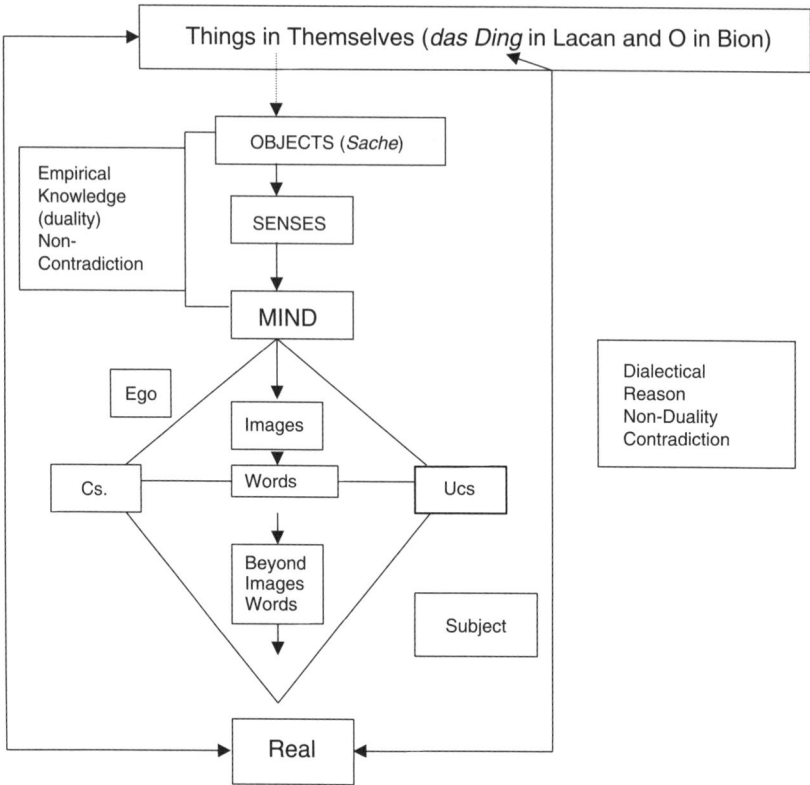

The ego in Freud's theory

As I have argued elsewhere (Moncayo, 2008), the relationship to the environment or to objects is initially primarily narcissistic but narcissistic as distinct from egoistic. Egoism is given by identification with the fantasy object of the other. Following Freud, I have called the latter relative primary narcissism (Moncayo, 2008). During the transition from absolute primary narcissism to relative primary narcissism, the Nirvana principle is also transformed into the pleasure principle. What was a principle of quiescence or of energy in a bound or condensed state (Nirvana principle) becomes a principle of excitation and of defenses against excitation (pleasure principle). Relative primary narcissism is inaugurated by the relationship to the partial object and is ruled by the pleasure principle that organizes both drives and defenses against the drives. At the stage of hallucinatory wish fulfillment, defenses are no more than the tendencies to avoid unpleasure.

Eventually, and after the establishment of the specular image or ideal ego (secondary narcissism), the ego's identification with the father, or the figure of the law, leads to the establishment of the super-ego and the ego-ideal. Both the ideal ego and the ego-ideal become more elaborate forms of both pleasure/desire and defenses against pleasure/desire.

But the basic point is that the rational ego, which is governed by the reality principle rather than the pleasure principle, requires the prior formation of the super-ego and the ego-ideal.

Just like the super-ego was formed through a type of ego identification and involved a modification within narcissism, the so-called rational reality ego presupposes the prior establishment of the ego-ideal. The ego before the super-ego and the ego after the super-ego are not the same ego.

So why does Freud (1914, 1923) speak of the super-ego as a grade or differentiation within the ego, instead of vice versa: the rational ego as an outcome of the development of the ego-ideal? Certainly the adult or mature ego depends on the identifications that concern the ego-ideal, with the qualification that these identifications have become ego-syntonic rather than ego-dystonic (as in the case of the super-ego). Once the ego identifies with social ideals, then the ego is transformed accordingly and these ideas are perceived as emanating from the ego itself. I have argued that the proper name and the patronymic are the first models for this process. Nomination as a paternal metaphor anchors the social form of language for a particular individual rather than simply as the subject of a sentence. Other than the name, the subject as an individual is identical to the subject of a sentence.

The proper name as an identification is recognized as emanating from the ego itself, yet it is the outcome of differentiations/modifications that have already occurred within the ego. The ego-ideal is a differentiation within the ideal ego (not the rational ego), although at the same time the ego-ideal is not a separate agency within the ego. The function of paying attention, for example, is hardly separate from the ideal of paying attention. In addition, the rational ego is also differentiated and evolved under the influence of the ego-ideal. So is there really a difference between the two once the ego-ideal is established? Is there really justification for continuing to speak about the two as being distinct agencies or two separate things?

The identifications that comprise the ego-ideal precipitate differentiations and maturations that strengthen the capacity for attention and rational symbolic thought. But as I said, this capacity is not the same ego that existed prior to the development of the ego-ideal, or is it?

It is difficult to distinguish the ego-ideal from the ego itself, since the ego is also explained as formed by processes of identification with the object or the other.

According to Lacan, the subject is a signifier of the Other, and is inhabited by language and a social, sexual, and cultural history. So why is the ego-ideal a differentiation within the ego if the ego-ideal was not there before? If we think of the ego as emerging from the ideal ego and from the *objet a* prior to that, the ego-ideal as a differentiation within the ego would not make a whole lot of sense. It is the subject of language and culture that re-signifies the ideal ego and the *objet a*.

Perhaps the solution to this dilemma is to think of the proper name as actually linked to the ideal ego and the specular image since most mothers address the child (in front of the mirror) by the child's name. At the same time the specular image and the name could be construed as the mother's imaginary phallus, unless a lack within the image is also formulated. The ideal ego/specular image as the mother's imaginary phallus explains the character of omnipotence associated with the ideal ego. The child is what completes the mother and threatens to make the father expendable.

Once the child moves past the specular image in search of the signifier of the mother's desire, the ego-ideal appears in the horizon of the subject under the Name of the Father. The father as a signifier of the mother's desire now replaces the mother as the object of the child's desire. The child wants what the father has but has to give up the mother and the imaginary phallus in order to get it. This transaction inaugurates the entire realm of substitution and gift giving linked to the symbolic order, and it constitutes the vertex of the phenomenon of identification. From this point of view the ego-ideal is another name for the patronymic or the paternal metaphor as a unary trace that over time re-signifies the bodily and mental states of the child with a new inscription. The subject and the ego-ideal (the paternal metaphor/name) become signifiers within language.

The ego can be understood as the reified name for something that is actually an energetic bodily and mental state that endures across time in the form of a trace or an inscription. In this sense I argue that the ego is the same as the name of the subject. Beyond the name, the ego is simply an aggregate of functions that, to one degree or another, exist in all human beings: attention, memory, thinking, perception, and consciousness. These functions are organized within a symbolic order and the metaphoric order of language.

The energy for these functions arises from the Real It rather than from the Id or the ego. The division between the mind and the body and the division of the mind and the subject is laid down on an undivided Life drive that strives towards greater unities or that "grows together," as Freud says. The Id or the drives evolve out what I call Infinite Life in a way that I will explore in an upcoming section of this chapter. The It or *das Ding*, as the no-thing, is consistent with what Lacan called the pre-subject or unbarred subject and that I will represent as S_0 and the subject of the Real.

The answer to the question of what to call the "maturation point," commonly referred as the ego, ultimately comes from the Real and not from the symbolic or linguistic subject. The Real here is represented by a modality of *jouissance* that was an integral part of absolute primary narcissism and that represents the energetic origins of the ego. And, unfortunately, Freud's ego psychology here becomes haunted by the specter of Jung's theory of the libido. According to Eigen (2009), Winnicott spoke of an unexcited state and of a background of quietude as an original or primary state of the infant, which is unpatterned and unplanned but not chaotic. A radiant and quiescent innocence describes the moment after birth and many momentary experiences of an infant. This is consistent with an undifferentiated state between subject and object.

A reader could object at this point that I have retrogressed to a pre-Freudian and quasi-spiritual and romantic notion of childhood innocence. I don't think so. For one thing, the mythical notion of the innocence of childhood is used to defend against and deny the fact of childhood sexuality and the condition of polymorphous perversion described by Freud. Second, there is a difference between an infant and a child. The state that I was alluding to, as containing energy in a primary bound or quiescent state, refers to an infant and not necessarily to a child. Third, I will follow Lacan's (1964) elaboration of Freudian theory where he distinguishes between perversion and the polymorphous perversion of childhood. It is the presence or absence of the ego of narcissism that differentiates between these two conditions.

In perversion the ego plays a prominent role since the *objet a* is prevented from disappearing by the ego occupying the place of the *a: a*→$ (feces or urine, stand in for the ego, for example). The *a* does not complete the ego as in neurosis, or threaten the ego with aphanisis, disappearance, or malevolent depersonalization, as in psychosis, but, rather, occupies the place of the ego function itself. In the primary state of a beginner's mind or of a radiant and quiescent innocence, the ego and the object are altogether absent. It is this state that explains two things:

1   The energetic origins of the ego-ideal.
2   That there can be differentiation and further development beyond the ego-ideal and towards the Lacanian subject. The Lacanian subject returns full circle to the pre-subject in the form of the subject qua nothing.

The rational reality ego is actually a subject that includes the pre-subject, before the object/ego differentiation, and that can be defined as either self or non-self. It is the subject that retroactively and proactively reaches towards non-duality and the principle that over-includes contradiction, not the ego. Finally, the subject differs from the Jungian concept of the Self because it also functions as a metaphor in language and not only as an archetype of the imagination. The question of the imagination will be addressed in the final chapter of this book.

The ego and the identification with the *sinthome*

In the seminar on the *sinthome*, Lacan says that the registers of experience (RSI) support a bone or an object bone, an *os*object, which characterizes the letter as an *objet a*.

The letter as a different form of writing with the body comes from a different place than the signifier: it comes from the unary trace, or the infinite straight line that Lacan says is equivalent to a circle. This equivalence can be observed in a drawstring bag or sack. The string points to something that lies at each point of a sphere or a circle and that ties the circle together. The many points or holes found along the circumference of a circle point to the pointillist and discontinuous reality of a circle rather than to its imaginary totality.

Related to the question of the letter as a form of writing with the body, in the seminar on the *sinthome*, Lacan also examines the function of the ego in the work of novelist James Joyce. Joyce was an Irish writer considered to be one of the most influential writers of the 20th century. *Ulysses* (1922) is his best-known work. According to Lacan, Joyce was able to avoid psychosis by using his literary work to construct for himself a new ego and a new name. The function of the ego in Joyce and in the *sinthome* plays a different role than in most cases. Usually the function of the ego is involved in writing and in the image of the body that is tied to the ideal ego (i[a]). But the body in the case of the new ego of the *sinthome* is only a *quanta, a q'bit*, a string or trace of *jouissance*. The letter as *a* (as a trace) has been separated from the total image of the ideal ego (i[a]) thanks to the discontinuity and the cuts found within the signifying chain.

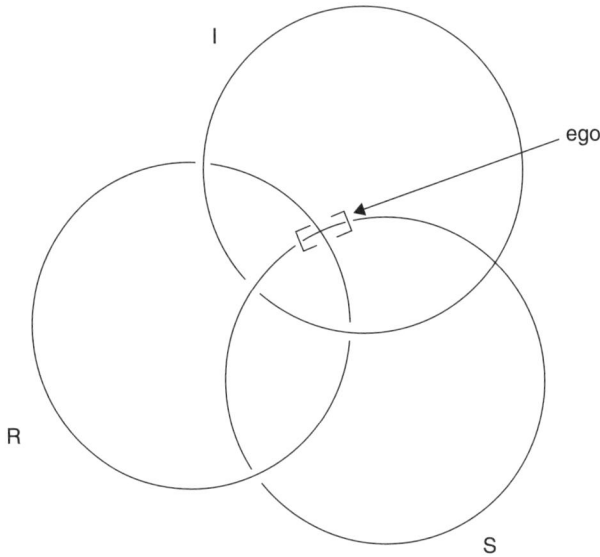

It is the enigmatic function of the ego, as a unary trace or as an infinite straight line, that has a reparatory function. The infinite straight line, or unary trace, is the line that is found inside the brackets that represent the cutting or unknotting of the knot (see above diagram).

Lacan also links the Real with the ego of primary narcissism that is not necessarily without a subject but where there is no discreet relationship between the inside and the outside. There is no relationship in the sense that two terms have not been differentiated that could have a relationship with one another. But the absence of a structural relationship does not mean that the inside and outside are isolated from each other. The unary trace is a trace of the One prior to a differentiation of an inside from an outside. The unary trace constitutes a pre-subject that is recovered or produced (going around a circle twice) via the *sinthome* and the Name of the Father as a new letter or signifier/signification of *jouissance*.

The symbolic subject is produced and reproduced via the signifier and the process of representation. It is in this sense that the subject is an effect of speech and language. The logic of the sentence holds the subject together. And here the signifier is the signifier that, according to Lacan, is ruled by the pleasure principle as the principle of repression and defense (the avoidance of unpleasure). In this instance, the signifier and the subject have some equivalence with the ego-ideal and the super-ego, with the exception that the ego-ideal and the super-ego also have an imaginary dimension, or better still, actually constitute the imaginary dimension of the signifier, the symbolic, and the father.

The purely symbolic signifier is consistent with a definition of the subject in the strict sense outlined by Lacan. The Lacanian subject can also be differentiated from Freud's ego and ego-ideal. If anything, the subject comes closer to the definition that Freud gives of an evolved ego ruled by the reality principle. The signifier is logically organized and is the site of reason or of the cogito. The subject is the ego without the narcissistic dimension of the ego or as a fourth-degree differentiation within narcissism. The second- and third-degree narcissism of the ego fall under the rubric of the ideal ego and the ego-ideal.

Lacan discovers an imaginary dimension of the signifier in the function of meaning and metonymy, or the endless displacement of the word, that never hits the target of invoking a particular form of *jouissance* in the Real. This displacement could be called an imaginary dimension of the rational ego: the more the ego speaks, the less the ego says. This is in fact a definition of the ego-ideal, wherein thinking or speech is confounded with the imaginary project of becoming someone worthy of the recognition of the Other.

The symbolic aspect of the ideal ego and ego-ideal is found in the function of three anchoring points: the specular image, the proper name, and the patronymic. The patronymic, of course, is a reference to the Name of the Father, and to the naming of the subject by the Other. Without this symbolic and unsubstantial dimension of the anchoring point, the subject could not acquire a stable identity within a particular context. I say unsubstantial because the image and the name speak for a subject that otherwise remains indefinable and that has the structure of a Real hole or emptiness. The image and the name are devoid of substantiality (they are a topological bubble and a letter, respectively), or, in other words, the true subject is no subject, and the no subject is a true subject as a bubble and a letter.

In Seminar XXIII, Lacan proposed that Joyce's literary work was his *sinthome* or his way of "making a name for himself" and of supplementing a deficit in his father's symbolic function. The *sinthome* functions as the Name of the Father and as the fourth ring in the Borromean knot. Joyce made a body and a name for himself through his work. In his work, Joyce speaks about the body in great detail, against convention, at the same time that he subverts the rules of the colonizing English language.

Lacan notes that Joyce's name is related to joy, and to *jouissance*, and that it is this *jouissance* that is evoked and comes through in his text and in his deviant use of the signifier and signification.

I argue that when Lacan thinks of the *sinthome* as an ego he is referring to Freud's third form of identification that Lacan called the *einziger Zug* or unary trait. The ego, subject, or self, as a body or a symbolic body, corresponds to the figure of its own negation. Both the ideal ego and the ego-ideal have to be first established and later abandoned in order for the subject to realize its being as a subject (*son être du sujet*). The ideal ego is replaced by the *objet a*, and the ego-ideal is replaced by the signifier of a lack in the Other. The unary trace, as the third form of identification, is the something or the residue of Life that remains as a result of the process that Lacan called subjective destitution. The One, or the unary trace, is the most that can be said about the Real. In addition, the Real is intrinsically linked to transformations between different types of *jouissance*.

The *sinthome* allows or facilitates rather than represses the flow of *jouissance*. In contrast to this, the ego and the signifier repress *jouissance*. A symptom also constitutes a destructive form of the *jouissance* of the Other, or of meaning. The *sinthome* implies a transformation of *jouissance* that renders *jouissance* sublimatory rather than destructive or inconvenient. In some ways this would be the equivalent of Freud's "where id was, ego shall be." Lacan already redefined this formulation by stating "where It was, I shall become." What is at stake now is the status of this I. Lacan says that the knot needs to be undone, in order to get past the imaginary dimension of the Symbolic, represented by S_1–S_2. "The knot must come undone. The knot is the only support conceivable for a relation between something and something else" (Seminar XXIII, lesson of 9 December, 1975: 9–10).

In this imaginary dimension of the Symbolic the subject in the Real always falls into the structure of a synaptic gap in-between the chain of signifiers. Lacan initially conceived of this hole as a kind of traumatizing and senseless absence of self and meaning that haunts the words of those who speak. The Real was construed as disruptive of the symbolic order.

> In a fabulatory manner, **I propose that the real**, as I think it in my pan-se (homophony between *penser* and *panser* or to bandage) **is comprised really** – the real effectively lying – **of the hole which subsists in that its consistence is nothing more than the totality of the knot which ties it together with the symbolic and the imaginary**. The knot which may be termed Borromean cannot be cut without dissolving the myth it offers of the subject, as *non-supposé*, in other words the subject as real, no more varied than each body which can be given the sign speaking-being [*parlêtre*]. Only due to this knot can the body be given a status that is respectable, in the everyday sense of the word.
> (Seminar XXIII, lesson of 9 December, 1975: 10; bold and bracketing added)

At the end of his work Lacan arrives at a new conception of the Real:

> In any case, it is very difficult not to consider the Real as a third, and let us say that all that I can solicit by way of a response has to do with a call/appeal

to the Real, not as linked to the body, but as different. At a distance from the body there is the possibility of something I termed last time resonance or consonance. In relation to its poles, the body and language, the real is what harmonizes [*fait accord*].

(Seminar XXIII, lesson of 9 December, 1975: 11)

Lacan finds the new ego of the Real most clearly in the scene of Joyce where young Stephen is "beaten" by his peers. Lacan points out that Joyce describes Stephen as literally "emptied out," as having no relation to his body at all.

It is not immediately obvious what would be harmonizing about the beating of the body, unless the beating of the body resulted in a dropping of the imaginary/symbolic mind, in a movement from thinking to non-thinking and then to a different form of thinking that emerges from the leaning on and beating of the meaning-making body. A Jewish mystical story described the experience of emptiness or no self that a Chasid had after receiving an anti-semitic beating. This is precisely what would have infuriated Freud, given his memory of witnessing a Gentile exercise his privileged right of way and dominion of the sidewalk by forcing Freud's father to step down from the curb. The Zen tradition has many stories of Zen teachers slapping or hitting their students in order to wake them up from their slumber and complacency. Japanese Zen teacher Dogen referred to the experience of waking up or realization as the dropping of body and mind. In another related story, Japanese Zen teacher Ryokan

> lived the simplest kind of life in a little hut at the foot of a mountain. One evening a thief visited the hut only to discover there was nothing in it to steal. Ryokan returned and caught him. "You may have come a long way to visit me," he told the prowler, "and you should not return empty handed. Please take my clothes as a gift." The thief was bewildered. He took the clothes and slunk away. Ryokan sat naked, watching the moon. "Poor fellow," he mused, "I wish I could give him this beautiful moon."
>
> (Reps, 1985: 27)

In the unknotting of the Borromean knot, what is bracketed or "desupposed" are both the total ego and the total Other. Both forms of totalization and knotting divide the subject and force the subject of the Real to haunt the symbolic order. It is the barring and bracketing of the Other that produces a new subject: "Where id and ego, Imaginary and Symbolic were, the unary trace or the One shall be." What lies inside the bracket [. . .] or [---] is the unary trace that appears in a hole within the Symbolic and that reconstitutes the Symbolic and symbolizes the imagination. The signifier is now composed of letters or traces that are inherently empty. By virtue of this emptiness the differential structure of the symbolic order is maximized/harmonized, precipitating thereby an outflow and transformation of *jouissance*.

> To produce a true hole, it must be framed by something resembling a bubble, a torus, so that each one of these holes is outlined by something which holds them together, for us to have something which could be termed a true hole.
>
> (Seminar XXIII, lesson of 18 November, 1975: 7)

The true (w)hole that Lacan says is not hooked up to the Freudian unconscious is distinguished from the lacuna or gaps that lead to repressed signifiers. The true (w)hole represents Being beyond signification. Wondrous being resonates with senseless traces of *jouissance* contained within the letters that circumscribe a beyond signification.

The *sinthome* is unique to each subject and follows after the traits or marks that characterize each subject. The universal is in the particular, the absolute within the relative, the abstract within the concrete. The traits of the ego, the ego-ideal and the super-ego are transformed into *sinthomic* unary traces. S_2 is returned to S_1, and S_1 is returned to S_0 as part of a structural re-knotting and reorganization/harmonization of the Borromean knot.

Identification and the *objet a*

So far I have considered how Lacanian theory links the unary trace to the ideal ego or the specular image, to the Name of the Father, the ego-ideal, the problem of the letter as distinguished from the signifier, and to the phenomena/noumena of *jouissance*. Now I must consider how Lacan also considers identification with the *objet a* in a way that goes beyond the imaginary dimension of relative primary narcissism already mentioned.

> Identification (identity) can only happen in relation to what the subject imagines rightly or wrongly to be the desire of the Other. In the normal, neurotic or perverse subject it is always a matter of identifying oneself in accordance with or in opposition to what one thinks is the desire of the Other. As long as this desire can be imagined, fantasized, the subject will find there the necessary reference points in order to define himself, either as the object of the desire of the Other or as an object refusing to be the desire of the Other. In either case he will be able to locate himself, to define himself.
>
> But from the moment when the desire becomes something mysterious, indefinable, the subject discovers that it is precisely this desire of the Other which constitutes him as subject; what he will encounter faced with this void is his fundamental fantasy. To be the object of the desire of the Other is only bearable in so far as we can name this desire, can shape it in terms of our own desire. To become the object of a desire we can no longer name, is to become oneself an object without a name having lost all possible identity: to become an object whose insignia no longer means anything since they have become undecipherable for the Other . . .
>
> (XVIII: 11)

It is by articulating in the most precise fashion this *a* at the point of lack of the Other, which is also the point where the subject receives from this Other, as locus of the word, its major mark, that of the unary trait . . .

(XXIV: 11)

In Seminar XI, Lacan (1964) defines the *objet a* as the index of a void. At first Lacan located the *objet a* in the Imaginary (as the object of fantasy), whereas the later Lacan (1969) linked the *objet a* to the Real. The first definition is related to the object of fantasy cause of desire, and the object of the drive, whereas the later is exemplified by the agency of the analyst in the theory of the four discourses. The *a* is first the breast that the infant identifies with and that will lead his/her search for the specular image or ideal ego. Once the child realizes that the *a* is also absent from the specular image, this realization will turn the object back into being an object of the other rather than of the ideal ego. Now the ego will look for its own object (which originally represented the part-object of the mother) in the other or the sibling/peer of the ego.

The Imaginary and Real aspects of the *objet a* are also related to two other distinctions within Lacanian theory: that between *das Ding* as the archaic maternal Thing, and *das Ding* as the no-thing. The no-thing before the breast, or before the subject–object or self–other differentiation (inaugurated by the presence of the breast), bears no mark whatsoever. The no-thing can only be recaptured under the signifier when the subject itself finally becomes a signifier of nothing or "What" represents the signifier for another signifier. In the practice of analysis, the *a* of the agency of the analyst is the subject qua-nothing. It is the latter that allows for the other (the analysand), to identify (S$_1$) and relinquish (rather than identify with) the primitive *objet a* subject of their unconscious identifications.

In the quote above, Lacan first establishes the connection between identification and the desire of the Other. Freud's super-ego, for example, is predicated on the desire of the Other. Most school children know that their parents want them to do well in school. A child may choose to identify with or against this desire of the Other. In the second paragraph, Lacan moves to consider the desire of the Other as an unconscious desire that now has more to do with sexuality than the law. Since, for the most part, this desire is unspoken, it remains invisible or void, and it is in this void of the Other that the subject will construct fundamental oedipal fantasies.

When a girl, for example, feels she is the intense object of desire of her father, she may name this desire the "great big bear." Thanks to the metaphor of this animal, a girl may now have identified her desire in relationship to her father's desire and her father's desire may have become bearable and bear-like as a unary trait. This may be the common origin of the teddy bears found in the beds of many homes. In this instance a teddy bear would be an example of a unary trait, a signifier, and an *objet a* contained within a transitional object (teddy). The letter "b" stands for the unary trace, whereas the "ear" represents the voice of the Other.

The word bear is the signifier, and the actual teddy bear is the transitional object. The fact that the bear represents the desire of the Other (father), as a love object or lover, also conveys traces of phallic *jouissance* and of *sexuation*, making this a girl rather than a boy.

The question of the identification with the *objet a*, or the unary trace that comes from the other, also raises the question of the relationship between this identification and the identification with the signifier.

The identification with the signifier is mediated by nomination and the Name of the Father. But in Lacan's paternal metaphor, the Name of the Father is an S_2 that replaces the S_1 in the sense of the child as the mother's imaginary phallus. The *objet a* represents a movement from the child to the mother, and the identification of the child with a partial object of the mother, whereas S_1-S_2 represents a movement from the parent to the child and the capture of the subject in a net of identifications coming from the Other.

In the imaginary register, the *objet a* is replaced by secondary narcissism and the unary trait of the specular image. In the Symbolic and in language, it is the S_1 or phallic signifier that will give rise to the divided subject.

"The signifier is essentially different to itself, namely that nothing of the subject can be identified to it without excluding itself from it" (Seminar IX, 1961–2: 12). In this quote Lacan proposes that the signifier replaces/excludes the subject from herself.

If one identifies the subject with a signifier that represents the subject ($\frac{S_1}{\$}$) then the subject is excluded from it (\$). This exclusion or erasure/cancellation of the subject can mean either the subject of the Real/Void **or** the subject that is subjected to the Other or to the signifier. The bar on the subject can either have the usual meaning of the divided subject, a subject divided by the bar of repression, or the bar can have a similar meaning to the bar on the Other (Ø). The bar on the Other signifies the lack or emptiness of the Other. In the same way the bar on the subject has the double meaning of subjection/division as well as the emptiness of the subject within the Symbolic.

The emptiness of the subject within the Symbolic recuperates and symbolizes the void that was the subject prior to identification with the partial object under relative primary narcissism. Absolute primary narcissism is reborn under the signifier and in the form of the subject qua nothing. This is exactly the new meaning that the divided subject will represent at the end of analysis. The division of the subject remains but acquires a new signification. However, the subject must be first alienated in the S_1-S_2 chain of meaning and subjection.

I propose that the subject of the Real should be written as S_0 or δ, as a double zero or the redoubling of zero where the Real is the first zero, and the subject the second. There is a zero for the Real and a zero for the subject. It can also be conceived as the splitting of zero, of one zero into two zeros: a zero for the Real and a zero for the subject. The splitting of zero produces a one zero or zero as a differentiated unit, with zero value, and then two (zeros), meaning zero as the absence of a particular unit or something, and zero as the absence of any unit whatsoever, including zero.

Zero as a number or unit, and zero as the absence of a unit larger than zero, is different from absolute zero as the absence of zero or of any unit whatsoever. Arithmetically, there is no absence of zero since it would be the absence of the absence, and the absence of the absence would be a number larger than zero, therefore the presence of something as distinct from the presence of zero. Zero is the presence of absence rather than the absence of a particular presence. Zero points to the fact that absence or non-manifestation exists and that emptiness is the origin of the unit and of the One.

Lacan says,

> Sign, sign of What? He is precisely the sign of Nothing. If the signifier is defined as representing the subject for another signifier – indefinite referring on of meanings – and if this signifies something, it is because the signifier signifies for the other signifier this "privileged thing" that the subject is qua nothing.
>
> (XIV, 1961–2: 8)

The signifier is what represents a subject to another signifier. This formula represents the subject as metaphor but also metaphor as a subject. The subject is nothing, yet without this nothing, which is not someone in the usual sense, the signifier could not be something in speech. The subject as nothing is essential to understand the unary aspect of the signifier.

The Symbolic in order to be established needs to have something of the Real in it. Something of the Real means something of the order of zero, and it is written: $S_0 \rightarrow S_1 - S_2$. This action takes place in the form of primary repression that establishes mental structure or the structure of the psyche. In actuality, however, primary repression may also come in two forms. In other words, there are two primary forms of repression. One is philogenetic, the other ontogenetic. The first concerns the history of the species, the second the development of the individual.

In the first type of primary repression, S_0 becomes S_1 as a signifier of zero or zero as the signifier of One:

$$\frac{S_1}{S_0}$$

Symbolization erases or represses at the same time that it represents. Thoughts and letters represent an erasure of the original relationship to the object. The thought/letter is the death of the object. This is the negative function of the thought/letter that then is preserved as pure erasure without an object. The negativity of a thought/naught and the letter points to emptiness and senselessness as an absolute value.

The letter represents a form of erasure that does not preserve a link to the object that was erased. The letter or S_1 now represents the void rather than a repressed act/trace. Instead of representing the repressed object of an iconic sign, or of a step or action, the void replaces the object, and the mirror/screen, or the blank paper or the sand, on which the letter is written, in turn, represents the void. The act or object now is transformed into perception or writing with erasure, and the act of erasure is not only preserved in the writing but also in the void represented by the blank slate of paper. The feelings or *jouissance* that accompanied the erased act or object are now in the ink as the very element of expression. It is the paper as void, or the ink, that makes letters a symbolic One of the Real. Ink and paper links letters, the same way that letters link words.

As mentioned earlier, Lacan taught that the vocalization of the step/action erases the step (trace of *pas* is transformed into *pas* of the trace) and eventually transforms the step or the action into made-up stories. The voice represents the void, *voi* or O, the unary trace that reveals/conceals the step or act, the S_1 that then will pair up with S_2 to constitute speech.

The second definition of primary repression involves a definition of S_1 as the first signifier but not as the signifier of zero or of the void. Here zero does not become zero and is not redoubled as One. Rather, zero becomes something, a thing more than the presence of absence or no-thing. The subject as zero is replaced and becomes represented as the absence of the S_1 signifier rather than as the presence of the absence. This process formative of the Freudian unconscious is identical to Lacan's representation of the master's discourse where S_1 becomes a master signifier that subjugates the subject:

$$S_0 \rightarrow \frac{S_1}{\$}$$

The difference between the two types of primary repression is that the first type is philogenetic and affects the symbolic cultural order and the preconscious or the collective storehouse consciousness of humanity. The second type of primary repression is ontogenetic and affects the individual personal history or the repressed unconscious.

The master signifier is the imaginary phallus as the signifier of the mother's desire and of the primal father. In the first phase of Oedipus, the subject becomes a phallic object for the mother. Why do we call a beautiful baby a phallic object? Do Lacanians and psychoanalysts like to objectify people? First of all, and on a phenomenological level, the baby was conceived via the phallus, which provided the link and coupling during intercourse. From a structural perspective, the baby had a prior existence as an equivalent signifier in the mother's unconscious symbolic equation, and as a signifier in the mother's own oedipal structure. Secondly, and also from a phenomenological perspective, the baby replaces the father/phallus in the relationship between the mother and the father. The mother is now complete with her baby and no longer has the same desire for sex with the father. Once the baby is born, the baby becomes a real obstacle in the way of the sexual relationship and the relationship between the parents, period. If the reader is not convinced by this, then please do a careful empirical investigation of what happens between couples once a baby is born. That is, if you are let into the bedroom and intimacies that in a family go beyond what the ideological self-reports may be (during interviews and surveys). Psychoanalysis has learned about these matters in the intricacies, dreams, and disclosures that transpire in psycho-analytic sessions over an extended period of time.

When the subject unconsciously identifies with the imaginary phallic signifier he/she causes a division between ego identity/strength, as the place of the agent (upper left-hand corner of the formula below), and the subordination or weakness of the ego, as the place of truth for the subject ($). We see this in the *matheme* or symbolic formula for the master's discourse $\frac{S_1}{\$} \rightarrow \frac{S_2}{a} \quad \frac{the\,agent}{truth} \quad \frac{the\,other}{production}$

In this *matheme*, S_2 in the place of the other represents the servant. The ego, as the identification with S_1, relates to his/her own division through the servant (S_2). In contrast to the formula for the master's discourse, in the paternal metaphor, S_2 stands for the Name of the Father and is in the place of the agent: $\frac{S_2}{S_1}$.

In the four discourses S_2 represents knowledge rather than the Name of the Father.

In the first moments of Oedipus, and in the master's discourse, S_1 becomes the signifier for the absence of one or for the minus one, rather than for the presence of zero. The presence of zero is transformed into an S_1 and its absence into the subject ($). S_1 becomes a signifier for a minus one or what the divided subject lacks. The unit that is something rather than nothing becomes the one of the imag-inary phallus, or the S_1 of the master's discourse, and the zero becomes the bar placed on the divided subject.

Eventually the $-\varphi$ (phi: imaginary phallus), instead of representing the absence of something in the Imaginary, becomes the presence or the S_1 of the symbolic phallus as a negative category. The symbolic father has the imaginary phallus because of his subjection to the law. He can have it because he has already lost it. This is a good example of a negative dialectic: the synthesis between the thesis of the imaginary phallus, and its absence in the minus phi, is resolved not in a positive presence but in the presence of a symbolic absence, the negation of the absence, that returns the imaginary back into the Real of zero. The symbolic phallus is a non-identity rather than an identity. The negation of the imaginary phallus returns the subject to the One of negation itself.

The Name of the Father in the paternal metaphor adds a second bar to the subject and converts the imaginary phallus into a minus phi and allows for a de-identification with the master signifier of the mother (*mater*) and the primal father. The identification with the phallic mother and the primal father has now been barred.

$$S_0 \rightarrow \frac{S_1}{\$} / \frac{S_2}{S_1} S_0 \rightarrow \frac{S_1}{\$} / \frac{S_2}{\$}$$

In the paternal metaphor, the Name of the Father replaces the desire of the mother in the child's mind, a signifier replaces another signifier, and the phallus as the first signifier (of the desire of the mother) takes the place of signified in relation to the new signifier (the Name of the Father).

Name/Law of the Father	S_2	Signifier	order of language
Desire of the Mother	S_1	Signified	phallus

S_2 or the Name of the Father establishes S_1 (the signifier of the mother's desire) as a missing phallus which the subject is seeking within the order of language and what this signifies to the subject (\$). Within the symbolic order of language inaugurated by the Name of the Father, the subject seeks the object cause of the mother's desire.

In the formula above, the barrier between the Name of the Father (S_2) and the signifier of the imaginary phallus (S_1) is a vertical instead of a horizontal line. In the denominator we still have the overall divided and repressed subject. If we added the two lines together, then we would have the money sign with two bars representing the subject.

Now what is missing from the *matheme* for the subject $\frac{S_1}{\$}$ and the one for the paternal metaphor $\frac{S_2}{S_1}$ is the *objet a* as the fourth element found in the formula for the four discourses. This fourth element will bring us back to the Real dimension of the *objet a* (and to the subject as S_0 or the subject of the Real).

In the Lacanian theory of the drive, the drive or the libido begins with what is lost with sexed reproduction. What is lost is infinite or long-lasting life. What is missing from this model is the place of the *objet a* as the representative of unborn life. At this level of the unknown of the body, the *objet a* appears as a unary trace in the form of what Lacan called an infinite line or string. Unary trace, infinite line, or string takes the place of what Freud called the affective representative of the drive. According to this perspective, the *objet a* precedes the phallus, although this is a circular argument since, under ordinary circumstances, you can't have sexed reproduction without the phallus.

As aforementioned, this object can be found in the formula for the discourse of the master $\frac{S_1}{\$} \rightarrow \frac{S_2}{a}$

However, juxtaposing the discourse of the master and the paternal metaphor

$$S_0 \rightarrow \frac{S_1}{\$} / \frac{S_2}{S_1}$$

leads me to the following reflections and conclusions. In the paternal metaphor, S_2 has ascendancy over S_1 whereas the reverse is true for the master's discourse ($S_1 \rightarrow S_2$). In the latter, the servant is compelled to produce the good object to compensate the master for the loss of the a. In the paternal metaphor, the a is lost under the phallus and stays non-manifest in its non-phallic aspect other than within the subject in the Real as a potential and latent meaning of the barred subject. The imaginary objects a of the drive are in a relation of compensation to the loss of the imaginary phallus. On the other hand, the imaginary phallus also compensates for the loss of the *objet a*.

However, the discourse of the analyst has the analyst in place of the a, and in the place of the agent, and the analysand as divided subject, and as other, has to find within itself the S_1 or phallic signifiers that will signify the a. The a over S_2 represents unknown-knowing or unconscious knowing rather than the knowledge that is typical of the S_2 of the university discourse.

$$\frac{a}{S_2} \rightarrow \frac{\$}{S_1}$$

Here the signifier, as symbolic phallus, as an absence or the signifier of a lack, points back to the *objet a* of infinite life. S_2, in the discourse of the analyst does not function as a bar (as in the paternal metaphor), but rather as the place of truth, which undergirds the agency of infinite life. In the discourse of the analyst the divided subject goes back to zero and to the *objet a* via the master signifier now re-signified as unary trace or senseless signification.

The Name of the Father, as a function, now grounds the *objet a* in the place of truth in the Real. With this in place, the divided subject as the symbolic Other, and the servant, can produce the signifiers or unary traces of the a of long-lasting life.

This formulation also illuminates another important problem raised by Lacanian theory. How is it that the Name of the Father for Lacan is not simply a signifier of the symbolic order but rather what organizes and grounds the symbolic order? Moreover, for Lacan the Name of the Father does not come from the Symbolic but rather is a manifestation of the Real. The Name of the Father is not only what organizes culture and even *a*theism but also what returns culture to its source in the Real.

The Name of the Father is what remains of the Real within the Symbolic, just like steps or actions are negations or vanish under the process of representation. These actions remain as the negative function of language or signification. The symbolic Name of the Father is a unary trace or an infinite straight line with the void all around it.

The Real appears in two forms: as *objet a* representative of unborn life, and as the Name of the Father as a unary trace within the Symbolic. But this unary trace is not I(O) because the latter represents the ego-ideal and the identification with ideas of the father or of ideology, "my father always told me" kind of thing. The super-ego and ego-ideal are imaginary and symbolic. The Name of the Father is the traceless trace or nameless name appearing within the lack in the Other as a place empty of designation, and as the place of permutation and transformation of the structure at the same time.

The symbolic phallus operates in the intersection of the Real and the Symbolic. In the subject in the Real there is no subject, only the Real of the drive. In the subject of the Real, the subject is the agent of transformation, whereas the lack in the Other is the potential for transformation inherent to the structure. Thanks to emptiness or the lack within the structure, the structure is in constant motion, although the set of elements remains the same (the more it changes, the more it remains the same). The dynamism of the structure constitutes a different level of change from the change associated with the emergence of new elements. The subject of the Real has to do with the possibility of the emergence of new elements via the lack in the Other.

The symptom, the unary trait, and the *sinthome*

Freud described the phenomenon of identification as a process by which a subject assimilates an aspect or a trait of another subject. In the process, the subject becomes transformed in the likeness of the other. At the same time, by the very same process of identification, the subject becomes differentiated from the other by virtue of the fact of the partiality of the identification. The unary trait becomes incorporated into the rest of the character structure, making the latter both similar and different to the other at the same time.

Freud used the unary trait (*einziger Zug*), as a type of identification associated to the formation of hysterical symptoms. A partial identification, as an unconscious process, is used to identify with and construct an unconscious partial object of fantasy. This differs from the identification process used to construct the ideal ego and the ego-ideal. The unary trait involved in the type of identification used to construct a symptom is similar to the earliest form of identification with the breast/*objet a* that I have defined as a relative form of primary narcissism. This *objet a* is the same object involved in the formula for the unconscious fantasy ($\$\lozenge a$) and can also be brought into relation with the concept of oral incorporation.

A clinical example of this would be the case of a hysterical cough or a tic that is acquired by identification and represents, for example, both a desire to suck the mother's breast and the father's imaginary phallus and a punishment for the same. What remains of the imaginary phallus is simply a cough of the father that the daughter (or son) is identified with. At the same time the cough, as a metaphor for the phallus, also reveals the father's lack or imaginary castration. Another example, would be the case of a man (male or female) who identifies with certain intonations, gestures, or words used by an idealized figure of authority. All of these traits could be used to convey forms of aggressiveness towards the other as well as the self.

The unary aspect of a symptom is also linked to a difference between Freud and Lacan, as well as to a difference between the early and later Lacan. The early Lacan followed Freud in considering the symptom as a symbol, and as having a symbolic meaning, therefore. However, since the early development of the psychoanalytic movement, the increasing accumulation of clinical experience began revealing the limited efficacy of interpretation as an intervention constructed on the basis of the understanding of a symptom as a symbol. The later Lacan came to understand the symptom as a form of *jouissance* in the Real rather than from the Real (the distinction is mine).

This understanding of the Real aspect of a symptom also led Lacan to develop his notion of the *sinthome*, which together with the Name of the Father became the fourth ring of the Borromean knot that tied the other three together. The symptom as the *sinthome* explains two things: why a symptom endures and is immune to interpretation, and that there are also good reasons for this being the case. With the concept of the *sinthome*, pain becomes linked to sublimation, and growth through strife and effort. This conceptualization also answers the question/fear that artists often have that analysis or the cure of the symptom will be the end of their creativity. Artists have no need to worry about this since the symptom will not be eliminated that easily.

The concept of the *sinthome* can also be linked to Jung's (1935, 1957) notion that a symptom also represents future purposes and intentions (Lacan's future anterior and his definition of sublimation with a twist: "Where the (ego) symptom was, I shall become"). The *sinthome* highlights positive as well as Real dimensions of a symptom. The ego is a symptom in the sense that it is meant to cover a hole, in the same way that a delusion is meant to cover a hole in the signifying chain. Jung's concept of individuation, as a humanistic striving towards wholeness, can be understood as an imaginary attempt to close the hole within the whole. The only possible way to close the hole within the whole is to leave the hole open and empty. In other words, self-realization is the same as the realization that there is no enduring self, only a series of processes and transformations held together by a unary trace (as already amply discussed).

The symptom is a traumatic S_1 or signifying letter/signifier stuck to the Real or in the Real. Here the signifier is functioning as a letter rather than a signifier in the following specific sense. Although letters are linked to other letters in the same way that words are linked to other words, letters by themselves are senseless. In addition, as aforementioned, letters constitute an erasure of the relationship to things outside language. The sensual aspect of a letter that was linked to a particular animal, for example, is lost. What remains in lieu of the erasure of the animal or of an action is simply a void. This void is traumatic, since an animal's ghost or voice haunts it. But the void, and *jouissance* as an experience outside language, is not only traumatic or inconvenient. A trauma, a symptom, or even a delusion can represent a form of illumination. The aspect of the *sinthome* that is positive or not only traumatic is the aspect of the symptom that is not <u>in</u> the Real but rather is <u>of</u> the Real.

The symptom as representing a repressed form of *jouissance* or pleasure/pain can also be recognized as having a similitude with the oppositional or contradictory aspects of identifications. To become himself/herself the subject must not only follow but also oppose the other by following and follow by opposing. Freud compared the resistance of the symptom to the way in which children rebel against the parents by failing or hurting themselves.

The *sinthome* as a form of identification constitutes a refusal of the symbolic order or the order of words and language. However, this refusal need not be seen as a form of maternal challenge of the law of the father or as a form of psychotic foreclosure of the symbolic order and the Name of the Father. More than refusing symbolic links, the unary trace is a form of *jouissance* and a place of openness to new meanings or to what Ricoeur (1991) called peculiar predication and semantic innovation.

The Symbolic is split in two between two types of S_1: symptom/symbol and unary trace/*sinthome*. There is a difference between signifiers as they are related to each other in the production of meaning (S_1–S_2) and signifiers insofar as they are related to a One, a signifier that resists any linking (S_1–S_0). This split, Lacan (1975–6) says, is a false hole. Symbols appear to be seeking a symbol or signifier that remains elusive, and the latter would also be seeking symbolization, but this is not the case. The unary trace links to the Real rather than to other signifiers. Signifiers are looking for other missing signifiers that are repressed in the Real of the unconscious, but this unknown has two forms:

1   Repressed signifiers/speech that are also looking to become associated. This is what I called the ontogenetic repressed unconscious.
2   The unary trace that simply links an element of the Symbolic order to the One void of the Real and not to other signifiers. It appears as a false gap or hole that leads to the repressed unconscious but instead simply leads to the void or the unconscious in the sense of the unknowable.

With the help of the unary trace, any signifier is capable of becoming auto-referential, taking on the function of the *sinthome* that opens up the signifying system. Like the Jungian symbol, the signifier here is only related to itself, not as relative but rather as an absolute difference in the sense of the Real. There is something of the Real in the Symbolic that resists the Symbolic. Lacan calls it a pure, radical, or absolute difference. This piece/trace of Real also erases meaning within the order of language.

Let us say that the Law has repressed S_1, or a phallic signifier. Within the order of language, S_1 would be replaced by S_2 in the same way that previously S_2 (Name of the Father) replaced S_1 (imaginary phallus). S_2 here stands both for the function of metaphor in language and also for the primary repression under the Name of the Father that installed the metaphoric order to begin with.

The S_2 substituting for an S_1 signifies that the S_2 wants to become S_1 in the same way that S_1 wants to become S_2. Words look for the missing/repressed words, and repressed speech looks for signifiers to emerge from repression. The imaginary aspect of language and of the Name of the Father seeks to close the gap left over by the two types of primary repression described above. With the unary **trait**, defined as a distinctive distinction, the S_1 is a master or narcissistic signifier (the narcissism of small differences) that totalizes the symbolic order by closing the gap or void of the Real within the Symbolic. The S_1 of the master signifier, or unary **trait**, links by subordinating other signifiers to a ruling idea or signifier. However, by the same token, the ghost of an imaginary void that threatens to destroy the order of the system haunts a closed symbolic system. In this way the S_1 of the master signifier becomes linked to an inconvenient or destructive form of *jouissance*.

In contrast to this, the S_1 of the unary **trace** is not linked to other signifiers but rather to a modality of *jouissance*. S_1 or the symbolic aspect of the Name represents the emptiness of the symbolic order. This S_1 reveals rather than conceals the void. With the S_1 of the unary **trace**, the void or emptiness becomes an ennobling form of *jouissance*, the luminous human face of the void. The unary trace is of the Real and not in the Real: like the *sinthome* or the Name of the Father (in the later Lacan), it ties the RSI knot together. In the same way the Name of the Father is not of the social-symbolic order itself.

The unary trace resists binary linking that divides the One and destroys *jouissance*. The unary trace or the One manifests the plenitude of the Real in the form of a benevolent *jouissance*. When dual or binary linking is resisted and the lack is left open, then out of the empty navel of the Real emerges or evolves the Name of the Father, as a nameless name, or a unary trace, that re-links the registers to one another. This name is nameless because there is no repressed signifier that could give the name its signification: it is because it is.

References

Adorno, T.A. (1966). *Negative Dialectics*. New York: Continuum, 1973.

Bachelard, G. (1940). *The Philosophy of No: A Philosophy of the New Scientific Mind* (C. Watson trans.). New York: Orion Press, 1968.

Barthes, R. (1984). *Image, Music, Text*. New York: Hill and Wang.

Benjamin, W. (1936). The work of art in the age of mechanical reproduction. In H. Arendt (ed.), *Illuminations*. New York: Schocken Books.

Derrida, J. (1982). Differance. In J. Derrida (ed.), *Margins of Philosophy*. Chicago: University of Chicago Press, pp. 3–27.

Eigen, M. (2009). *Flames from the Unconscious*. London: Karnac.

Erikson, E. (1968). *Identity: Youth and Crisis*. New York: Norton & Norton, 1992.

Freud, S. (1914). On narcissism: An introduction. *SE*, 14: 67–102.

Freud, S. (1919). Lines of advance in psychoanalytic therapy. *SE*, 17: 159–68.

Freud, S. (1920). *Beyond the Pleasure Principle*. New York: W.W. Norton, 1961.

Freud, S. (1923). *The Ego and the Id. SE*, 19: 1–66.

Freud, S. (1937). Analysis terminable and interminable. *SE*, 23: 209.

Habermas, J. (1968). *Knowledge and Human Interests* (J.J. Shapiro trans.). Boston, MA: Beacon, 1971.

Irvine, A.D. (2009). Russell's paradox. In E.N. Zalta (ed.), *The Stanford Encyclopedia of Philosophy* (Summer 2009 edition). URL http://plato.stanford.edu/archives/sum2009/entries/russell-paradox/.

Joyce, J. (1922). *Ulysses: The Classic Text: Traditions and Interpretations*. Milwaukee: University of Wisconsin, 2002.

Jung, C. (1935). The Tavistock Lectures. *CW*, 18: 389, 1950.

Jung, C. (1957). Psychiatric studies. *CW*, I: 132.

Lacan, J. (1961). *The Seminar of Jacques Lacan IX: On Identification* (Cormac Gallagher trans.). London: Karnac.

Lacan, J. (1964). *Seminar XI: The Four Fundamental Concepts of Psychoanalysis* (Alan Sheridan trans.). New York: W.W. Norton, 1978.

Lacan, J. (1969). *The Seminar of Jacques Lacan: Book XVII: The Other Side of Psychoanalysis*. New York: W.W. Norton, 2007.

Lacan, J. (1971). *The Seminar of Jacques Lacan XVIII: On a Discourse That Might Not Be a Semblance*. London: Karnac, 2002.

Lacan, J. (1972–3). On feminine sexuality, the limits of love and knowledge. *Encore, The Seminar of Jacques Lacan, Book XX*. New York: W.W. Norton, 1975.

Lacan, J. (1975–6). *Seminario 23: El Sinthoma* (Ricardo Rodríguez Ponte trans.). Unpublished.

Macey, D. (2000). *Dictionary of Critical Theory*. London: Penguin Books.

Moncayo, R. (2008). *Evolving Lacanian Perspectives for Clinical Psychoanalysis: On Narcissism, Sexuation, and the Phases of Analysis in Contemporary Culture*. London: Karnac.

Reps, P. (1985). *Zen Flesh, Zen Bones*. Boston, MA: Charles E. Tuttle.

Ricoeur, P. (1991). *From Text to Action*. Evanston, IL: Northwestern University Press.

Thatcher, M. (1987). Interview 23 September 1987, as quoted by Douglas Keay, *Woman's Own*, 31 October 1987, pp. 8–10.

Zizek, S. (1989). *The Sublime Object of Ideology*. London: Verso.

Chapter 2

Semblance and the luminous face of the void

Semblance or "the semblant" is a word/concept that has two different yet related meanings. The first refers to the classical distinction between appearance and reality. The second acceptation refers to the face or countenance. Appearance and face are also related through the concept of the mask and the Jungian concept of the persona. Mask and persona point in the direction of social appearances and norms and the imaginary ego. These are in contradistinction to the psychic reality of desire and the subject of the unconscious.

Appearance and person also have semantic links in different languages. In English the word a-pparent is homophonically related to being a parent, and the word person refers to each son (per-son). Between a parent and a son there is a relationship of kinship that in Spanish is written with the word *parentezco* that connotes a likeness or similarity of appearance (*parecido*) usually reflected in the semblant or face. Between a parent and an offspring there is a likeness or kinship or relationship of identification that is usually reflected in the semblant.

Likeness or resemblance represents the reflection of a reflection, or the semblance of the semblant. Conversely, a son could also represent the appearance of difference. A son could embody an appearance in the sense of appearing to be without a parent (a-parent: where the privative *a* is used to negate the noun). Finally, the word resemblance bears a relationship of similarity to the word/concept of representation. Ordinarily a representation has a resemblance to what it represents. A re-presentation represents the beginning of a chain or a lineage where the second presentation is the re-edition of a semblant.

The letter and the signifier

In his seminar "On a Discourse That Might Not Be a Semblance", Lacan (1971) worked on two related themes: that the signifier/representation is nothing more than a semblance (1/13/71, I: 9) and at the same time he established a distinction between a letter in the Real and a symbolic signifier (12/5/71, VII: 14). With the latter distinction Lacan reflects on the possible existence of a discourse based on the letter and its relationship to the littoral (*lituraterre*). The semblant points to the intersection between the Symbolic and the Imaginary, whereas the letter lies between the Symbolic and the Real.

A littoral is the meeting place between two elements (water and land, *jouissance* and language) that mutually circumscribe each other. A letter is what the Other has left behind, the alliterations and obliterations of speech, and the portal through which *jouissance* both enters and escapes language. Every discourse is discursive but a discourse can also be used in a non-discursive fashion or as speech via its senseless pieces or component elements. An example of this would be the above scansion of the words apparent and person to produce new significations/knowledge related to the question of the semblant. Syllepsis and catachresis are other examples of *litterality*, as a meeting place between the signifier and *jouissance* within language. In syllepsis, the expression "She lost it," for example, refers both to a woman's temper and to whatever object "it" could indicate or be an index of. Black sun is the catachresis that bears the title of Kristeva's (1989) book on depression. Alternatively, and conversely, "luminous hole" could be used to describe the experience of mania or euphoria.

The question of the letter and the possibility of a discourse that would not be a semblance implies that the letter, perhaps, then, would not be a semblance or at least would be more substantial and Real than a signifier. The signifier would represent an appearance and the letter something Real. This formulation or conclusion, however, runs the risk of replacing the duality between appearance and reality with a duality between the signifier and the letter. Nevertheless, such conclusion is already refuted by the Lacanian aphorism that truth or reality has the structure of fiction. The Real does not represent reality for the symbolic semblant and the symbolic semblant is not the reality for an imaginary appearance. The semblant or the signifier is already an appearance, and the appearance (or the Imaginary) is already symbolic.

> There is confirmed the fact that the truth only progresses, only progresses from a structure of fiction.
>
> (5/19/71, VIII: 6)

Every letter is erased by the effect of a flux/*jouissance* or the disruption of a flux/*jouissance* that at the same time is represented by the One of the letter or the letter O(ne) as a unary trace. Just like words represent objects that are absent, or represent the death of the object, a *jouissance*, or an energetic intensity, represents the erasure of a letter, at the same time that the letter as a One, or unary trace, becomes an S_1 representing a *jouissance* outside signification. *Jouissance* returns a letter to a form of cessation or emptiness ($S_1 \rightarrow S_0$) and at the same time this S_0 can only be represented by an S_1 in a state of erasure.

In the Spanish translation of his paper on the Thing, Heidegger (1950) also links the void within a jar to scansion in the Spanish acceptation of the word as a gift or a pouring forth or outwardly flow. In Spanish the word scansion (*escancion*) applies both to the segmentation of poetry and language and to this outpouring or evacuation of the void and vacuity. Scansion is associated with literality, and represents the transformation of the signifier into the letter. The segmentation or scansion of the signifier back into the letter precipitates the outflow of the Real contained within the letters.

In contrast to the letter, the signifier, or the word, is replaced rather than erased. Another signifier replaces the signifier. It is this S_2 that attempts to close and conceal the S_0 represented by the letter. S_2 turns the letter into a signifier, into something Imaginary, a cock and bull story. When the letter becomes the signifier, a signifier also becomes a semblance. Yet without S_2, the letter would not be a signifier proper. With S_2, S_1 becomes a signifier of a lack/gap/hole that is stitched over by S_2. Without S_2, S_1 becomes a letter indicative of a One *jouissance* beyond signification.

The signifier is a semblance or organized fiction of a common object or of another signifier. The letter instead is a non-systematic semblance of *jouissance*. This distinction between the semblance of the signifier and the semblance of *jouissance* is based on the definition that Lacan (1972) gives of the *objet a* as a semblance of being. Furthermore, Lacan also says that S_1 (without S_2) is also the place of the semblant. This solitary S_1, as a letter or a form of non-sense, is singularly related to the *objet a*.

The *objet a*, as a semblance of being, can be differentiated from the signifier, defined as what represents a subject for another signifier. The signifier excludes the Real being/unbeing of the subject at the same time that it represents the subject within the Symbolic order. Historically, when the signifier excludes the child from being the imaginary phallus of the mother, the Imaginary dimension of the Real (the drive objects and energetic intensities that operate prior to linguistic signification) is transformed into what is Real about the Symbolic and being becomes *unbeing* (*desetre*).

Transformation or conversion is a manner of speaking because in actuality the *objet a*, as what Lacan calls the *lamella* and unborn life, had already been covered over by the imaginary phallus as a source of relative primary narcissism. The signifier helps to reveal or unveil *unbeing* at the same time that it conceals it. Only the *objet a* and S_1, in the sense of the One, are semblants of unbeing. With the advent of the signifier, S_2 functions as semblance of S_1, and the letter is semblance of *jouissance*.

Lacan's first conception of the semblance was built on the classical distinction between false appearance and true essence or reality. The Imaginary represented a kind of wall or blockage of the Symbolic. At the end of his teaching Lacan articulated the concept of the semblance in continuity rather than opposition to truth, reality, or essence.

What is confusing about the concept of the semblance is that the levels of analysis can be homogeneous and heterogeneous, contradictory and non-contradictory at the same time. For example, there is an Imaginary semblance that represents the apparent objectivity of the external world and of real images. On the other hand, the Imaginary also represents the fantasies through which we perceive the external world.

For Lacan truth and reality have the structure of fiction. Real images are also semblances of the gaze as an *objet a*: the object world is the eye of the Other. In the same way, the real image of the body represents the specular image that in turn represents the primary object cause of desire. Lacanian theory breaks with the classical and modern distinction between appearance and reality. The two sides of the duality are like the two sides of the Moebius strip that in reality is only One. The Imaginary of visual perception and the Imaginary of the fantasy is the same thing.

Language is the third symbolic dimension that articulates both sides of the Imaginary while not falling entirely on one side or the other of the subjective–objective relationship. In this way, the signifier is found in the semblance itself. But if the Imaginary includes the real image as much as the virtual or fantasized one, and the signifier is found in the objectivity of real images, then what is the signifier a semblance of?

The signifier is a semblance of another signifier (S_1–S_2), but the letter, as the elementary unit of the signifier, is semblance of being/unbeing (S_1–S_0). The Imaginary and the Symbolic, thing-representation and word-representation, mutually exclude or contradict one another. In addition, representation and the Real also have the same relationship of exclusion. The relationship between the registers/dimensions is organized by both formal and dialectical logic, a principle of non-contradiction or exclusion, and a principle of interdependence or contradiction.

The Imaginary excludes the signifier because in visual perception the world of objects or of dream images appears to be independent from language. In actuality, it is language that determines visual perception. The signifier excludes the Imaginary because the signifier erases the relationship to the object or the thing and replaces the object with a signifier that from now on will represent the subject for another signifier. But the object that is replaced and the subject that is represented reappear once again in the phantasm ($\$\Diamond a$).

Semblance, the *sinthome*, and the Name of the Father

The same apparent duality with regards to the registers and the semblance (signifier/letter) can be transferred to the relationship between the *sinthome* and the Name of the Father. Is the *sinthome* a semblance for the Name of the Father or is the identification with the analyst a semblance for the symptom? What exactly is the relationship between the semblance and the *sinthome*?

The *sinthome* is a way of approaching and coping with the *jouissance* in the symptom. Given that the symptom can represent a form of partial identification with the other (unary trait), other schools of psychoanalysis (ego psychology, object relations, etc.) formulate the identification with the analyst as a model for the end of analysis and the resolution of the symptom. A semblance replaces another semblance, and a reflection is the reflection of another reflection. But in the case of the identification with the analyst, the analyst and the analysis become the symptom of the subject.

Lacan instead proposes the alternative formulation of the identification with the *sinthome*. The symptom appears in the place where the desire of the mother or the function of the father fails: instead of a father, there is a symptom that reveals/conceals the *jouissance* of the Other. In Lacanian psychoanalysis the desire of the mother and the name or function of the father are both subsumed under the paternal/parental metaphor.

Otherwise, Lacanian psychoanalysis appears to focus exclusively on the father to the same extent that the object-relations school focuses exclusively on the function of the mother. In Kleinian theory the body of the mother contains the father's penis and in Lacanian theory the paternal metaphor contains/formulates the desire of the mother as the denominator for the name/numerator of the father.

Within Kleinian theory the penis could be considered a symptom of the theory (the phallus is not theorized other than as a penis contained within the mother), while for Lacan, via the paternal metaphor, the desire of the mother is a *sinthome* to the same extent as the Name of the Father. Given that Lacan says that the *sinthome* is one of the forms of the Name of the Father, and that in the paternal metaphor the desire of the mother is the denominator within a symbolic equation (the Name of the Father is the numerator), the *sinthome* can be said to articulate the lack of the m(O)ther for which the Name is a signifier. As the symptom reveals/conceals the *jouissance* of and the lack in the mother, the *sinthome* reveals/conceals the lack of the Other.

Lacanian theory includes the *sinthome* as an aspect of the theory, but Kleinian theory does not recognize what is symptomatic about the theory. In Lacan the related aphorisms of "desire is the desire of the Other," or "the unconscious is the discourse of the Other," both include the mother's desire and the unconscious signifier of the mother's desire, as well as the desire of the father for the *objet a*, and for the Law.

It is well known that in the seminar on the *sinthome* (1975–6) Lacan renders the Name of the Father and the *sinthome* as two aspects of the fourth and final ring of the Borromean knot that re-knots the other three together. The *sinthome* is a way of converting the symptom not into a substitute for the actual father but into the very function of the name.

If the Name of the Father is one of the forms of the *sinthome*, then the question arises as to whether identification with the *sinthome* would still represent a form of identification with the Name of the Father or a re-appropriation of the same. How would this differ from sublimation, the renunciation of a deadly form of *jouissance* or even the identification with the analyst as a new version of the paternal metaphor?

The key point is that the re-appropriation or re-signification of the Name differs from identification with the father or with the analyst. Rather than identifying with the analyst, the analysand has to re-signify the Name for himself/herself with the help of the aspect of the *sinthome* that implies a transformation within *jouissance* itself: from the *jouissance* of the Other to the Other *jouissance*, from the plus-de-*jouir* (the *jouissance* of the Other) to *jouissance* plain and simple, either in the form of phallic/feminine *jouissance* or sublimation.

In contrast to the identification with the analyst or with the imaginary father or mother, the identification with the *sinthome* does not close or suture the opening of being or the gap of the lack or of the void. The void of absence, or the anxiety-producing nothingness, or the anxiety-producing presence of the object, is trans-formed into the presence of a luminous and benevolent void.

In this way, the Name of the Father, as a *sinthome*, is linked to the symbolic dead father, the lack in the Other, and the Real face of the *objet a*. The Name of the Father is a unary trace that links the Symbolic and the Real by symbolizing a dignified void at the center of the Real. This aspect of the Name and of the *sinthome* differs from what Oedipus represented for Freud, given that Lacan considered Oedipus a dream of Freud.

Freud owed his fame, or the fame of his name, to Oedipus and Sophocles. The name or dream of Oedipus is a *sinthome* that represents what the subject constructs as a substitute for, and to cover the faults, lack, and emptiness of, the Other. By using the Name that clears rather than closes the opening of unbeing, the *sinthome* transforms the quality/modality of *jouissance* itself.

The imaginary aspect of the Name of the Father, or the identification with the imaginary father, or the S_1–S_2 as a cock and bull story, covers the lack of and within the subject and the Other. As a *sinthome*, the symbolic function of the name is a letter that represents the One of infinite life. The latter opens the subject towards empty being.

To summarize, I submit a grid of the relations among Semblance and the Void, the letter and the signifier, and the Semblance, the *Sinthome*, and the Name of the Father.

Formal Semblance of the Signifier.	Semblant in a non-systematic State of Erasure. The S_1, the letter, and the *objet a* as Semblances of Unbeing.
The Symptom as a Metaphor or Signifier.	The *Sinthome* as *Jouissance*.
Imaginary identification with the analyst or with the Name of the Father that sutures the gap of being and the lack in the Other.	The Symbolic function of the Name as a letter or One that opens being to Unbeing. The *Sinthome* and the Name are semblances of *Jouissance* and its transformations.

Psychotic delusions, or the ideologies of perversion, are symptoms but not *sinthomes* because they represent attacks and reinforcements of either foreclosure or disavowals (correspondingly) of the metaphor that links and knots signifying connections within language. It is the *sinthome* that can re-knot the registers/dimensions of experience.

Cultural forms and symbolic thought formations are *sinthomes* the way that Oedipus was for Freud, Freud was for Lacan, and Freud and Lacan are for the rest of us. But for the *sinthome* to stop being a symptom or erase itself as a semblance, and take the step that crosses over from being to unbeing, the name has to be used to unlock the mysteries of *jouissance*. The semblant or the face no longer masks anything: the knot, the no, and the name (nom), are in fact the luminous face of the void (naught).

The semblant, the face, and the mask

The word erasure can also be interpreted as a form of effacement. The verb to efface points to the face as a semblance or how the semblant masks, erases, or substitutes for the face. The signifier as a semblance masks or substitutes for the face, whereas the letter effaces the semblance from the semblant. In everyday language we find such expressions as "Tell it to her face," "To face someone," "To be cheeky, barefaced, or bold-faced, to save face, to face the consequences, to face up, or to lose face."

A discourse or the letter (a character), as well as character (sounds like *cara* or face in Spanish), are in the face or in the semblant. The duality of the signifier as S_1–S_2 and S_1–S_0 is reproduced or redoubled in the relation between the mask and the face. But the letter is not like a face behind a face nor is the signifier a mask in front of a face. The semblant of the semblance (resemblance) is not found elsewhere other than in the very same semblant that is One and Other at the same time.

The Other here does not represent the like-minded member of the same species. The Other is the cultural Other and the *objet a* as both a presence and an absence, or better the presence of an absence rather than the absence of a presence. The *a*, as partial object, functions as a One letter of the Real and in the Real of the organism but not as an imaginary signifier of the body. As far as the semblant is concerned, the *objet a* functions as a unary trace. The unary trace is the little empty part (the not-All) that contains the All.

The face or visage in Latin is associated with the eye (*visio*), but the imaginary eye with its genotypic characteristics is not the gaze through which the bodily ego sees itself and the other. In the gaze, the Other through which I see myself, is seeing. When the gaze sees, seeing is seeing in and through me. The gaze represents the Other, as the symbolic eye that mediates the look of the eye, but it also represents the looking glass or clear mirror, as well as the possibility of anything functioning as a mirror for a reflection (the infinite mirror). I only identify or locate myself in relationship to everything else.

The different genotypic components of the face have two perceptual characteristic: they are seen as independent from each other, and at the same time they are invested with a narcissistic charge that turns them into a unary trait more than a trace. Green eyes or blond hair, for example, become bodily signifiers of the beautiful object that fills the lack of and in the subject.

In actuality, the meaning of the different components of the face is given by differences within language. The unary trace is something else that represents each part as independent in a Real rather than an Imaginary sense. The Real of the unary trace is also different from schizoid fragmentation of the body image or postmodern fragmentation of the symbolic body. With the unary trace, the nose knows, and a smile is a simile for something more than lips and teeth. The mouth is an opening of being and of the Real as a vacuum plenum. In its emptiness, and singularity, each part of the body, linked to an erogenous zone and to *jouissance*, can embody the entire universe.

The semblant can represent either the grimace or the smile of the Real. The semblant can reveal what is most me about myself, the unrepresentable it-self or the thing in itself, or it can represent a mask as a formal or painful marking of *jouissance*. From this perspective the semblant represents the reversible perspective (Bion's [1992] concept) of the Möbius strip. In relationship to the face, the mask represents the multiplicity of the face. The mask can represent the formal social gesture or the previously suppressed emotions, as seen in the examples of Greek and Japanese theatre. The ordinary face of everyday life can also represent the same spectrum: from *la belle indifference* and/or phallic narcissistic grimace of the hysteric, to the tight upper lip, and angry face of the obsessive character.

The expression "to lose face" can mean either to be unmasked or to lose one's dignity or nobility. Conversely, "to save face" can mean either to keep the social mask intact or to maintain the half-smile of true composure and ease. Which would be the true mask or semblant in this context?

In the seminar on the semblant, Lacan defines truth as a form of *jouissance* of semblance. Truth is half-said between *jouissance* and the semblant. The first half of truth is the unsayable *jouissance*, whether pleasant or unpleasant. Truth may be silently spoken and half-said by the face/semblant or half-concealed by the mask (also a form of semblant). The first semblant is a semblant of *jouissance*; the second, a semblance of the signifier and of the law of the code. These two aspects of truth and of the semblance interact and mutually determine each other. The two types of semblance (of the signifier and of the letter) interact with the three types of *jouissance*.

The signifier refuses *jouissance* (the *jouissance* of the Other), but by opposing also facilitates a different form of (phallic) *jouissance*. But as a unary trace, the letter itself is a form of *jouissance* (feminine *jouissance* and the Other *jouissance*). The latter can be seen in the semblance of ecstasy of St. Therese in the statue by Bernini figured in the Spanish version of Seminar XX (Lacan, 1972). The smile and gaze of the angel that precipitates her *jouissance*, however, represents the second half of truth. In this instance, the signifier (as law and word) has become a phallic form of *jouissance*.

The semblant in the transference

To conclude I will address the question of the semblant in the transference and in the person of the psychoanalyst. Lacan (1961) affirms that payment with one's person is one of the three payments of the analyst. The analyst abandons the social mask and listens more than he/she speaks. Does this mean then that the analyst functions more according to reality and is less fooled by appearances? If this were the case, then we would be back to the duality between appearances and reality or essence.

Lacan (1960) also speaks of the "tactical vacillation of the analyst's neutrality." An analytic act is not guided by the poker mask/face despite Lacan's (1961) reference to the closed face with lips sewn shut characteristic of the place of the dummy in the game of bridge. The closed semblant would be an example of the semblance of the signifier as a law of the code that we already know stimulates rather than simply eliminates *jouissance*. It is as if, with the closed face, the analyst was saying this is not funny and I am not enjoying this at all. With the seriousness of the face, rather than being humorless and uptight (the tight upper lip associated with the sewn lips of repression), the analyst is pointing to the semblance of unbeing, and the *jouissance* of the letter.

The desire of the analyst, which together with the unconscious of the analysand directs the treatment, is not an ascetic desire not to desire, but rather a desire to relinquish the desire to be desired or admired by the analysand. The analyst knows that the analysand is not there to satisfy the analyst's personal demands. By the same token the analyst expects the analysand to forward a love demand to the analyst. Since transference love is fundamental for the treatment, the desire of the analyst is what gives the analyst the ability or capacity to work within the transference relationship.

The desire of the analyst is what allows the analyst to function with something more than cold neutrality or the poker face semblance. The analyst stays composed and cool rather than cold and indifferent. Neutrality is better understood as equanimity rather than as aloofness or indifference. Equanimity, as a transformation within *jouissance*, over-includes both the seriousness of the semblant and the warm interest and empathic (*Einfühlung*) understanding that Freud (1913) thought was fundamental to establish a positive transference relationship, especially at the beginning of the treatment. In contrast to a closed poker face, the open face of the semblance of unbeing, and the half-smile of the analyst, and even the tone of the voice, as strategies within the transference, help generate a desire in the analysand to formulate a demand for analysis and to commit to the length and costs associated with the treatment.

In the first phase of analysis, the analyst represents a semblance of knowledge through the positive transference to the subject supposed to know what the analysand appears to ignore. Eventually the analyst has to become a semblance of being (the *objet a*). It is the love dimension of knowing that serves as a transition and facilitation between knowing and being and eventually between being and unbeing or emptiness.

But in order for transference love to have a facilitating function, the analyst has to give what he/she does not have rather than what she/he has or what the analysand demands. Because the analyst does not believe in the imaginary and symbolic dimensions of transference love (the illusions and lies of love), and is not identified with the object of fantasy, he/she can keep his/her desire empty and therefore lead the analysand through the phases of transference and on to the logical end of the analysis. At the end of the analysis, the analysand is no longer identified either with his/her unconscious object or with the figure of the analyst.

But the emptiness of desire or of the desire of the analyst is neither a manipulation of the transference nor a semblance or fabrication of the signifier: it is a form of *jouissance* or an experience beyond experience or beyond feelings. *Jouissance* is a feeling yet it is not a feeling; it is something more than a feeling. The Other *jouissance* is a semblance of unbeing and therefore can manifest as either an open or a serious dispassionate face. In the end, the desire of the analyst is a desire without a fixed object or cause. The desire of the analyst represents the emptiness of the presence of the analyst, rather than the analyst as the presence of the lost objects of the analysand. Because the analyst no longer represents either the presence or the absence of the unconscious object, the emptiness of the analyst generates the dynamism that converts the analyst into a dispensable and recyclable waste product.

At the end of analysis, the analyst no longer represents a semblance of knowing or of the *objet a*. The analyst remains alone, although not lonely, and represents the semblance of unbeing or emptiness in the sense of the vacuity of the Other that led to both new significations within the subject and the vacuity of the subject cause of his/her *jouissance*.

References

Bion, W. (1992). *Cogitations*. London: Karnac, 2005.

Heidegger, M. (1950). The Thing. In *Poetry, Language, Thought*. New York: Harper & Row, 1971 (Spanish translation available at: http://elpsicoanalistalector.blogspot.com/2007/09/martin-heidegger-la-cosa-das-ding.html).

Freud, S. (1913). On beginning the treatment. In J. Strachey (ed., trans.), *The Standard Edition of the Works of Sigmund Freud*. London: Hogarth Press, Vol. 12, pp. 123–44.

Kristeva, J. (1987). *Black Sun: Depression and Melancholia*. New York: Columbia University Press, 1989.

Lacan, J. (1960). Subversión del sujeto y dialéctica del deseo en el inconsciente freudiano. *Escritos II*, p. 804.

Lacan, J. (1961). *The Seminar of Jacques Lacan IX: On Identification*. London: Karnac.

Lacan, J. (1971). *The Seminar of Jacques Lacan XVIII: On a Discourse That Might Not Be a Semblance*. London: Karnac, 2002.

Lacan, J. (1972). On feminine sexuality: The limits of love and knowledge. *Encore: The Seminar of Jacques Lacan, Book XX*. New York: W.W. Norton, 1998.

Lacan, J. (1975–6). *Seminario 23: El Sinthoma* (Ricardo Rodríguez Ponte trans.). Unpublished.

Chapter 3

On the aim and end of analysis in the Lacanian school

> The termination of analysis occurs when one has gone around a circle twice;
> that is to say, to rediscover that which holds one captive.
>
> Jacques Lacan (1978)

Introduction

The question regarding the end of analysis implies something beyond the final moment of a process. In fact, the way the final phases of analysis are conceived influences the direction of psychoanalytic treatment from the very beginning.

In Spanish and English the same word is used to describe an aim or objective (fin/end) and the end of something (fin/end). Thus, it is the aim or objective concerned which allows for the definition and/or the termination of an activity. For this reason, in this chapter both of these themes will cross-fertilize and interact with one another: the aim of analysis and the termination of analysis. Depending on how the aim is defined, the aim and the end may be similar or different.

For example, if the aim of analysis is to build the identity of the ego and the therapeutic alliance, then, given this premise, it is not surprising that psycho-analysis would end with the identification with the analyst. In the case of the object-relations school, if the aim of analysis is the development of secure attach-ment (Bowlby), good-enough mothering (Winnicott), or the acquisition of the alpha function (Bion), then it is not surprising that analysis would end with the identification with the good object (the Kleinian analyst).

In contrast to these perspectives, within Lacanian psychoanalysis, the aim of the analysis of identifications is the end of the identification with the analyst.

> Any conception of analysis that is articulated – innocently or not, God only knows – to defining the end of the analysis as identification with the analyst, by that very fact makes an admission of its limits. Any analysis that one teaches as having to be terminated by identification with the analyst reveals, by the same token, that its true motive force is elided. There is a beyond to this identification defined by the relation and the distance of the *objet petit a*

to the idealizing capital I of identification . . . This crossing of the plane of identification is possible.

(Seminar XI; Lacan 1964: 272)

Any one who has lived through the analytic experience with me to the end of the training analysis knows that what I am saying is true . . .

(1964: 273)

For the fundamental mainspring of the analytic operation is the maintenance of the distance between the I – identification – and the *a*.

(1964: 273)

It is in as much as the analyst's desire, which remains an *x*, tends in a direction that is the exact opposite of identification, that the crossing of the plane of identification is possible, through the mediation of the separation of the subject in experience.

(1964: 274)

The aim of the desire of the analyst is to eventually work himself/herself out of a job by becoming dispensable rather than indispensable. When the analysand no longer identifies with the analyst, the analyst becomes dispensable and the analysis has reached its logical conclusion. Lacan argues that at the end of a Lacanian analysis the analysand identifies with the *sinthome* rather than with the analyst.

Psychoanalysis goes around the circle of identification twice. Identifications have to be first recognized and deconstructed and then relinquished, or taken away. This process is part and parcel of the path by which the desire of the subject is recognized and differentiated from the desire of the Other or from the desire to be recognized by the Other. When identifications (with the analyst and other significant figures) are abandoned, the subject finds his or her identity in the larger symbolic structure and the wondrous emptiness of unbeing (*desetre*, according to Lacan, 1966–7).

I have linked the concept of unbeing and what Lacan called the *sinthome* to the third form of identification defined by Freud and that Lacan called the unary trace. Lacan has called the *sinthome* a new form of ego but I do not find this to be a necessary feature of Lacanian theory. One can think of the unary trace, and the third form of identification, as a type of ego, but this categorization may be misleading since a trace represents a partial form of identification in contrast to the usual conception of the ego as a total or whole object (representation).

If anything, the unary trace may be better described as a form of non-self or non-ego (rather than ego or self) that nonetheless undergirds and re-knots the symbolic functioning of the subject. The unary trace is a form of identification based on non-identification (zero as One and One as zero). What remains of the ego after a critical analysis and deconstruction of identifications can only be articulated in the form of the negative. Following Lacan, I have also linked the unary trace, to the letter, to the *objet a*, to transformations of *jouissance*, as well as to permutations of the Name of the Father.

Terminable, interminable

Given Lacan's call for a creative return that retroactively re-founds the meaning of Freud's work, I will begin by examining Freud's approach to the subject. It is important to remember that Freud's discussions with Ferenczi regarding Ferenczi's "active technique" played the role of a precipitating event in motivating Freud to write "Analysis Terminable and Interminable" (1937). In the history of psychoanalysis, the question of introducing technical modifications is often linked to attempts to abbreviate the process of the cure. The criteria used to determine the termination of analysis becomes a question of the utmost importance.

In my opinion, the meaning of Freud's title establishes the guidelines of a clinical program. Freud does not propose an option or alternative, but quite the contrary: he emphasizes that an analysis is both terminable and interminable. And this does not apply to some analysands and not to others but to each and every one of them. On the other hand, an analysis has to have an end because otherwise it would be interminable. And if regular sessions end, how can analyses can be interminable?

Freud remarked that when he began his psychoanalytic practice he did not know what to do in order to have his analysands conform to what he termed an analytic or therapeutic pact. Conversely, once Freud had fine-tuned the analytic situation he did not know what to do in order to terminate the analysis.

> In the early years of my psycho-analytic practice I used to have the greatest difficulty in prevailing on my patients to continue their analysis. This difficulty has long since been shifted, and I now have to take the greatest pains to induce them to give it up.
>
> (1913: 130)

In "Analysis Terminable and Interminable", Freud proposes two criteria by which to determine whether a treatment can be ended and considered successful: if the symptoms have been resolved and whether enough unconscious material has been evoked and resolved in the treatment and the transference relationship so as not to have concerns about possible relapses in the future. The latter point is important because only if the treatment has had a therapeutic effect on the symptoms could one consider the treatment as having produced robust and long-lasting effects. Otherwise, the symptoms could have temporarily resolved for reasons unrelated to the treatment. In this case, the analysand could remain prone to relapses in the future.

However, Freud stops short of claiming that a treatment could have future preventive power. Although the treatment produced the remission of the symptoms, the analyst or psychoanalysis cannot predict accidental or environmental factors that could have an adverse or regressive effect on an analysand's condition in the future. Psychoanalysis has an effect on symbolic causality but not on causality in the real (*automaton* and *tuche*, respectively, according to Lacan [1964]).

According to Freud, the resolution of the symptoms is directly related to two factors: either the strength of ego defenses or the weakness of the drives. The reverse is true for the persistence of the illness or the failure of the treatment: they are due to the weakness of ego defenses or the strength of the drives. What is ambiguous in Freud's description is the meaning of the strength or weakness of defenses. By the weakness of defense, Freud means not only the absence of necessary defenses, but also the predominance of unconscious defenses.

Paradoxically, unconscious defenses weaken the ego, although unconscious defenses emanate from an unconscious part of the ego. Based on the same premise one could make the opposite argument: the ego is so strong that it has roots in both conscious and unconscious processes and it is this strength that is responsible for the development of symptomatology. Freud was a believer in conscious and rational forms of repression or of "mastery" of the drives. He only rejects unconscious forms of repression as being counter to healing and the therapeutic aims of psychoanalysis.

In this Freud is a traditionalist and his work is co-extensive to the more general process of secularization of religious principles characteristic of modernity. Freud pictures the ego and the drives in equivalent terms to the distinction between good and evil. However, we also know from his theory that ego defenses can also be problematic and that not much happens in life without the drives. In addition, the repressed amounts to more than simply the drive as a kind of evil inclination that needs to be tamed by morality and reason.

Freud's theory is more nuanced and less moralistic/dualistic when he speaks of the repressed in terms of repressed conflicts, traumas, or developmental fixations. In this context he emphasizes the principle of undoing rather than redoing ego-repression and how the repressed needs to emerge and be resolved/worked through in the course of the treatment. The more the unconscious played a central role in the treatment, the more likely the resolution of the symptoms will be. However, in my opinion, the unconscious encompasses both the unconscious of the repressed and the unconscious of the repressive.

When symptoms are not resolved, then this is due to the intensity of the symptom or to the *jouissance* of the symptom (pain/pleasure linked to it). The *jouissance* of the symptom in Lacan is equivalent to the intensity of the drive in Freud's work. Freud attributes the failure of the treatment to either the *jouissance* or the strength of the drive or to the failure of defenses. The first is what leads Lacan to develop the notion of the *sinthome* tied to the *jouissance* or the Real or drive dimension of the symptom. For Lacan, since the drive cannot be extinguished, the symptom continues after analysis in the form of the *sinthome*. However, the *sinthome* also has an aspect of defense built into it. The *sinthome* allows *jouissance* but also contains it by re-knotting the three dimensions of experience (RSI: Real, Symbolic, Imaginary).

Before proceeding on to the analysis of the question of ego defenses an important point must be made in relationship to the question of the stubbornness or the insistence and repetition of the symptom. This point is usually made to invalidate psychoanalysis as a form of effective treatment. The case of the Wolf-man is often cited as an example of a fraudulent or false claim on the part of Freud. It is claimed that Freud claimed that he had cured the Wolf-man of his symptoms when in fact his symptoms persisted throughout his life. However, Freud was clear on the process by which and how the Wolf-man returned to treatment, with him and others, and had a way of accounting for the successes and failures of the treatment. The Wolf-man spent over 70 years in analysis, and this example is used to discredit psychoanalysis as a form of medical or psychological treatment.

What is often overlooked is that there are plenty of examples of failed treatments in other psychiatric treatment modalities. Experienced clinicians know that medications are never as effective as reported in empirical or controlled statistical studies. Symptoms of depression and anxiety persist despite years of anti-anxiety or antidepressant medications, not to mention the case of antipsychotic medications. Medications are less expensive but not necessarily more effective than psychoanalysis. The same can be said of behavioral treatments. If one focuses attention on the patient and the symptom, by writing down the symptom as it manifests on a daily basis, for example, or seeing the patient several times a week for the purpose of suppressing the symptoms via various kinds of behaviors that strengthen defenses (exercise, entertainment, relaxation, etc.), then this intervention will indeed have an effect on the symptom, but the question is for how long or how robust the modifications will be? It is kind of unbelievable that behaviorists think that symptoms can be reliably eliminated for good without any consideration given to the patient's history, family, relationships, sexual life, or passions.

The analysis of ego defenses: obstacle or treatment?

According to Freud, when the ego is "crippled," regular ego defenses cannot defend against anxiety, explosiveness, addiction, or depression, just to name a few examples. Freud attributes the intensity and the pathogenic nucleus of these symptoms to the quantitative factor of the drives. But the question that follows from this assumption is whether the build-up of healthy defenses reinforces unconscious defenses or allows for them to be undone and modified? Freud answers this question when he says that the better is the enemy of the good. If by building healthy defenses the analysand feels good, he/she will not want to do the painful work of undoing unconscious defenses. It is ego strength not weakness that is an obstacle to the cure.

When considering the obstacles to effective treatment, Freud asks what are the obstacles to building stronger defenses rather than what are the obstacles to undoing repression or to revealing/disclosing the truths about the subject's desire.

He considers that he had already done the latter with limited success in the early period of psychoanalysis (if you can't beat them, then join them). Lacan (1955), for his part, wants to go back to the early Freud but does not address the legitimate reasons that Freud gave for his later focus and theorizing on ego defenses. However, when focusing on the defensive process rather than the repressed content, Freud is more interested in strengthening ego defenses than in finding a new way of working with or undoing unconscious defenses and resistances. Of the initial group of early analysts, Reich (1933) was the one notable follower of Freud who focused on ego defenses to undo rather than strengthen them (the technique of character analysis). Lacan's answer to Freud's interest in (strengthening) ego defenses was to shift the analysis of resistance to the analyst. I shall return to this further on.

Freud writes as if generosity and kind-heartedness, for example, were qualities associated with the alleged harmony of the ego, whereas miserliness and hostility are quantities of the id. In the developed character, the strength of the ego prevails over the strength of the id. This refers to the question of identification involved in the formation of the ego-ideal. According to Freud (1900, 1923), the ideal qualities of generosity and kindness are formed by identification with what is opposite to the tendencies/quantities of miserliness and hostility that have been abandoned. A child identifies with the generosity and kindness he/she is shown by his parents. However, such generosity and kindness may have been there all along since Freud grants that at the beginning the ego and the id evolve out of a single matrix. The actions of parents strengthen certain traits and weaken others.

The duality between the ego and the id is never completely attained, and if it is, it still remains in relationship to a non-dual dimension between them. The ego is never pure and undefiled and the id is not only impure and defiled. Often there is more honesty in the id and in desire than in the presumptions of the ego, tainted as they are with narcissistic forms of self-love and self-righteousness. The ego lives by the fantasy of being the master of his/her own house. It is this phantasm of being or becoming someone important, of replacing or vindicating the father, which represents an attempt to close or suture the gap in the ego. It is this attempt that leads to a division rather than a unity of the subject. The ego lacks the object that would make him/her a master. The true master is not a master or is the emptiness above the crown of power, political, administrative, or otherwise.

But to get to the emptiness beyond the crown of power, the subject has to work through the quantitative factors that were associated with the imaginary projects of the ego: anxiety, loss, lack, grief, and anger. Although these quantitative factors divide the ego, they contain useful and pure qualities needed to produce a psychic state that does not spontaneously occur within the ego or at least is usually found obstructed within the imaginary dimensions of the ego. It is the combination/ amalgamation between the quantitative id factors and the qualitative factors associated with the ego that taken together lead the subject towards the emptiness of both ego and object.

I link the qualitative factors in the ego to what I call "It" (*das Ding* or the no-thing) as the emptiness of the subject of the Real that reveals or gives access to symbolic understanding and new permutations/realizations of the symbolic structure. As Lacan pointed out, following Lao Tse, within the Symbolic the subject knows without knowing that it knows. This unknown-knowing of the subject or of a non-ego differs from the unconscious part of the ego of the defenses.

Both ego identifications and the identifications with the partial objects of the drive equally close the gap within the ego and produce an imaginary form of unity. These two forms of identifications represent two of the three identifications outlined by Freud. The third form of identification is the unary trace that I examined in chapter 1. The unary trace is a form of dis-identification, or non-identification, and a form of undoing the "entification" of the id (id-entification as signifying a form of reification of the id). In the "It" of the unary trace, the subject becomes a metaphor, rather than an ego identification, and the object becomes a form of *jouissance* linked to the same metaphor, instead of to an infantile derivative of the drive or the primal objects.

Freud was optimistic that better, shorter, and less expensive treatments can be achieved by giving more help to the ego. The latter signifies to strengthen the ego. However, better therapy that will strengthen the ego is the therapy that suppresses/represses the symptom, or masters the drive, in the style of common sense and behavioral interventions. Ego psychology goes hand in hand with behaviorism or cognitive therapy. Freud intends to replace pathogenic unconscious repression with current, flexible, rational, and healthy defenses.

But can better repressions be developed without conjuring up the repressed? Does treatment fail because better defenses cannot be built due to the weakness of the ego or because repression has not been undone?

Ego defenses do not allow pain and want displeasure over in the shortest amount of time. So how is it then that a stronger ego is good for treatment? Would a stronger ego tolerate more pain or would it want the pain over in the shortest amount of time? This is another contradiction. In fact it is the ego that needs to be let go and replaced by a different organizing principle.

It is the symbolic order and the subject that can allow for the signification of desire, for its manifestation and clarification, and at the same time for symbolization that places desire squarely within the dimension of the Law. One could object that this is a square desire and argue in favor of the romantic and postmodern notion of drives and desires that are independent of any law. However, this leads to postmodern chaos, catastrophe, early deaths, and suicides, if not perversion. The borderline and narcissistic conditions are ample evidence that such notions lead to problems with impulse control, unbridled individualism, and the illusions of a sexuality not determined by the regularities of social or natural laws.

How can the ego be the part of the analysand that the analyst can ally with in order to further the cause of the treatment, if the ego is one of the biggest obstacles to the cure? Related to this is whether the ego works under the pleasure principle or the reality principle and how the pleasure principle is defined: as the organizing principle of the drives or of the ego? The notion of the therapeutic alliance, for example, relies on the link between the ego and the reality principle, not between the ego and the pleasure principle.

Freud defined the reality principle as the temporary tolerance and acceptance of displeasure in order to achieve a more lasting, stable, long-term satisfaction. But this definition contradicts the definition of the ego as being intolerant of displeasure. The desire to avoid pain interferes with the possibility of more long-term solutions to mental problems. The ego has to be willing to put up with some temporary pain in order to be released from suffering. The ego is an obstacle to this objective.

The ego of the defenses is also the ego of narcissism because the pain involved in making the unconscious conscious necessarily involves the recognition that the ego is not the master of the psyche. It is a mistake to think of the ego as the dominant mental agency. This is what Lacan (1969) called the master's discourse that interferes with the discourse of the analyst and the aims of psychoanalytic treatment.

The undoing of the defenses requires the recognition that the subject does not know a lot about himself/herself and that some of the historical fictions/memories/narratives may be incorrect or at least fantasized and that the symbolic Other is also required to restore continuity to experience.

The challenge for psychoanalytic treatment is how to achieve the twin goals of helping the analysand accept suffering as part of the analytic process and at the same time maintain a positive transference in the analytic relationship. There are some built-in gratifications in the transference that make this tolerable or possible. The analyst does not provide recognition or support for narcissistic identifications, and the empathy with ego defenses needs to be short lived. But what takes their place? The answer lies in the dynamics of transference love, another aspect of the practice of analysis that Lacan widely illuminated. I will return to this in a section up ahead.

Another requirement of this therapeutic task is not only the suspension of ego defenses, or the tolerance of a narcissistic injury, but also the deconstruction of the super-ego. By this I mean that whatever the analyst does it should not be intended as a form of punishment, since this is what the illness is thriving and depending on.

Freud established equivalence between the ego and a text, when in fact the better comparison may have been between the unconscious and a text. Lacan calls the unconscious "the discourse of the Other" (1957a, 1957b: 163). It is this discourse that is "riddled" with holes, allusions, avoidances, distortions, etc. In *The Interpretation of Dreams*, Freud (1900) used the example of a censored public text to explain the workings of the dream censor in the production of a dream. However, in "Analysis Terminable and Interminable", Freud only thinks of censorship in terms of either the ego or the pleasure principle.

In addition, both Freud and Lacan ignore the fact that Freud early on used the pleasure principle to explain the sexual drive and the tendency towards wish fulfillment. It is this double aspect of the pleasure principle that is related to the unconscious as a discourse. The unconscious and the pleasure principle not only represent and organize drives but also the unconscious tendency towards symbolization and censorship.

For Freud pathogenic defenses weaken the ego or produce what he calls an ego-modification that affects and interferes with the course of treatment. Pathogenic defenses cripple the ego or healthy ego defenses and function. This formulation would work if it were not for the fact that pathogenic defenses are also fixated at the level of the ego or, more strongly, emanate from the unconscious ego, according to the Freud of *The Ego and the Id*. It is a case of the ego crippling the ego. So, again, do we want to strengthen or weaken the ego to further the cause and success of psychoanalytic treatment? One possible answer that Freud gives is that we want to weaken the unconscious ego and strengthen the conscious ego. This would also work if it were not for the fact that the conscious ego is also an obstacle to the treatment. The ego says: "I'm fine, I am not so bad after all, I am feeling better now, and I would rather not talk about that."

Both the unconscious and conscious ego and super-ego need to be deconstructed and replaced by the subject of the unconscious and the subject of the Real that I have identified with the unary trace. The beyond the ego is the beyond the pleasure principle, whether one thinks of the beyond as the suffering that needs to be accepted instead of repressed, or of the pleasure of the good and sublimation rather than the good of pleasure in terms of an inconvenient *jouissance* or a destructive pleasure.

Bion (1970) speaks of this in terms of the negative capability as a capacity for patience, faith, and the tolerance of frustration. This capacity is also beyond reason or at least certain types of reason or certain logical types, as discussed in chapter 1. However, Bion does not posit a self, ego, or subject linked to this capacity. Bion and his followers speak of it in terms of a quality of the analyst as an analyst of achievement or as a psychic state or reality linked to intuition. Here intuition is a human mental capacity or psychic function that is the non-understanding side of understanding, or the side of understanding that allows human beings to perceive and access a dimension of experience or beyond experience that is beyond understanding.

The intuitive psychic state is a function or a place where human understanding intersects or meets a larger dimension of mind that is beyond conscious understanding. This larger dimension knows without knowing that it knows. In this sense we can speak of an unconscious function or at least of a function beyond consciousness, or a beyond a sense of self or ego that can also be recognized as a locus of truth-value.

However, as soon as this function is recognized as a true or Big self in a relative sense, then it becomes a major fiction like the ego was for Freud. Big mind or the unconscious, and even the self, is best described as no-self. Of the three categories of self, ego, and subject, the subject is the one that best captures the sense of the human subject being something temporary or impermanent, evanescent, and insubstantial. In this I believe that Lacan was essentially correct, and for this alone I can call myself a Lacanian.

The analysis of the formations of the repressive unconscious

Symptoms persist due to the *jouissance* at play, that is to say, the pleasure involved in even the most horrible forms of psychic pain. A person wants to both cling to the pleasure in the symptom and avoid the pain in the same, a kind of impossible (Real) state of affairs. It is the avoidance of unpleasure that constitutes one of the main motives behind defenses. On the other hand, it is the seeking of pain that constitutes the second opposite motive for preserving the symptom. The ego wants to suffer for two reasons: to cling to pleasure or *jouissance* and to satisfy the need for punishment or pain. The latter represent two aspects of *jouissance* and of the super-ego: the demand to enjoy and the equal demand to suffer, two aspects of passion or pathos (suffering).

One of the key manifestations of ego defenses is denial, or defensive rather than creative negation. The ego says, "I rather or I don't want to talk about that, and if you insist I can make life very unpleasant for you." The patient routinely avoids talking about certain subjects (topics and people) to the point where the analyst finally gives up asking and begins to collude with the patient's defenses. This leads to stagnation and interrupted or partially successful/unsuccessful treatments. This example underscores the convergence of the aim with the end. If a treatment is going nowhere, the treatment may end without having reached its logical end point. In this sense, termination refers to a phase in treatment that comes after a significant amount of unconscious material has been evoked and worked through. If a treatment ends without having passed the beginning or middle phases of treatment, then this is not an end in either sense of end as aim or conclusion. The end simply means the stopping of the sessions.

It is always unclear in Freud's texts, as in life, whether the problem/obstacle is the strength or the weakness of ego defenses. Sometimes Freud writes as if the treatment would have been more successful if the ego defenses were stronger and the ego was able to successfully suppress a symptom, the *jouissance* and impetus of the drive, or the Oedipus complex. In this, Freud's approach to treatment is quite similar to common sense and to behavioral treatments that depend on various successful defenses against symptoms. Sometimes Freud also writes as if pathological defenses/repressions in childhood had altered the ego's ability to use healthy defenses. Unconscious repression stemming from childhood alters the ability of the ego to use conscious or rational defenses against the symptom/drive. At other times Freud refers to the need to alter the ego defenses in the treatment. Here he attributes unconscious repression to the ego rather than identifying the ego with health, rationality, and consciousness or self-awareness.

In my opinion, this is what led Lacan to reject the analysis of ego resistances altogether, and to identifying the latter with an unsuccessful attempt at repression, and social conformity, equivalent to behaviorism and adaptation to the environment. In *Variants of the Standard Treatment*, Lacan (1955) critiques the analysis of resistances in so far as it relates to the school of ego psychology and the analysis of the ego. He believes that this variant of the treatment ignores the analysis of the formations of the unconscious that truly represents the right treatment for the symptoms.

Lacan emphasizes that the analysis of resistance is always within speech and that defenses are taking place within discourse with all its distortions. Lacan contrasts the analysis of speech and discourse from what Fenichel (1941) said when he wrote "the understanding of the meaning of words is particularly a concern of the ego" (p. 54). For Lacan the truth-value of words is found in unconscious desire and not at the level of the ego.

However, Freud's ambiguity with regards to the ego and to defenses may continue to be a source of exploration and of new discoveries that may advance the course and future of clinical psychoanalysis. In this regard, Lacan may have thrown out the baby with the bath water. I agree with Lacan that the problem is the strength and not the weakness of the ego, and that the imaginary ego needs to be deconstructed and let go in the process of analytic treatment. However, I believe that, precisely for this very same reason, the analysis of defenses remains a crucial aspect of analytic treatment and of an analytic understanding of suffering (psychopathology).

A clinical example can help to illustrate this point. In the example provided by a new case of a supervisee of mine, the analysand told him that he'd had sex with a different man every day since his last session. The supervisee did not know what to do with the material and feared correctly that a transference interpretation would increase the defenses against the analysis.

At the same time the analyst candidate did not want to say something that would make the analysand feel judged by the analyst. I suggested that he needed to ask the analysand simply to speak about what he thought or felt about what he told the analyst. In this instance, the analysand may tell the analyst that he feared or was angered by the possibility that the analyst could judge him for his "acting out." In response the analyst could help the analysand explore how the analysand himself felt about his actions. In turn the analysand could become conscious of how he has some judgments about his actions and how he projects his own judgments onto the Other (for the analysand the Other represents a social authority). Via the projection, his own desire for the Law becomes the desire of the Law or of the Other.

This example helps illustrate how desire is acted out, or repressed by "expression," and in turn what is overtly repressed is the repressive activity of the analysand's own conscience and unconscious censor. The analysand may also be provoking the analyst to make a transference interpretation so that the analysand could tell the analyst all about his sexual fantasies with the analyst. Here possible unconscious fantasies with a father figure are being acted out rather than repressed or are being repressed by acting instead of remembering. In this example what needs to be addressed first is the repressive rather than the repressed unconscious. But is there a difference between unconscious judgments and the workings of the unconscious censor, or between the repressed super-ego and the repressive unconscious?

As Freud himself acutely observed, all the dream work censor does is use the same processes involved in language and judgment to confuse the relations among the terms. The terms don't change but their location does. Self is replaced by other, love for hate, and inclusion for exclusion, just to name a few. In addition, the structure of judgment, unconscious censorship, and the symbolic order of language are all co-extensive to one another with only one exception.

The exception involves the drive or the affective component of judgment or censorship that justifies carving out a separate category for the super-ego. The repressed and unconscious repressive super-ego is the same as the repressive unconscious with the exception that the super-ego is angry with the subject. The super-ego is the personal and drive dimension of unconscious judgment. Personal here refers to lived experience, but paradoxically personal also refers to the impersonal death drive working through the laws of the Code.

The difference between the analysis of the repressive unconscious and Reich's technique of character analysis is that despite the common objective of decon-structing ego defenses, Lacan does not believe that desire can exist without the Law. In contrast to this, Reich believed it was possible to reach an unrepressed desire buried under social prohibitions and defenses. For Lacan the prohibition of desire generates desire at the same time.

Lacan often emphasized how desire is intrinsically intertwined and entangled with the function of the Law. The Law for Lacan functions unconsciously and unconsciously produces the effects of repression. The Law not only conceals but also reveals and produces desire. We want what we can't have and don't want what we have or can have. The formations of the unconscious, or mental forma-tions, are compromise formations between unconscious desire and unconscious defenses.

When an analysand omits or refuses to speak or symbolize something, not only he/she refuses a particular wish, thought, or emotion, but also refuses to recognize a narcissistic injury resulting from the loss of an object: a loss that is central to the constitution of the subject. Lacan associates this misrecognition with denial or negation (*Verneinung*) as an unconscious function of the ego (ideal ego/ego-ideal).

Now for Freud denial, as a defense, and as a form of negation, was not uncon-scious. Unconscious repression utilizes denial, and denial is a form of the nega-tive, but in denial the repressed is intellectually accepted and unconsciously negated at the same time. The ego can recognize his/her division and the existence of repression but deny that it applies to the ego at a particular circumstance. In denial, negation is not unconscious since it requires a deliberate action/decision, a judgment or choice by the subject. The ego says: "I am fine, I am not lacking anything, have not lost anything or anybody, I am not 'less than,' and I don't want anything that I can't have."

When the ego says, "I am fine, I am in control," although these statements are conscious affirmations, that deny their opposites, the fact that they are denying their opposites is preconscious, while the fact that the ego is protecting a narcissistic injury resulting from the castration complex is entirely unconscious.

The alteration of defenses in treatment depends on the ability/capacity to alter pleasant and unpleasant feelings and to accept or seek what is or is not true within experience, or within the subject or the object. The analysis of resistances is not an ego analysis per se, because the actual question is to analyze the repressive unconscious, or unconscious repression, and not only the repressed and the return of the repressed. The analysis of resistances or of defenses is not only a question of undoing rather than strengthening ego defenses, but the so-called ego defenses may be unconscious linguistic formations rather than ego processes.

In his paper on negation, Freud (1925) describes a defensive reflex and repression under the pleasure principle as preliminary forms of judgment. The pleasure principle or what he calls the original pleasure ego attributes a good or bad quality to something, and "wants to introject into itself everything that is good and to eject from itself everything that is bad" (p. 237). The decisions of the pleasure principle or the pleasure ego thus play the decisive role in operations determined by instinctual factors such as swallowing and spitting that are also motor operations that establish the first distinctions between inside and outside.

However, the decisions of the pleasure principle can also be understood as the laws of the unconscious. And in this regard, the laws of the unconscious and the pleasure principle are equivocal: they serve both the purposes of wishful thinking or pleasure and object seeking, and the defensive moves of pain/anxiety avoidance and of unconscious displacement and distortion. Seeking pleasure is the other side of avoiding pain as well as vice versa.

This is the archaic aspect of the unconscious that organizes the primitive relationship to the mother and the partial object (breast). However, early on, and via the paternal metaphor, the unconscious becomes embedded with the structure of desire, the Name of the Father, and the structure of language. "Repression may without doubt, be correctly described as the intermediate stage between a defensive reflex and a condemning judgment" (Freud, 1905c: 175).

The process of affirmation and negation at work in language seems to be intrinsically related to the acquisition of language via emotional and symbolic parent–child relationships. It is the parent as Other that affirms or denies certain actions of the child, which are then found duplicated in the child's own relationship to itself. The identification with the opposite, as a union of opposites, is internal to the process of identification. Objects are abandoned or negated/repressed through the process of identification at the root of the formation of the ego-ideal.

> I have asserted above that dreams have no means of expressing the relation of a contradiction, a contrary or a "no." I shall now proceed to give a first denial of this assertion. One class of cases which can be comprised under the heading of "contraries" are, as we have seen, simply represented by identification

– cases, that is, in which the idea of an exchange or substitution can be brought into connection with the contrast.

(Freud, 1900: 318)

Separation is achieved via identification with a parent, but the identification is the affirmation of a contrary wish or desire to that which is being negated/ repressed via the identification. The boy represses his hostility and homoeroticism towards the father by identifying with the Name of the Father. If the mother rejects the Name of the Father, then it is the hostility towards the father and the Law that will prevail. The girl identifies with the Name of the Father by accepting the absence of the imaginary phallus and identifying with the symbolic mother and suppressing the hostility and homoeroticism towards the same. The identification resolves the opposition between parent and child but also the opposition between contrary feelings held by the child towards the parent. Instead of homosexual love, for example, there will be a love for ideals or ideas. Instead of hostility, there will be a hate of contradicting ideas. In the case of homosexuality, the same could be said for heterosexual love. The ideals substitute for the parent, but also for the censored love and hate felt towards the parent of the same or opposite sex.

The child and the parents are figures for the dialectical movements of matter and mind at work within instinctual reflexes, within wishful thinking, seeking and avoiding pleasure and pain, within the unconscious structure of language, and within the acts and decisions associated with conscious speech and the function of judging the subject matter of thoughts. When someone using conscious negation as a defense, says no, this is not my mother or father, here the yes becomes no, or something that I rather forget or repress, and the no becomes a way of saying yes to repressive identifications with the opposite.

Freud also distinguishes between repression and negation by saying that negation is the way that censored thoughts can make their way into consciousness. Negation facilitates the undoing of repression by allowing a thought into consciousness and denying it at the same time. But the act of conscious negation is a repetition of the similar unconscious act that led to repression. The affirmation and negation that takes place in judgment are similar in form to the affirmation and negation that takes place in language and in the dream-work. The latter represent the interplay of the primary forces of being and non-being, life and death, from which the conscious intellectual functions of judgment originate.

Dream distortion and dream displacement, for example, are due to the agency of unconscious censorship. Dream censorship is an integral part of dream representation, the same way that negation is an integral part of linguistic representation. In a psychoanalytic conception of symbol, a symbol represents something that has been repressed/negated. In language, negation works differently: there is a substratum of negation or erasure of the relationship to the object at the same time that the object is represented. The object is not repressed. The object elephant, for example, is represented in absentia by the signifier elephant, but is also partially represented or misrepresented as a difference in relationship to other words. But within letters there are primitive relationships to objects that the letters no longer refer to. These objects have been erased or repressed. For example, certain letters initially bore an iconic resemblance to a particular animal. The spirit of the animal passes onto the letter and comes to animate the energetic sparks contained within the letters. The relationship to the animal has been replaced by the question of the Real or what exists or does not exist in reality independently of images and language.

In dreams this process is reversed: instead of words replacing images and objects, it is images that negate dream thoughts and words. The same happens with conscious perception of visual reality. The world is perceived as existing out there and "as if" names were contained within the essence of things. How naming and language conditions perception remains ostensibly unconscious.

The human mind/psyche, or spirit, is constructed by dialectic of negation and affirmation, between words and images, the Imaginary, and the Symbolic. Affirmation represents the desiring aspect of the dialectic or psyche, whereas negation, repression, or censorship represents the ethical dimension of the same. At the same time, the two are interdependent or mutually condition one another.

The unconscious or conscious aspects of the mind are two figures, metaphors, or opposites that manifest the same dialectic found in the paternal metaphor (Name of the Father over the desire of the mother), and the relationships between parents and children. The unconscious can represent either the repressive or repressed force, and the same is true for consciousness.

Freud gave contradictory accounts of how the unconscious represented repressed desires and consciousness represented the power of ethical repression or conscience. In the same way, he said that there was no negation in the unconscious, but then was forced to explain how repression took place unconsciously. He gave accounts of how the super-ego, as the unconscious repressive force within the ego, could itself be repressed by the ego, and at the same time distinguished a form of unconscious that was not repressed. This latter form of unconscious approximates his view of the preconscious as being unconscious in a descriptive sense (Freud, 1915).

The dialectical movements between desire/drive and the Law, between conscious and unconscious experience, between the repressed and the repressive, parallel the unconscious structure of language. The act or the decisions of speech involve the same choices and judgments of affirmation and negation that reveal or conceal the truths about thought, words, and desire.

Language reproduces the symbolic functions of Culture, the Law, and the paternal metaphor. The prohibition of incest and the rules of kinship, grammar, and logic are all interrelated. Although in one sense the dream-work can be identified with the primary process of energy in dreams (free flow of energy–immediate satisfaction–unlimited condensation and displacement) characteristic of the repressed unconscious, in another sense, condensation and displacement, as the laws that regulate the dream-work in the unconscious, are the laws of the unconscious censor or of the repressive unconscious.

The repressive unconscious is another name for the laws of the signifier or of the word, of the Other, the symbolic father, and the locus of the Code, as Lacan called it following the linguistics of Jakobson. A code is a system of constraint and possibility, or inhibition and facilitation, that exists within language, the psyche, the brain, and the family. In addition, the laws of the Code, or of the Other, are not necessarily within the subject, but rather are a Third Dimension between sender and receiver, dream thoughts and dream images, thoughts and words, self and other. Lacan considers the signifier as ruled by the pleasure principle, because he considers the pleasure principle as the principle of defense and repression and not as what stimulates the sexual drive as a craving for pleasure/ pain or for *jouissance*. Instead, he associates *jouissance* with the death drive. *Jouissance* is linked to both pleasure and suffering, and suffering is linked to both the craving for pleasure and the repression of desire.

The Law is a transitive experience, since the subject is both the subject and the object of repression. The decision to say or not to say something is co-extensive or parallels the process of symbolization and of affirmation and negation in the unconscious.

In *The Ego and the Id*, Freud wrote that "the faculties of self-criticism and conscience – mental activities, that is, that rank as extremely high ones – are unconscious and unconsciously produce effects of the greatest importance" (1923: 26). Yet in other texts Freud writes that unconscious repression is only a preliminary form or stage of judgment. The question at stake here is not only whether unconscious repression involves the faculties of self-criticism and conscience, but also Freud's conception of conscious and unconscious repression. I have pointed out that Freud regarded conscious repression as necessary and positive or rational, and unconscious repression as irrational and negative. It is unclear in his quote whether he regards an unconscious conscience as something rational or irrational akin to his concept of a malevolent super-ego.

Freud derives his belief that "in unconscious thinking no process that resembles judgment occurs" from the fact that in dreams a term can be transformed into or be represented by its opposite. A similar word can be used to express antithetical meanings. Freud does not consider Hegel's concept of "sublation" or "*Aufheben*," whereby something is eliminated only insofar as it has come to situate itself in a unity with its opposite. Freud does not consider the operation of negation in sublation and therefore claims that there is no negation in the unconscious. The determinate being of an element in the dream image is the unity in which its opposite has been preserved/negated.

In other texts Freud seems to be acutely aware of this process when he writes:

> Contrary thoughts are always closely connected with each other and are often paired off in such a way that the one thought is excessively intensely conscious while its counterpart is repressed in the unconscious. This relation between the two thoughts is an effect of the process of repression. For repression is

often achieved by means of an excessive reinforcement of the thought contrary to the one that is to be repressed.

(1905a: 200)

The transformation of a dream-thought into its opposite in the dream-content is precisely a way of repressing that presupposes the activity of negation. The element in the dream-content is affirmed at the same time that the censored dream thought is negated. Moreover, the function of affirming or negating applied to a pair of opposites is extrinsic to the opposition itself. The attribution of a quality or value (positive/affirmative versus negative) will depend upon the meaning given to the terms by a wider associative context or assemblage. "Old" could be strength or weakness/lack and represent either having or not having something. The same could be said of the signifier "young." Whatever signifier comes to signify lack will be negated, and its opposite affirmed. With human beings the pleasure principle is modified by cultural and linguistic modifications that will reduplicate the duality found within the pleasure principle. Both desire and defenses will be unconsciously signified within language and visual perception.

Finally, although the analyses of unconscious defenses, narcissistic injuries, and formations of desire are crucial for the treatment and elimination of symptoms, and for improving the social, sexual, and productive function of the subject, the structure and division of the subject and of the psyche will not end or disappear with the ending of the treatment. This is the interminable aspect of analysis. However, analysis also allows the subject to experience the division and duality of the psyche in the non-dual way of the One that includes the not one, the not-all, as well as the Other. A metaphor of this would be the Moebius strip where the inside goes into the outside, the conscious into the unconscious, the law into desire, as well as vice versa. The subject becomes capable of perceiving from more than one register or perspective at a time. And perhaps this is what the psyche or psychic structure had been doing all along, except that now the subject is adverted with respect to and actually enjoys the phenomena that determine his/her functioning. The subject may now traverse the terrain that goes from the subject of the enunciation to the subject of the statement.

Narcissistic injury and resistance

Lacan associates the misrecognition of the division of the ego with denial or negation (*Verneinung*) as an unconscious function of the ego. The ideal ego and the ego-ideal in their own ways both attempt to cover over or conceal the basic division of the subject. The ideal ego covers the division by using body images, whereas the ego-ideal does it using ideas and words. Although division and splitting is common to all subjects, it nonetheless constitutes a narcissistic injury since narcissism is always represented by an ideal of unity/fusion, completion, and even perfection. From this perspective, narcissistic injuries and defenses are not exclusively or intrinsically linked to so-called pre-oedipal phases of development. In addition, early injuries to the ideal ego are not necessarily due to lack of maternal empathy or mirroring behavior, as is commonly believed.

The specular image, as a body image, and as the ideal ego, incorporates and resolves the intensities of the life and death drives that were linked to the absence and presence of the breast. The body image replaces the presence of the object and compensates for its absence.

At the same time, the life and death drives continue to be revealed and manifest through the ideal ego as a new mental formation. The absence of the *objet a* will appear in a blank spot, defect, flaw, or something missing within the body image. If the absence does not appear, then this leads to a grandiose self-image, linked to an idealized good breast and to the mother's imaginary phallus. The absence of the absence also leads to developmental arrest because the self does not move in the direction of the Other. Absence of the object, together with a prior presence, lead to the formation of the ideal ego, as a necessary body image, but the absence of the object within the image also stabilizes the body image and prevents it from becoming a grandiose image. In papers published by the International Psychoanalytical Association, the differences between the ideal ego, the ego-ideal, and the grandiose self are often confused and all explained in terms of fusion states with the mother (Lichtenberg, 1975; Hanly, 1984).

In addition, fusion with the mother, leading to a grandiose self, is also confused with neglect, deprivation of "emotional sustenance," or the lack of maternal desire for the child. The lack of maternal desire is also confused with the mother's conditioned desire for a fantasized object. All of these factors are seen as determining either a form of depressive ego-weakness, or a defensive grandiose or false self.

The absence of a specular image, as an ideal ego, fixates the ego at the level of the partial object and renders it subject to the *jouissance* of the Other and to persecutory psychotic anxieties as well as primitive forms of fusion with the partial object. There is no self or subject at this point. This condition can be produced either by privation of maternal desire or by the foreclosure of the Name of the Father in the mother's mind. Either too much or too little amounts to the same result in this regard.

The denial of the division of the ego takes two forms: one related to the ideal ego, the other to the ego-ideal. The first includes the denial of any bodily or physical limitations or flaws. The denial can also take the form of narcissistic overestimations of the body in all its glory. An example of this would be the case of an analysand who dreamt that she was a superwoman. Her associations included a sense of the great dexterity of her body and a memory of her father recognizing her as the "birth of perfection."

The second denial of the division of the subject is linked to the ego-ideal. Here the subject finds its unity via identification with ideas, ideals, and relationships that seem to complete the subject. An example of this is an analysand who considered her relationship as idyllic and a source of great happiness, and yet had a repeated dream where she was with different men and feared that her partner would find out and risk losing the relationship. She denied that she had any ambivalence about her partner and feared exploring the possibility that she might be too dependent or fused with the partner. Any exploration of ambivalence immediately translated into a fear that the analysis could cause an end to the relationship.

In general the division of the subject appears when the other does not recognize or misrecognizes the identifications of the ego either with bodily or specular images or with the mass or aggregate of ideas that constitute the ego-ideal. It is important for the analyst not to be fooled by the strength or unity of the ideal ego or ego-ideal. At the same time the analyst needs to be able to be empathic with the defenses in a purely strategic sense. The judo-style flow with ego defenses, while preserving the awareness of their defensive purposes, enables the analyst and the analysand to work with and through the divisions of the subject. The apparent support of ego defenses is purely strategic for the purposes of their eventual dissolution and transformation into the symbolic functioning of the subject.

Castration

In "Analysis Terminable and Interminable", Freud (1937) also points out how the joint efforts of the analyst and analysand to recognize and work through resistance run aground upon the rock of castration.

Although castration is prefigured in the loss of the breast, the hole in the image of the ideal ego, and the loss of feces, strictly speaking, the fear of castration is what triggers the development of the super-ego and the ego-ideal. Retroactively, castration can also determine the meaning of the loss of the breast, and the lack in the body image. An example of the first, and of identification with the partial object of the drive/desire, would be the sense of loss and dispossession that small breasts can trigger in women, and the castration anxiety that the small breasts of a lover can trigger in some men. The example of people who go to medical doctors requesting the removal of a hand or arm would be a glaring example of castration producing a retroactive effect on the body image. The super-ego retroactively affects the image of the body as described in the Bible: "If your hand causes you to sin, cut if off" (Gospel according to Mark 9:38–48). It is interesting to note how although the pre-modern cruel super-ego has disappeared from the ideals of the culture, its unconscious effects re-emerge via developments of new forms of psychopathology. In traditional biblical culture, there was a direct correlation between cultural ideals and the pathologies of the primitive super-ego. In postmodernity, traditional ideals or super-ego formations that have been suppressed in the culture return from repression via new forms of psychopathology.

According to Lacan, Freud discovered the existence of a true complex when he came across what has been called the problem of castration. It is well known that, by using that term, the founder of psychoanalysis attempted to account for a threat that in fact is never fulfilled. Castration as a developmental complex has nothing to do with emasculation or an effective bodily loss. But, then, why is castration so decisive and marking, to the point that Freud calls it the living rock that signals the unsurpassable limit of any analysis?

Castration is effective by virtue of being a symbolic condition. Symbolic here refers to a theory or to what Freud calls the sexual theories of childhood. Freud says childhood theory, not fantasy, fiction, or lie. Freud presupposes that childhood sexual theories regarding the difference between the sexes are an invariable step in the constitution of the subject. Castration does not arise from the inside as a phase or an ontogenetic stage of development but rather comes from the field of the Other. The mother is perceived as lacking something that she wants from the father, and the same is true for the father. The mother lacks the imaginary phallus, while the father lacks the *objet a* (of love and drive) the mother is perceived as having.

For the child the *objet a* had already been lost prior to the encounter or missed encounter with castration. The child had been an *objet a*/phallus for the mother, and the breast, as well as the specular image, had been an *objet a* for the child. At the time of castration the *objet a* will be transfigured into a phallic object that causes the difference between the sexes. However, the mother does not disappear as an object of love, since she is also the father's love object. In addition, the father through the gaze and into the ego-ideal also figures as an *objet a*. The father has what the mother wants but also the recognition that the child wants. In fact with castration, in the case of heterosexuality, the child represses the aggressivity and homoeroticism towards the parent of the same sex while at the same time both parents are preserved as love objects.

The Other is revealed as both complete and incomplete. The complete or imaginary aspect of the (f)Other is the one that threatens castration, or in other words, the one that generates the lack or loss that refers to the anecdote of the castration threat. The Other will take something away from or reveal a lack in the subject. On the other hand, the (m)Other herself is perceived as incomplete, inconsistent, or as having something missing which refers to the anecdote of femininity as the absence or lack of the phallus.

Given this, what does the Freudian limit of castration imply? According to Freud's understanding, the analysis of the male (I would say masculinity) does not go beyond a point the passing through of which would signify a giving in, a submission into passivity before the father. Said conflict would be equivalent to the castration complex provoking all the consequent duels, challenges, combats, rebellions, and ingratitude that usually are expressed as stagnation and a worsening of the analysand's condition. Correspondingly, the analysis of the female collides with the demand for the phallus, the impossibility of which makes for varied dissatisfactions and complaints, if not for plain depressions.

Castration is beyond Oedipus

According to Lacan castration is a genuine complex. Based on Freud's writings on femininity, Lacan argues that castration is the logical premise that then and only then as a defensive consequence generates what before Lacan had been called the Oedipus complex. From a Lacanian perspective Oedipus becomes a myth and no longer a complex. Moreover, in Seminar IX "On Identification," Lacan (1961–2) states that Oedipus is a dream of Freud and should be interpreted as such. What is implied? Oedipus is repressive before it is repressed. The Oedipus story and the rivalries and passion concerned conceal the truth that desire is established as a function of the law and prohibition – the incest prohibition being the paradigmatic example of all prohibition. As it is written in the Gospel of Paul:

> The sinful passions aroused by the law were at work in our bodies . . . I would not have known what sin was except through the law. For I would not have known what coveting really was if the law had not said, do not covet.
>
> (Romans 7:7)

In the case of Paul, the Law is rejected for causing the very problems that it is invoked to cure. On the other hand, the rejection of the Law also causes the elimination of desire, and therefore raises the severity of the Law to a level previously unprecedented within the Jewish religion (for example, the absence of a celibacy ideal for the priesthood within Judaism). Castration and the prohibition flowing from it compel one to desire. In addition, the fact of the partiality of desire imposes a limitation that the subject finds difficult to accept. The resistance to desire appears to follow from a neurotic conflict, between the law and desire, but, in fact, it is a desire not to desire because the law of castration itself causes desire. In this sense the very posing of a conflict between the law and desire may be seen as defensive in and of itself. I shall return to this later on.

Can one go beyond castration?

The answer is yes. Lacan with legitimate ambition proposes to go beyond castration. This new aim is associated with a central tenet of Lacanian clinical practice: the question of the resistance of the analyst. The analysand is teaching us that the person is not resisting via the symptoms but that something is resisting through them. Desire as a primordial definition of the subject is resisting. And desire must resist in disguise before the rule of censorship because in general terms desire is systematically reduced, negated, inverted, retroactively undone, attributed to somebody else (the other), and so on and so forth.

The resistance of the analyst is something else: it is resistance to listening, to intervening (the horror of the act, as Lacan calls it) and especially it is resistance to set aside the wish to function as the analysand's wished for ego-ideal. The analyst instead functions not with his/her ego-ideal or his/her formal professional identity, but with what Lacan calls the "desire of the analyst." The desire of the analyst is neither the countertransference nor the vocational desire to work as an analyst. Rather, it is the difficult attainment (which is no-attainment) of a psychic position that is characterized by the intention of directing the desire of the analysand first towards the analyst but then turning it towards others. The desire of the analyst is something like a second-degree desire that differs from the common and "human all too human" (Nietzsche, 1878) "desire of being desired." What is at stake here is that the analyst, on the basis of his or her desire, succeeds in overcoming the resistance to work in favor of becoming dispensable to the analysand and working through the mourning thereof.

The beginning and middle phases of analysis

The end of analysis is played out and prepared from the beginning in accordance with the aim of the analyst. If the aim of analysis is not resisted, then analysis will be regulated by the desire that defines the analytic position and the psychic state of the analyst.

The desire of the analyst is the function or capacity that enables the analyst to work with the transference of the analysand, and to redirect transference love both towards as well as away from the analyst. Ultimately it is the desire of the analyst that carries an analysis to its end beyond the rock of castration.

Lacan (1974–5) says that the neurotic "believes in his symptom" (Seminar XXII). The neurotic understands that the sign/symptom is trying to say something not yet understood. The symptom is an enigma, therefore. Put differently: she knows that there is something she does not know and is certain that if that "knowing" were to be known, the cure would follow. The analyst therefore is localized in Lacan's terms as the subject supposed to knowing (the *Sujet supposé Savoir* or the S.s.S. position)[1] what the analysand ignores. It is the unconscious knowing of the analysand that is being attributed to the analyst. Contrary to what would be expected, the neurotic is not looking for the person of the analyst but for that "knowing" that he/she ignores. The analyst becomes the subject attributed to knowing, but it could also be a magician, astrologer, alchemist, healer, shaman, etc. in so far as they present themselves as carriers of a "knowing" that is lacked by the subject. And as soon as a subject is being attributed to knowing, the basis for the transference has been established. Therefore, the transference is defined by "unknown-knowing" and not by conscious knowledge or by feelings or affective states. Affects are subordinate to knowing according to the following characterization: I love, whom I presuppose to be a subject of knowing; I hate, whom I withdraw this supposition from (Seminar XX; Lacan, 1972).

To assume the analytic position, the analyst must first ignore[2] or not be attached to what he/she knows in order to apprehend the singularity of a new analysand and second, with respect to what he ignores, intend to understand it. This double game reveals one of the richest paradoxes of analysis: although the analysand supposes the analyst knows many things about him or her, in truth the analyst ignores everything about it.

The unknown-knowing is situated within the analysand. Granted that without the analyst, the unveiling of the unknown becomes impossible. Such is then the *via di levare* (by way of extracting or taking away) that Freud (1910) talked about: namely, to be like a sculptor who chips away the stone in order to make the appearance of the sculpture possible by following the lines of the material itself rather than the designs of the artist. But the analysand (and suggestive/behavioral treatments) is searching for the *via di porre* (way of superimposition or putting on). The analysand offers/gives his/her self as a canvas upon which the analyst may draw or offer some brilliant designs. The analysis installs the analyst in both the S.s.S. position and that of the ego-ideal. Just as in love, one loves in the other that which one lacks in oneself in order to reach one's own ideal. The other of love is who allows the subject to deny the lack. I am referring to a narcissistic type of bond or union that reveals what is deceiving about all love. In truth, ordinary dual love is to want to be loved. And if I am loved by an ego-ideal, then I am an ideal ego. This follows what Freud said regarding the childhood desire to be one's own ideal. This is an aspect of the relationship between the ideal ego and the ego-ideal.

Thus, when Kohut (Kohut and Wolf 1978; Baker and Baker 1987) notes that some narcissistic analysands did not experience him as a separate object or even a separate body, he is only discovering a narcissistic characteristic of love or Eros itself. The object or the other is expected to be an extension of the subject precisely because such other has been situated in the place of the ego-ideal or ideal ego. The ideal ego or the alter ego, as they refer to object love, can be conceived as a mental image of this or that body. Thus, this other body, which is an extension of my body, is what allows me in the imaginary to complete what I think (albeit unconsciously) I lack in my own body. In the love of the object, the other as object is what the subject desires in order to conceal his/her own incompleteness of being. To put it differently: the desire and love of the object as it relates to sexuality cannot escape what has been called a narcissistic type of bond or union. This would not be a characteristic of "self-object needs" only found in narcissistic character disorders.

In addition we are referring here to a fundamental lack of being, which in Freud's theory is intrinsically interwoven with sexuality, the castration complex, and the symbolic function of the phallus. In this case the concern with failure has more to do with the inevitably lost object of metonymic desire (not need) which becomes symbolized as a loss at the level of the subject than with whatever symbolic object-love historical parents had or did not have to give or not give.

But the most decisive point has not yet been made. A neurotic is a specialist in the art of becoming the object of the demand of the Other – of course, that without being willing to pay the price for it or recognizing that this demand of the other is unconsciously emanating from the neurosis itself. Therefore, the defining formula of the neurotic is that he/she situates the demand of the other uppermost. And what does he/she think this Other wants from him/her? That he/she be just like the Other to the point of nullification. From this follows the decisive character of the identification that the analysand comes to look for in the analysis. And if one falls into the trap of neurosis by offering to give what one has that the other seems to be lacking, one is – despite all good intentions – only aimlessly swimming in the depth of the neurosis without further recourse. In summary, the identification with the analyst that many believe to be a formula for the final phase of analysis implies nothing but the stagnation in one of the stages of the process. In this scenario the analysis becomes interminable.

Ego identification with the analyst has more to do with the neurosis itself than with what Greenson (1978) called a realistic object relationship characterized by the empathic alliance with an analyst achieved during the initial stages of an analysis. Greenson states that humanness consists of giving insight and understanding in an empathic and serious fashion. But as shown with Lacan, this knowing and understanding is a basis for the transference.

From another perspective, empathy and the alliance with the analysand runs the danger of becoming an imaginary reinforcement of the defensive ego which analysis is supposed to deconstruct. The suffering of the analysand is commonly connected to secondary or false presenting problems, which often function as some of the repressive substitute ideas that keep repressed and unconscious contents away from consciousness. In this context the <u>demand</u> made upon the analyst is to be empathic and understanding of the analysand's problems as presented by the analysand and his or her ego defenses.

In addition, the patient initially wants to speak about what she or he wants to talk about; an empathic analyst should respect the patient's agenda or the defensive selection of material. Thus, it should be remembered that the alleged alliance is being established with the ego of the defenses themselves. Finally, if the demand of the analysand is actually about being loved and recognized, the task of the analyst does not end with an offering of the image of the analyst as an auxiliary ego and an explanation of where the parents of the analysand failed.

Therefore, if the demand of the analysand directs the transference towards identification with the ideal, the desire of the analyst should attempt to break up such a situation. The analyst has to cultivate a meditative state or thinking beyond the crown of power and authority represented by the ego-ideal. In his/her own analysis, the analyst has to have reached a state beyond the ego-ideal in order not to wish to be such for the analysand. Transference love represents the analysand's resistance aimed at erecting an ego-ideal or a complete Other in the figure of the analyst. This transference resistance defends against the lack in the subject as well as in the Other.

When the ideal (I[O]) is deconstructed back into a relationship between the subject and the *objet a* in the fundamental fantasy ($\$ \lozenge a$), then the subject becomes capable of accessing his/her own symbolic knowing. Eventually, the ego-ideal (I[O]) is replaced by the figure of the fantasy, and when the fantasy is traversed it transforms into the signifier of the lack in the Other (S[Ø]), or the *objet a* as a letter, and ultimately into the figure of the double torus (8) representing the Real emptiness of subject and Other alike.

When the analyst renounces to be in the place of the ideal and does not respond to the demand of the analysand, then in that void the analysand's fundamental fantasies will become apparent. The analysand not only wants that the analyst tells him/her what to do or not do, a demand of a demand, but also demands that the analyst give him or her the signifier of the phallus as well as the object of love and of the drive. Finally, the analysand also wants to become and give the analyst the object that the analyst desires, lacks, and needs. The analysand wants the analyst to demand this object from him/her.

It follows from the above that the analyst's position/state is that of the silence of the Buddha, or of the stoic who does not respond (*ataraxia*),[3] and/or that of who responds in surprising or unexpected manner to the many ways in which the analysand unconsciously sets up the analytic situation so as to widen the reach of his/her demand.

It is well known that Freud (1912) prescribed the fundamental rule of free association as well as different forms of advice regarding the direction of the cure. The latter consist of a limited series of restrictions as to not to educate or legislate or impose sublimations or have sex with the analysand and so on and so forth. But having said all this, he then subscribes to Ferenczi's (1928) elasticity principle, where obviously one finds included the sticky question of the length of the sessions.

Freud (1913) established a distinction between advice (*Ratschlage*) and rule (*Regel*). With respect to the direction of the cure, two different factors are discernable. First, a series of variables (counsel, advice) that allows a certain margin of uncertainty, indefiniteness, and creativity. Second, the formulation of what is non-negotiable and constitutes the foundation of psychoanalysis: the rule of free association. If this distinction is read retroactively, one discovers that advice does not acquire the character of being fundamental. What is fundamental? The term does not only indicate that something is important, but also clearly connotes a reference to the foundation of a structure. Contrary to indications or varied forms of advice that may or may not be more or less negotiable, the rule of free association constitutes the founding rock of psychoanalysis.

The analyst should not even ask the analysand to speak about himself but simply to speak openly without holding anything back. Even worse, speak and say whatever foolishness may come to your mind. Analysis creates an original situation where foolishness (*bêtises*) may be neither criticized nor made marginal. Here we find the equivocal genuine trap of the analyst: speak foolishly because through foolishness the core of your being will be revealed. What is fundamental arises not out of a conscious intention but out of whatever speech element may break the homogeneity of the conscious ego. The fundamental rule establishes an analysis as the practice of listening for the *jouissance* that speaks between the spaces of what the prattle is intending to communicate.

But what does the analyst offer of himself by prescribing the rule of free association? For one thing, the analyst transmits to the analysand two things: (1) I know so much that whatever you say I will interpret; and (2) I love you so much that I do not require of you even the most minimal form of verbal performance. Put differently: according to item 1, the analyst lays the foundation for exercising the S.s.S. position. According to item 2, already being loved for his/her "knowing" the analyst becomes a perfect *Erastes* or lover relating to a beloved *Eromemos* or analysand.

Lacan (1960–1) uses the Greek categories in Seminar VIII, on the subject of transference, in order to account for what he calls <u>the metaphor of love</u> as it occurs in the psychoanalytic cure. If I speak of metaphor, I am speaking of substitution with respect to the reciprocal substitution that takes place between analyst and analysand in relation to the places of *Erastes* and *Eromenos*. In other words, the lover must become lovable or beloved (analyst) and the beloved turned into a lover (analysand). The analyst/ego-ideal becomes *Erastes* or lover by the prescription of the fundamental rule as if it were a love declaration. But how does one emerge from this situation in order to work in the direction of the end of analysis?

In *Group Psychology and the Analysis of the Ego*, Freud (1921) establishes a very close link between love and hypnosis. Since the psychoanalytic cure can be viewed as a love story – as genuine and deceptive as any other – how avoidable is the conclusion that hypnosis has an important role to play in such a process? The servitude of love requires that love be demanded just as the hypnotized is begging to be ordered, healed, or satisfied. Thus, one becomes subordinate when elevating a needed Lord to a position of control and domination. Hypnosis, like the proverbial serpent, is a recurring presence that must be mastered in order to avoid being fascinated by its power. Again, the question becomes how to renounce the power granted by the cure and the fine-tuning of the analytic situation.

Herein lies the end of analysis that (beyond castration) can be rendered effective on the basis of the analyst's desire. The desire of the analyst leads to the suspension of certainty, the relativity of the senses, and towards the founding senselessness/emptiness that originates us. The frustration of demand and the ending or cutting of sessions is also part of this process. Last but not least, interpretations should not be pedagogical explanations that attempt to inflate a "small ego book" by means of defensive psychological recipes. Interpretations are surprises that make room for what is equivocal. Interpretation is a type of true intuition not requiring of the analysand's skill, ability, or schooling. However, it does depend on how the analyst turns and returns to such work in the transference.

By means of the above the analyst separates himself from the ego-ideal of identifying, like the child, with the father in order to occupy the place of what Lacan denominates the *objet a*. Here the ego-ideal reverts to the ideal ego, and the ideal ego reverts to the partial *objet a* that was a residue/substitute for **unborn infinite Life**. With birth the fate of infinite life is to be lost and for its substitute object also to be lost (*objet a*). Such object represents loss and separation in so far as this is necessary for the constitution of the subject. In this way, the analyst will be stripped away from the place of the father, the S.s.S., the ideal and the indispensable *Eromenos*.

Thus, it is possible to understand that the conflict with which the analysand entangles the analyst by means of the transference neurosis and the Freudian limits that point to castration and its accompanying rivalries, arguments, dissatisfactions, ingratitudes, etc., do not yet constitute true limits. The conflict still continues a theme and a plot that allow for the concealment of a Void or Emptiness that Lacan (December 10, 1959) calls the <u>pain of existence</u>. In this respect the imaginary fixation to the wish to murder the father or mother serves the purpose of avoiding contact with the abyss of the Real as Emptiness. Emptiness is not to be "a-voided" but rather accepted and realized as true being or unbeing rather than as absence (relative nothingness).

The experience of the pain of existence does not lead to nihilism or skepticism. On the contrary, the circular experience of emptiness, of perfection and imperfection, finitude and infinity, wholeness and incompleteness or *"holeness,"* leads towards the One, energizing the possible word or unary trace of all who speak. It becomes possible then to set aside the pretension that one has been allocated the worst in the distribution of the *jouissance* of life. When mutating the subjective position, one abandons the myth of guilt and interdiction by accepting the impossibility of the *jouissance* of the Other. The latter *jouissance* implies the fantasy that the Other enjoys something inaccessible to the subject. For example: the mother in the oedipal myth.

To sum-up: what is especially or actually implied in forbidden *jouissance* (which otherwise may be possible if the prohibition is transgressed) is the confrontation with the fact that the *jouissance* of the Other as such does not exist. In addition, *jouissance* itself or the Other *jouissance* neither exists nor does not exist. *Jouissance* does not not exist, or immortal Life is beyond is and is not. Herein are joined the two fundamental determinants of psychoanalysis: sex and death.

To terminate: the interminable

When, how, and why an analysis ends? Let us return once again to our starting point in order to take this time another converging road. The analysand transforms into what at the end of analysis? Lacan gives a strange response to this question. The analysand transforms into an analyst. But does this mean, then, that after all the analysand did in fact identify with the ideal? Not if the analyst was able to let go of himself/herself by going beyond identity or identification via the deconstruction of the ego-ideal and the ego. The symbolic subject or the true turning word and the desire of the analyst imply a transformation of *jouissance* or sublimation in the consciousness/unconscious of the analyst. It is this transformation that facilitates a transformation in the *jouissance* of the analysand. In this sense there is a mind-to-mind transmission not based on identification that does not transform the analysand into a professional analyst. Rather, the analysand uses his/her own transformation of *jouissance* for whatever symbolic purposes or ideals they may have.

The analysand has attained the corresponding subjective position/state as well as the type of social linkage which the position/state of the analyst may generate. It is not that the analysand has identified with the analyst and decided to mimic his/her every gesture. It has more to do with the fact that the practice and work of listening to the ways of the Unconscious produces a similar subjective position/state in the analysand. Such subjective destitution (Lacan, 1967) or depersonalized psychic state is attained by a series of modifications, mutations, and permutations of ideational, affective, and bodily processes and activities. Nonetheless, the analysand has to discover this truth in his or her own psychic structure and not by mere identification with the analyst.

The possibility that the analysand may be able to listen in a singular way to himself/herself serves as a guarantee that the analysis may in fact be interminable. Therefore, if there is self-analysis, such only begins when an analysis with the Other has ended. All in all, this realization of senselessness, as a new metaphor of analysis by means of which the analysand becomes an analyst, succeeds in producing a subjective awareness able to re-cognize desire without confounding or hiding it behind the demand of the Other. The subject then may disregard the Name-of-the-Father precisely because he/she knows how to use it.

Notes

1 This is my translation of Lacan's *sujet supposé savoir*. Alan Sheridan (1977) has translated it as the subject who is supposed to know (Lacan, 1964). However, such translation does not underscore the fact that the subject is not the source of "knowing," or that there is no subject of knowledge; rather it is the subject who is being attributed a knowing. Sheridan's translation emphasizes the subject, whereas in mine the subject is secondary to knowing. As in the case of the English word "understanding," the subject is standing under this unknown-knowing. Lacan also distinguishes between what he calls the referential knowledge of science and what I am calling in this chapter the contextual "knowing" in the analytic situation. This latter form of knowing would not be characterized by cognitive or secondary ego-processes.

2 This attitude is in agreement with what Medieval philosopher and theologian Nicolas de Cusa denominated *docta ignorancia* and contemporary Korean Zen teacher Soen Sa Nim termed "don't know mind."

3 A calm or imperturbable mind. Equanimity or impassivity in the sense of inner-mastery or freedom from being controlled by disturbing emotions or an inconvenient form of *jouissance*.

References

Baker, H. and Baker, M. (1987). Heinz Kohut's self psychology: an overview. *American Journal of Psychiatry*, 144: 1.

Bion, W.R. (1970). *Attention and Interpretation*. London: Tavistock Publications.

Fenichel, O. (1941). Problems of psychoanalytic technique. *The Psychoanalytic Quarterly*.

Ferenczi, S. (1928). The elasticity of psycho-analytic technique. In M.S. Bergmann and F.R. Hartman (eds.), *The Evolution of Psychoanalytic Technique*. New York: Basic Books.

Freud, S. (1900). *The Interpretation of Dreams. The Standard Edition of the Complete Psychological Works of Sigmund Freud*. London: The Hogarth Press and the Institute of Psychoanalysis, volumes 4–5.

Freud, S. (1905a). Fragment of an analysis of a case of hysteria. In P. Gay (ed.), *The Freud Reader*. New York: Norton and Norton.

Freud, S. (1905b). On psychotherapy. *SE*, VII: 260–1.

Freud, S. (1905c). Jokes and their relation to the unconscious. New York: Norton, 1960.

Freud, S. (1910). *Leonardo da Vinci and a Memory of his Childhood.* New York: W.W. Norton & Company, 1964.

Freud, S. (1912). Recommendations to physicians practising psychoanalysis. *SE*, 12: 111–20.

Freud, S. (1913). On beginning the treatment. *SE*, 12.

Freud, S. (1915). *The Metapsychology. The Standard Edition of the Complete Psychological Works of Sigmund Freud.* London: The Hogarth Press and the Institute of Psychoanalysis, volume 14, p. 109.

Freud, S. (1921). *Group Psychology and the Analysis of the Ego. SE*, 18: 67–143.

Freud, S. (1923). *The Ego and the Id. SE*, 19: 3–66.

Freud, S. (1925). On negation. *SE*, 19: 235–9.

Freud, S. (1937). Analysis terminable and interminable. *SE*, 23: 209.

Greenson, R.R. (1978). The working alliance and the transference neurosis. In *Explorations in Psychoanalysis.* New York: International Universities Press, pp. 199–224.

Hanly, C. (1984). Ego ideal and ideal ego. *International Journal of Psychoanalysis*, 65: 253–61.

Kohut, H. and Wolf, E. (1978). The disorders of the self and their treatment: an outline. *International Journal of Psychoanalysis*, 59: 413–25.

Lacan, J. (1955). *Escritos 1. Variantes de la cura tipo.* Mexico: Siglo XXI, 1985.

Lacan, J. (1957a). *El seminario sobre la carta robada.* In *Escritos 2.* Mexico: Siglo XXI, 1975. The Seminar on "The Purloined Letter." In *Écrits* (Jeffrey Mehlman trans.). *Yale French Studies*, 48 (1973): 39–72.

Lacan, J. (1957b). The instance of the letter in the unconscious. In *Ecrits* (Bruce Fink trans.). New York: W.W. Norton.

Lacan, J. (1959). *El Deseo y su Interpretacion.* Buenos Aires: Nueva Vision.

Lacan, J. (1960–1). *La Transferencia* (Ricardo E. Rodríguez Ponte trans., 1999). Unpublished.

Lacan, J. (1961–2). *The Seminar of Jacques Lacan IX: On Identification* (Cormac Gallagher trans.). London: Karnac.

Lacan, J. (1964). *The Four Fundamental Concepts of Psychoanalysis. The Seminar of Jacques Lacan. Book XI* (Alan Sheridan trans., 1977). New York: W.W. Norton.

Lacan, J. (1966–7). *The Seminar of Jacques Lacan XIV: The Logic of Phantasy.* London: Karnac.

Lacan, J. (1967). Proposition of 9 October 1967 on the Psychoanalyst of the School (Russell Grigg trans.). *Analysis*, 6 (1995): 8.

Lacan, J. (1969). *The Seminar of Jacques Lacan: Book XVII: The Other Side of Psychoanalysis.* New York: W.W. Norton, 2007.

Lacan, J. (1972). On feminine sexuality: the limits of love and knowledge. *Encore: The Seminar of Jacques Lacan, Book XX.* New York: W.W. Norton, 1998.

Lacan, J. (1974–5). *R.S.I.* (Ricardo E. Rodríguez Ponte trans., 1999). Unpublished.

Lacan, J. (1978). *Momento de Concluir.* XXV. Unpublished.

Lichtenberg, J. (1975). The development of the sense of self. *Journal of the American Psychoanalytic Association*, 23: 453–84.

Nietzsche, F.W. (1878). *Human, All Too Human: A Book for Free Spirits* (R.J. Hollingdale trans.). Cambridge: Cambridge University Press, 1996.

Reich, W. (1933). On the technique of character-analysis. In *Essential Papers on Character Neurosis and Treatment.* New York: New York University Press, 1989.

Chapter 4

Variable-length Lacanian analyses and the question of brief analysis

Raul Moncayo and Ayelet Hirshfeld

Introduction

Brief treatment can be viewed as an ideology of the consumer society of late capitalism. Clients are faced these days with an overwhelming variety of brief therapy products aimed at eliminating specific phobias, boosting self-esteem, combating depression, eliminating various addictions, and more. Brief therapy responds to a need to increase access to treatment, provide cost-effective treatments within the managed-care culture, and respond to the requests for evidence-based, efficient, empirically validated treatments (Levenson, 1995).

Studies documenting the efficacy of short-term treatment cannot capture the ends achieved by long-term treatments due to their complexity, sampling limitations, and research in this area being time-consuming. There is an inherent built-in difficulty in measuring the efficacy of long-term treatments empirically and using controlled statistical studies to measure the long-term efficiency of a treatment such as psychoanalysis. Thus, long-term treatments have to rely on case studies and consumer outcome approaches to measure effectiveness. Lacan's non-standard frame, or what Moncayo (2008) calls a multiform criterion for the practice of psychoanalysis, addresses the issues of effectiveness, duration, and cost of treatment. Among other things, a multiform frame allows for the possibility of variable-length treatments where these may be indicated due to the resistances/financial limitations of individuals and mental health systems. Finally, whereas the variable-length analyses concept being presented emerges out of considerations internal to psychoanalysis, brief analysis, as a shorter form of treatment, also becomes more amenable to being studied according to empirical methodology if, of course, somebody wanted to pursue this objective.

Brief therapy is differentiated from psychoanalysis because the former is aimed at symptom reduction whereas psychoanalysis addresses the psychic causality of the symptom and is not merely aimed at symptom reduction. Because brief therapy does not remove the causes and roots of the symptoms, the person may remain prone to relapses and to further episodes of treatment. However, this is not to say that unqualified long-term psychoanalytic treatment is an ironclad form of relapse prevention. In fact, there has been a fair amount of published criticism regarding the therapeutic ineffectiveness of long-term psychoanalysis. From within psychoanalysis, Lacanians in general point out that analytic treatments under the ego psychological standard frame and the object-relations holding environment became longer and longer, lasting up to 20 years or more. Lacan's constructive critique of the theory and practice of psychoanalysis after Freud can be used to target the ineffectiveness of a long-term dependence on the analyst. This is despite the fact that some of Lacan's own analyses tended to be quite long. Lacan provided the theoretical tools to evolve psychoanalytic practice in directions that were yet unknown to him.

Though the notion of a variable-length Lacanian analysis might appear contradictory to the notion of Lacanian psychoanalysis itself, we offer a short version of Lacanian analysis as a second-best practice to an entire course of Lacanian analysis. It is, therefore, not the optimal method of treatment, but a response to lack of financial resources, time, and desire to engage in a long-term course of treatment. In addition, in the first chapter of this book, Moncayo considered how psychoanalysis is organized by a logic and method of contradiction rather than the non-contradiction linked to formal empirical logic and methodology. What appears to be a contradiction may not be. Lacanians use a variable-length session, and in this chapter the variable length is being applied to the length of the treatment itself. Finally, even long-term analyses may in fact turn out to be of variable length, given that not all analysands stay to the logical end of their treatment. In any case, and as already stated, this model is not intended as a replacement for analysis proper. It is proposed as preparation and as an introduction to Lacanian analysis.

The following short Lacanian analysis model suggests 30–40 sessions in acknowledgment of the reality of the cost associated with the treatment. Often those who use the brief therapy model, driven by cost analyses conducted by the managed-care industry, would rather take the risk of offering the person many episodes of brief treatment (of 10–20 sessions) instead of offering long-term treatment from the start. Clients who finish a brief Lacanian analysis and desire further treatment would be offered a regular course of analysis for 3–4 years instead of the 30–40 sessions of the brief analysis model. This is notwithstanding the fact that a previous episode of short Lacanian treatment could shorten the length of a long-term analysis.

In fact this was the most common outcome of the cases that have been treated thus far with a brief Lacanian analysis. Initially the clients themselves were not interested in long-term treatment and wanted resolution of their symptoms and behavioral outcomes rather than more in-depth understanding/transformation of themselves or of their history. This presentation coincides with prevailing views of psychotherapy available within North American culture at large (professional and otherwise). However, after a brief analysis the clients consistently became more interested and more open to self-exploration and to redefining their views of themselves and the relationships to their families. As a result of the treatment, their productive capacity and income increased to the point that towards the end of their brief analysis they developed the desire to pay for a regular course of sliding-scale analysis with a frequency of two to three sessions per week.

The numbers 30 and 40 are somewhat arbitrary but are also entirely within the logic of Lacanian theory and practice. These numbers are being used as symbolic and logical integers rather than as probabilistic quantities. We intend to show that the efficacy of psychoanalytic treatment is maximized when the different phases/ faces or moments of oedipal structure become an integral part of the treatment in a systematic and differential fashion. We will be correlating the phases of treatment with the phases of Oedipus and of the transference relationship. Thirty to forty sessions can still be considered brief treatment, and a length of 3–4 years is shorter than the average length of psychoanalysis. In addition, the number 3 pervades the logic of the analytic frame. There are three phases of treatment, three forms of psychopathology, three forms of logical time, three phases of the transference, three phases of oedipal structure, three dimensions of time, and three registers of experience. Finally, the later Lacan added a fourth dimension to the Borromean knot, and Moncayo (2008) has formulated a fourth moment of Oedipus found implicit in Lacan's work as well as the possibility of considering the borderline condition as a fourth diagnostic group or borderline category intersecting the other three (neurosis, psychoses, perversion).

Although psychodynamic brief therapy in general has a thematic focus that could include psychoanalytic themes, a short analysis is differentiated from brief therapy because of the focus on unconscious fantasy life. But a short analysis is differentiated from analysis proper because in a short analysis there is no resolution of the transference neurosis and the question of traversing the fantasy – crossing of the phantasm – is not fully worked through. In a short analysis the phantasm is identified or recognized but is not traversed or worked through. The previous chapter quotes Lacan where he says that the end of analysis occurs when one has gone around a circle twice. Well, in a short analysis, one only goes around a circle once. An example of this would be the case of a client who initially wanted behavioral help in improving her level of functioning and decreasing her depression.

In the brief analysis she disclosed that she had been adopted by a couple who in fact turned out not to want to have children. She described how once she went off to college her adopted parents told her that they had made a mistake, that they should have never had children, and that, therefore, from then on, she was on her own and she should not expect them to remain involved in her life. The treatment identified this memory and biographical detail as a key traumatic element and loss in her life that was not yet a fantasy.

At the end of the treatment, however, it became clear that although the client wanted to work to be able to afford a regular course of analysis, she did not want to get a regular job, and was unconsciously demanding that the analyst demand from her that she get a job. She was setting things up (making the therapist make her get a job) so as to have the experience of being rejected for refusing to get a job and become independent. The rejection by her parents could also be interpreted as a response to her refusal to become independent and self-sufficient. She was not only enacting a repetition of the trauma but also revealing its fantasized dimension. It is the fantasized dimension of a trauma that is the effective cause of the repetition despite the empathy, understanding, and support of the analyst or trauma therapist/specialist. This is an example of what we mean by going around a circle once and recognizing the fantasy but without resolution or working through.

The notion of the phantasm in Lacan ($\$\Diamond a$) dates back to Freud's (1915a, 1916–17; see Laplanche and Pontalis, 1968/1973, p. 331) protofantasies or "primal phantasies," which included the question of the origins of sexuality or the seduction fantasy, the question of castration, or the origin of the sexes, and the primal scene, or the origin of human life. According to Freud (1915a, 1916–17), these universal structures exist in a fantasy dimension and are irreducible to personal individual experience. According to Lacan (1956–7) unconscious fantasy both sustains desire and defends against castration. The crossing of the phantasm or fantasy has to do with elaborating on these two aspects of the fantasy: how the fantasy sustains desire and at the same time defends against castration. In brief analysis there will be recognition of the function of how fantasies sustain desire and defend against castration, and this will suffice to affect the symptoms but will not be enough to prevent a future relapse or to work through or traverse the phantasm in the transference.

History of brief psychodynamic psychotherapy

Flegenheimer (1982) traced the origins of brief psychodynamic psychotherapy to the work presented by Freud and Breuer in *Studies on Hysteria*. Many of the techniques and selection criteria Freud employed in his early cathartic method are used today in brief therapy (e.g., therapist is highly motivated and active). Rank was apparently the first to advocate using a fixed time limit as a regular part of analysis. Ferenczi advocated "active" therapy as the exception to the rule of free association. Alexander stressed the therapist's activity, limiting the patient's regression to limit the patient's gratification, which he felt often prolonged treatment unnecessarily, and he allowed for regression only to the point where developmental trauma had occurred. Alexander focused on the central conflict and what he called the corrective emotional experience. After Alexander many authors have developed models of brief psychodynamic therapy. For an exhaustive review, please read Flegenheimer's (1982) book.

Analytically oriented brief psychotherapy requires a properly selected patient and appropriate therapist technique. Moreover, having a focus is critical, and it clearly sets brief therapy apart from long-term therapy. The focus, in the form of a circumscribed symptom or area of difficulty, is established at the start of therapy, although it may be modified as the therapy progresses. The focus should represent the patient's "nuclear conflict." In brief psychodynamic therapy, the transference neurosis is controlled by limiting the patient's regression and dependence on the therapist, while the therapist is much more active by making early interpretations of transference manifestations. Moreover, the bulk of the working-through process occurs after therapy has ended.

About Lacanian psychoanalysis

Whereas the standard frame predominates in the field of psychoanalysis these days (e.g., standard fixed session length, fixed number of sessions per week, etc.), Lacanian psychoanalysis proposes a case-by-case evaluation of the question of the frame, which is tailored to fit the singularity of each case (Moncayo, 2008). Lacan's clinical practices can also be considered an aspect of what he called his "return to Freud." In this case it would be a return to Freud's actual way of practicing. Freud did analysis and sessions of variable length and in different settings and formats. This way of working provides an analyst with more degrees of freedom in selecting the appropriate clinical treatment. In general the Lacanian multiform approach to the frame of analysis is a response to ineffective analyses and long-term treatment courses that stay stagnated within or limited to the first or second phases of oedipal structure.

The concept of time

In his paper on "Logical Time," Lacan (1945) divided time into logical and chronological. Chronological time moves from past, to present, to future. The distinction between logical time and chronological time is also consistent with the distinction between synchronic and diachronic time: the usual sense of the passing of time, and time in the present moment that is also a form of timelessness. The sense of the timelessness of the unconscious corresponds to the manifestation of time in the present moment. Although, like memory, the unconscious contains the past, it manifests or erupts in the present moment as more than simply a recollection of things past.

According to Lacan (1945) there are three moments of logical time that are at work in every session: the "instance of the glance," a "time for understanding," and a "moment of concluding." The "instance of the glance" corresponds to the opening and closing of the unconscious and as such contains all three dimensions of time. Something from the past is appearing in the present, the significance of which, according to Lacan, will not be fully understood until the future, and then only retroactively. In logical time Lacan reverses the relationship between the "time for understanding" and the "moment of concluding." In most therapies you understand first and then you conclude, whereas Lacan says that the "moment of concluding" precipitates the "time for understanding." Just like the three dimensions of time are included in the present, every session includes the three moments of logical time but they are not arranged chronologically. It is as if the passing of time was not from past, to present, to future, but from present to past and from future to present.

A similar point can be made with respect to the phases of Oedipus and the phases of treatment. Lacan developed the concept of the phases of Oedipus in Seminar V (1957–8), "On the Formations of the Unconscious". Each phase contains the other phases of treatment and of Oedipus, although at the same time they are differentiated. Layers, faces, or moments of Oedipus exist synchronically even though they may have unfolded developmentally or diachronically. The relation between phases of treatment and phases of Oedipus is not linear. For example, phase III of Oedipus can appear in phase II of treatment, but if it does it will not be the focus of treatment until the third phase of treatment. Although the faces/phases of Oedipus appear synchronically throughout the phases of treatment, they are not the focus of treatment until the appropriate phase of treatment. In different phases of treatment, analysts focus on a particular phase of Oedipus and ignore others. Psychoanalysis requires that psychic material is understood both structurally/synchronically and developmentally/diachronically. According to the logic of contradiction, psychic phenomena are both similar and different at the same time.

The logic of retroactivity also transforms linear diachronic time into synchronic circular time. What comes after redefines what came before, and what is linear becomes circular. Retroactivity is similar to logical time because the end of the session affects both the mid-point of the session as well as what transpires between sessions.

In addition, the concept of retroactivity is synchronically at work within language and not only within the phases of development. The last word in a phrase redefines the meaning of the phase/phrase that came before. A structure is composed of phases and faces, or synchronic and diachronic dimensions. There are themes/threads that run through all of them, such as loss/lack, for example, and at the same the type and agency of lack is different in each phase. Development evolves in spiral fashion in such a way that while streams/strings of being move through different circles/phases, in each circle/phase they go around similar themes and signifiers.

Each session contains non-standard personal time. Not only is a session a personal moment, but it also occurs in a length of time that is personal or unique to each individual. In addition, it is not standard or chronological because the dimension of the future is also present in the present (the ending of treatment in the ending of each session) and the present moment will not be the true present until the future. The present moment and the unconscious contents of our mind have a way of escaping us. These paradoxical notions suggest that the ending moment of each session is crucial and that the work continues outside of the analytic room. A significant portion of the understanding will take place in-between sessions.

There are three dimensions of time, three moments of logical time at work in every session, and three phases of the treatment (beginning, middle, and end). In the ordinary understanding of time the chronological phases of a session and of treatment match up to a significant degree. A session/treatment begins, then you understand in the middle phase of a session/treatment, and then you end (the session/treatment). But according to Lacanian logical time, the future end of treatment is present in each session not only to allow for understanding between sessions, but the awareness of the time limitation of each session also precipitates the opening of the unconscious in the "instance of the glance." In addition, the seeds of understanding are already present in the beginning moments of a glance. Thus, every session symbolically contains the three dimensions of time, and the three moments are present in each session (i.e., glancing, concluding, understanding) and are also at work within the logic of the phases of treatment (i.e., beginning, middle, end of treatment). The future dimension of the end of treatment, as articulated in the end of each session, is at work in precipitating the movement from the beginning phase to the middle phase of treatment.

About technique

The demand for analysis: client's demand versus institutional offering

As mentioned, a brief analysis is a second-best practice and is offered either as a time-limited treatment within the economic constraints of an institution or because it is the only treatment that a client can afford or is willing to engage in. It can also be used as an institutional/academic tool for empirical outcome research.

The presenting symptom and its rectification

Any complaint that brings the client to treatment will have to be ego-dystonic rather than syntonic and be capable of transformation into an analytic symptom. This is the necessary precondition to be able to link the symptom to unconscious fantasy as the focus of the treatment. Ego-dystonic refers to the subject taking responsibility for the symptom and to a desire to transform ego-defenses. Ego-dystonic implies a redefinition of the ego itself and does not simply refer to a description of impairments in ego or social and occupational functioning. The rectification of the symptom ties the symptom to a character trait as well as to an unconscious fantasy while stopping short of the overhaul of the character structure involved in analysis proper.

Sitting arrangements

Brief analysis could be done on a chair or on the couch. The chair arrangement will not be "face to face," to allow for the possibility of having or not having eye contact. This arrangement follows the principles that different structures require different things, and that the eye does not see what is essential to the eye (e.g., the organ of sight). Seeing is not seeing, and not seeing is seeing. The not seeing that is necessary for effective analysis can be embodied on a perpendicular chair arrangement or on the couch. Paradoxically, not seeing provides the psychic space for the analysand to speak about what ordinarily is not allowed to be seen or heard in society. This is particularly important for brief analysis since the focus of the treatment will be on unconscious fantasy.

Qualifications of the therapist

Strictly speaking, brief analysis is a treatment done by either analysts or therapists who have themselves undergone an analysis of long duration.

Difference between advice-giving within the context of the transference versus advice in disregard of the transference

Not to give advice is not a rule of the order of the golden rule of free association. Although the prescription not to give advice is commonly known as what differentiates psychoanalysis from other forms of treatment, most analysts give advice in one form or another. This leads many to think that people say one thing in the theory but then do another in the practice. This in turn leads to a push for treatments by manual, where clinicians follow the letter of the law with regards to a treatment practice. An alternative approach is to reconcile the theory and the practice by understanding the difference between advice within and outside the transference. Advice works within the transference to knowledge or to the "subject supposed to know(ing)." In psychoanalysis, we regard the knowledge that transforms as contained within the analysand rather than the analyst, though, at the outset of analysis, it is the analysand's perception of the analyst as the one who knows that initiates the transference relation. We work with the transference in such a way that unconscious knowing of fantasy life is brought to bear on symptoms, character traits, and relationships. But so long as the path of transference analysis lays wide open, and the clinician can move back and forth between their knowledge and the analysand's own knowing, then advice could also be used as an ancillary or supplemental tool of the treatment.

Length of treatment and of sessions and the frequency of sessions

In Lacanian treatment the sessions are of variable length, although the treatment at times could also include sessions of fixed length. The frequency of the sessions may vary as a function of the progress of the work and the remaining amount of time. Overall a brief analysis lasts 30–40 sessions.

In the pretreatment phase the client is told that in the treatment proper the length of each session may vary roughly between 20 and 55 minutes and will not have an exact, fixed duration. The model has the flexibility to fix the duration of sessions if for some reason the client cannot tolerate the variability or it is otherwise counterproductive. In such cases the session may end at a particular time within a range of

5 minutes, but the analyst will end the sessions thematically. Something is said by either party with regards to the content of the treatment that triggers the ending of the session. In any case the analyst does not end the session by saying "time is up."

One major distinction between brief analysis and analysis proper is that the analysand does not choose when to end the treatment, hence the analysis may not reach its logical end-point. A major feature of analysis proper, according to Lacan, is that the analyst ends the session but the analysand ends the treatment when the analyst is no longer needed or relevant. The analyst falls from his or her position as the "subject supposed to know(ing)" and is reduced to a mere surplus, a pure *object petit a* (Evans, 1996). "When he can speak to you about himself, the analysis will be over" (Lacan, 1954). This is a major disadvantage of a brief Lacanian analysis. However, the fact that the analysand does not choose when to end is somewhat offset by the fact that in some cases the analysand has chosen the brief version of analysis. Moreover, according to Evans (1996), an analytic course may be regarded as successful even if incomplete, as long as it leads the analysand to articulate the truth about his or her desire. For those cases where brief analysis is the only option available financially, this remains a major stumbling block. The end of analysis will be a forced termination. This reality requires even further skill on the part of the analyst to maneuver the treatment in such a way that the analysand somehow feels that he or she has had enough of the analyst and thus will not experience termination as a damaging form of rejection. This can only happen as a result of the uncomfortable intensity of the treatment and the transformations within the transference. The analyst cannot remain in the place of the beloved or of the subject supposed to know. This is a particular feature of Lacanian analysis that will be examined at further length below.

Free association and focused association on unconscious formations and dream analysis

Because free association can lead to defensive or idle speech, free association can be supplemented with the technique of dream analysis where the analysand is asked to free associate to different elements of the dream. The flow of speech can be interrupted and the analysand is asked to say more or what comes to mind about this or that word/phrase. Clients are regularly asked if they have had dreams and are asked to keep a dream journal. On the other hand, dreams can be ignored or by-passed if the analysand is obsessively focusing on dreams and taking all of the time of the session to give the analyst a minute recounting of various dreams. The focus on dreams can also be defensive.

Punctuating, the scanning/scansion of speech, and utilizing the resources available within language

The analyst employs punctuation and scansion of the analysand's discourse. Pauses that interrupt the flow of speech and open a particular sentence to a different meaning than the meaning that was going to be given by the last word of a sentence are an example of unconscious formations not mentioned by Freud. In this instance, the analyst simply repeats the sentence in its scand form. This allows the analysand to hear its different unconscious signification. Other uses of the resources of language include homophony, or the similarity of sound between words, and the holophrase, or a word that stands for a whole sentence, and using such words for interpretation or free association. In addition, words can be cut/ segmented to produce new meaning and the antithetical meaning of words is explored in both directions. Finally, the meanings of first names, last names, and pseudonyms, are also explored.

Lacan also linked punctuation to the scansion of the session, which as a concluding moment precipitates the time for understanding between sessions.

> It is, therefore, a propitious punctuation that gives meaning to the subject's discourse. This is why the ending of the session – which current technique makes into an interruption that is purely determined by the clock and, as such, takes no account of the thread of the subject's discourse – plays the part of a scansion which has the full value of an interventions by the analyst that is designed to precipitate concluding moments.
>
> (1953a: 44)

Facilitating progression and limiting regression

The cutting of the session and the scansion of speech facilitate treatment progress but also limit regression, which is particularly important for time-limited treatment. They both lead to separation or *separare*, meaning to give birth to oneself.

Work with affects

The following affects often appear and are the focus of treatment within sessions: love/hate; desire/aversion/fear; envy/jealousy; and anxiety/depression. According to Freud (1915b), affects can be suppressed in their development but are not typically unconscious. Affects are usually conscious and known and either ego-syntonic or ego-dystonic. Affects are commonly linked to false or imaginary triggers/causes. In treatment suppressed affects are revealed and made conscious. Affects that are already problematic for the client are verbalized, but then made ego-dystonic, and re-linked to unconscious memories and fantasies. Confronting both suppressed and false affects in the early assessment phase of the treatment can be a good indicator of whether the client will be able to benefit from a short analysis.

The practice of interpretation

Explanation is usually limited and more prevalent during the pre-treatment assessment phase. According to Lacan's "renewed technique of interpretation"

(1953b: 82), the analyst asks questions by using the analysand's words <u>verbatim</u>, while avoiding reframing to direct the analysand's attention to his/her own speech and facilitate him/her moving away from assuming that the "expert" knowledge of the analyst will cure him/her to understanding that the knowledge that will help him/her will emerge from his/her own speech. The analyst is governed by his/her desire to listen to the signifying chain that determines the development of the analysand's symptomatology. In interpretation we distinguish three floors/levels and regard the third as the proper analytic level:

1   *Going from the known to the known.* We do not focus on what a client already knows about his/her problems based on common sense or from what he/she has acquired from previous therapies, friends, or support groups. During the assessment phase this information is brought out and the client is asked what he/she has understood from previous treatment. The assumption is that if he/she continues to have symptoms, this means that there are dimensions/floors/levels of the unconscious that have not been affected or transformed by prior treatment.

2   *Going from the unknown to the known.* This category falls under what is usually understood as making the unconscious conscious by providing wholesale interpretations or explanations of unconscious conflicts. In this category the unconscious is reduced to ego processes or to what is already known. In Lacanian psychoanalysis, the analyst also limits this type of interpretation in favor of the analysand himself/herself arriving at the interpretation via the exploration of the signifying chain. Lacanian analysts regard this type of interpretation as imaginary and as meaning rather than signification. It is similar to when a client thinks that dream work is about him/her giving a global interpretation of the meaning of a dream. This level of interpretation also refers to the question of Lacanian analysts analyzing rather than interpreting the transference. If the analysand is talking about feelings or associations he/she has in relationship to somebody else (the so-called extra-analytic transferences), the Lacanian analyst tends not to say "and maybe you feel that way about me." The transference is analyzed only when the analysand speaks about it directly. Although it is not easy for many analysands to speak about their thoughts or feelings about the analyst, analysts have other ways to encourage their analysands to verbalize their transference experience. For example, an analyst could ask: "Is it difficult to speak to me about that?"

3   *Going from the unknown to the unknown.* This is interpretation proper. Lacan said that interpretation is found somewhere in-between a quote and an enigma, "The enigma and the citation constitute the two axes of analytic interpretation" (Nobus, 2000: 174). An interpretation is a symbolic reflection or mirroring back of those speech elements where analysands are not aware of what they are saying. "The less you understand, the better you listen" (Lacan, 1954–5: 141). According to Lacan and Bion understanding can be a problem in analysis. Instead of listening, the analyst is trying to reduce the

analysand's speech to what he/she already knows. Interpretations aim at disrupting meaning and reducing the signifiers to their "non-sense" (Lacan, 1964, cited in Evans, 1996). Enigmatic statements point to the subject of the enunciation rather than to the enunciating ego. They use descriptively unconscious or preconscious speech elements to affect repressed speech elements lodged in the unconscious or in the Real of unconscious experience. This is a key level of interpretation for the work with unconscious fantasy material.

Who can benefit from brief Lacanian analysis and assessment considerations/the preliminary phase of treatment?

The term "brief Lacanian analysis" will be used here to refer to the focus on unconscious fantasy, which usually is not addressed in brief psychotherapy. A brief Lacanian analysis course requires a preliminary thorough assessment of the client's history, symptomatology, and character. Obtaining a detailed psychosocial history, a history of prior treatment, and an assessment of the desire for treatment is of the outmost importance. Similarly, obtaining a detailed account of current and past symptomatology is crucial. Clients who struggle with substance abuse issues (who have not been clean and sober for at least 12 months, or 6 months if they are enrolled in substance abuse treatment), clients who suffer from psychosis, clients who endorse a trauma history (which was not addressed in a prior treatment course), clients with character disorder (unless symptoms are ego-dystonic), clients with antisocial personality or sociopathy, clients with criminal history, clients who have been hospitalized in a psychiatric unit, and clients with a history of and/or current suicidal and/or homicidal tendencies are ruled out.

Overview of the structure of a brief Lacanian analysis

	Phases of Treatment	Phases of Transference	Phases of Oedipus	Interventions
Phase I	Assessment and pre-treatment	The analyst is foreground lover and background beloved Subject supposed to Knowledge (S.s.K.); the analysand is a foreground beloved and background lover of Conscious Knowledge.		Explanation of the problem and the treatment. Imaginary empathy with ego defenses.

(Continued)

	Phases of Treatment	Phases of Transference	Phases of Oedipus	Interventions
				Clarification/ rectification of the demand for analysis and of the symptom.
Phase II	Beginning	The analyst is foreground beloved for their love and recognition of the analysand and background lover of the analysand as the transference may fulfill unconscious wishes of the analyst; the analysand is foreground lover (of the analyst) and background beloved (the pre-conscious gratifications of the transference for the analyst) of the analyst.	I	Interpretation of the known and Punctuation of themes of phase I of Oedipus. Scansion of the session. Imaginary empathy with the losses of the subject. Differentiating between the loss of not being the mother's imaginary phallus and losses related to privation and neglect; the technique of dream analysis is introduced.
Phase IIIa	Middle	Analyst is foreground beloved/object of desire and background (fantasized) sexual lover.	II	Not being the phallus. Having and not having the phallus. Symbolic empathy with the unconscious subject.
Phase IIIb		The analysand is foreground sexual lover and background beloved.	III	Going from the known to the unknown in the S.s.Kg (see p. 118).
Phase IV	End	Analyst lets go of beloved position but remains as lover of lack, not as object but as pure desire; analysand is the beloved and no longer the lover of analyst. The analyst as lover of emptiness supports the desire of the analysand for someone else.	IV	Desire of the analyst. Coming to terms with the lack in the Other and the subject. Going from the unknown to the unknown.

Phase I of treatment

Assessment and pre-treatment

As stated earlier, a brief Lacanian analysis necessitates a preliminary thorough assessment of the client's history, symptomatology, and character. Obtaining a detailed psychosocial history, a history of prior treatment courses, and an assessment of the desire for treatment is of the utmost importance. It is also crucial to obtain a detailed account of current and past symptomatology. Towards the end of the first assessment session an ego-dystonic symptom must be identified. The analyst will introduce the frame of treatment by presenting the variable-length session (the sessions will last anywhere between 20 and 50 minutes, depending on the work of each session) and the variable frequency of sessions over no less than 3 months and no longer than 12 months (i.e., intensity versus extensity in time: session frequency might change when deemed necessary by the content and will be brought up for the analysand's approval). A termination date is not established at the beginning, but the total number of sessions is (i.e., 30–40). The termination date will be introduced no later than at the onset of the termination phase (this dynamic will evolve within the course of treatment). Missed sessions are rescheduled unless there is no apparent reason for missing the session; or if the client abandoned treatment altogether, then a form of truncated treatment will evolve. Moreover, the "rule of free association" is given and clients are asked to pay special attention to dreams and to keep a notebook next to their bed to document them upon awakening. The analyst informs the analysand that when she/he suggests a time to end the session she/he will give the analysand an opportunity to agree to stop or produce more material. The analyst will end the session by saying something like "until next time" or until the specific day and time of the next session. If the analysand decided to end the session, the analyst will inquire as to the wish to end/cut before, or will agree to the cut (Moncayo, 2008).

Transference–countertransference

During the first phase of the treatment, the first phase of the transference relation is being initiated by the analyst and is operated through the analyst's functioning as a foreground lover of knowledge and as a background beloved "Subject supposed to Know" (conscious knowledge); by the same token, the analysand is established as a foreground beloved and a background lover of unconscious knowing. Within this model the "therapeutic alliance" (as is considered by the ego psychology school) would constitute the first/preliminary form of transference within the treatment. The ego psychology school differentiates therapeutic alliance from transference. Within the ego psychology school the therapeutic alliance represents the conscious work cooperation between the therapist and the client (e.g., agenda for the treatment, therapeutic contract, treatment goals). The proposed framework suggests that therapeutic alliance is constituted on the basis of the S.s.K. and represents a specific phase in the unfolding of the transference.

We will distinguish between "Subject supposed to Know" (or S.s.K.) and "Subject supposed to Knowing" (or S.s.Kg). This distinction was gained from the difficulty of translating the concept of S.s.S. (*Sujet supposé Savoir*). This diffi-culty in translation illuminated a distinction within the concept itself. Subject supposed to Know (S.s.K.) refers to the conscious knowing in the analyst, which is at play in the formation of the therapeutic alliance. The concept of Subject supposed to Knowing (S.s.Kg) addresses the unconscious relationship to know-ledge in the transference proper.

The therapeutic alliance is formed via the love of the analyst (wherein the analysand is a beloved), but what is the analysand for the analyst? The S.s.K. represents the conscious and professional knowledge of the analyst. The love of the analyst refers to his/her emotional engagement with the profession as well as his/her capacity for empathy. As most Lacanians do not use and reject the notion of empathy, the concept of empathy will be used here with the caveat of making a distinction between imaginary and symbolic forms of empathy. In addition, the fact that Lacanians reject the concept of empathy does not mean that they may not use it in their clinical practice. There is a video online on YouTube that features Lacan giving a lecture at a university in Belgium. A young man in the audience stands up and begins criticizing those in the audience and psychoanalysts. In a fertile moment Lacan responds to the young man by saying: "I understand" and the entire audience breaks into laughter. The joke was that Lacan was intervening as a psychoanalyst rather than giving an intellectual response. This "I understand" is a good example of therapeutic empathy because it does not mean that Lacan agrees with him but rather that he understands that the young man is upset and that there may be legitimate basis for his feelings.

The imaginary form of empathy is relevant for the pre-treatment and phase II of treatment. Symbolic empathy is relevant for phases III and IV of treatment. Imaginary empathy represents not only being empathic with the patient's feel-ings, but also being empathic with the patient's defenses. Symbolic empathy represents being empathic with the unconscious subject but not with the ego defenses. Imaginary empathy is used as a strategy during the early phase of treatment, and it continues with the development of the therapeutic alliance that activates the formula of the first phase of Oedipus.

Similarly, Racker (1960) distinguished between a concordant and a comple-mentary countertransference. In concordant countertransference the analyst iden-tifies with the analysand's current ego-representations or ego defenses. In complementary countertransference the analyst identifies with the analysand's repressed fantasies. The concordant countertransference can be viewed as an imaginary form of empathy with the analysand's pain and defenses, whereas the second type of countertransference can be considered as an imaginary identifica-tion with the analysand's fantasies. From a Lacanian perspective, the former is a purely strategic form of empathy, whereas the latter is a definite impediment to the treatment since it leads to unconscious collusions between analyst and analysand. Such unconscious complicities interfere with the recognition of a desire for recognition as well with the recognition of desire and the fantasized object cause of desire. Analysts are likely to experience more concordant countertransference reactions in phase I and II of treatment and a greater rate of complementary countertransference reactions in phase III and IV of treatment.

The analyst's professional identity is linked to his or her oath to help others as well as to the professional ethical code that regulates the relationship. Love functions within the transference relationship not only in transference love or the transference to the subject supposed to know, but also in the altruistic or the so-called mature object relationship that the analyst establishes with the analysand. The love dimension of the relationship affects the affective quality of cathartic emotional experience. On the side of the analyst, love is related to altruism and the liking of people, love of the unconscious object of desire, and a love of knowledge, all of which are embedded in a professional identity.

However, altruism and being of service to others is a suspect motivation and cannot be assumed naively. Altruism is implied in professional ethics, but professional ethics from a psychoanalytic point of view also has an unconscious dimension. The unconscious dimension of professional ethics is related to the connection between altruism and egoism or what in psychoanalysis is called the object versus the narcissistic orientation. However, object love or the love of the object is not a disinterested or selfless form of love/motivation. The object includes the subject, just as the Other includes the self. The ethical commandment "you shall love your neighbor as yourself," which Freud strongly rejected, has a double or non-dual meaning. The other is being loved as self in the sense that the object is being loved narcissistically. The other is loved as a self-object because the self is also loved as an object. This is true of most relationships and not only of the empathic failures that Kohut found in the histories of borderline and narcissistic personality disorders.

The object is supposed to be a "healthy total reality object," but a reality object is never a purely cognitive objective object independent from the subject. The object exists within language, and language always has a subject for whom the object is a signifier. Self-centered or an imaginary form of narcissism dissipates when the subject/object co-arise or are structurally interdependent within the process of signification.

Most people will present their intention to help others as purely based on altruism and are not aware of egoistic purposes structurally related to the unconscious object of desire. When the professional clinician is not aware of his/her unconscious love object, he/she will be more prone to use altruism as a form of pseudo motivation. Unconscious egoism in relationship to the object of desire becomes a determining factor in the clinician's transference to the patient. Invariably the analysand will represent an unconscious object for the clinician to a greater or lesser extent. This unconscious object could be money, love, and/or sexual interest. To the extent that the client embodies an unconscious object for the analyst, the analyst also finds his/her self in the Other or in the analysand. The professional persona is only the numerator for a symbolic equation. The denominator has to do with the transference and the subject's love for an unconscious object of desire.

The countertransference as containing the desires and motivations of the analyst is organized around both an object of knowledge and an object of love and desire. In a Lacanian reading of the countertransference, the therapeutic relation in variable-length psychoanalysis will be regulated by the desire of the analyst. The love object needs to be subordinated to the love of unconscious knowledge, and the love of unconscious knowledge needs to be subordinated to the desire of the analyst. The object of knowledge constitutes an object for the ego. The ego seeks the object that will gain his/her recognition in the gaze of the Other. The desire of the analyst is the desire **not** to be desired or loved by the patient for his or her knowledge. This is how the desire of the analyst regulates the search for unconscious knowledge.

The desire of the analyst provides a guarantee that the knowledge revealed belongs to the analysand rather than the analyst. The desire of the analyst is the fruit of the analyst's personal analysis. The desire of the analyst grants the analyst the necessary peace of mind needed to occupy the analytic function. It manifests in the interest in the analysand, in being nonjudgmental, in attentive empathic listening, the capacity to face unconscious experience, to recognize mistakes, and the acceptance of any speech element. The latter conveys a demand for the analysand's speech. From our point of view, authentic or genuine experience signifies a willingness to the fooled by the unconscious, a recognition of the transference and the limitations of the analyst (the lack in the Other), but not the mutual self-disclosure of analyst and analysand as recommended by the relational, humanistic, and existential forms of psychotherapy.

The wishes of the analyst also manifest in the provision of the service for a fee. There is a relationship between the object of desire and money as an object. The analyst is being paid for being the support for the transference, and for providing the rule of free association, both of which differ from providing a service for a fee. She/he is being paid to put up with being addressed as someone Other than whom she is, as well as for being blamed for things in the transference that are not of his/her own doing. Since wishes for union or merging with the client as well as sexual desires for the client are not permitted in analysis, these are commonly displaced in the direction of the desire for money or object of consumption. A desire for money is a legitimate interest on the part of the analyst who is providing a reimbursable service. However, the desire for money could also function as an obstacle for the treatment. It is ethical for the analyst to recognize this desire within himself/herself and prevent that it function as a guiding rule in the treatment. Analytic treatment should not be provided or continued or its frequency should not be determined solely for the monetary compensation. It is essential that analysts remain conscious of their desire for money and how it relates to their oedipal desires towards the patient. Lacan draws from Freud a notion of an ethic of desire of how ethical decisions are guided by examining one's own desires in relationship to the patient.

Because the analysand is searching for a master of knowledge who may understand something about his/her suffering, the therapeutic alliance is also established by the analysand's position as background lover of the conscious knowledge of the analyst (the analyst as the beloved). This emotional love for knowledge has the emotional impact on the analysand of feeling heard and understood by the analyst. The fact that the analyst appears to be knowledgeable in the analysand's eyes will endear the analyst to the analysand. Similarly, the analysand's relation to the knowledge available in the culture about psychology in general and/or Lacanian analysis in particular will mediate his/her view of the analyst as a S.s.K. It will also alleviate or increase his/her resistance to forming a collaborative therapeutic alliance and will set the emotional tone for the beginning of the treatment.

The analysand's relation to the knowledge that she/he is seeking in the analyst is mediated by her/his exposure to the knowledge about psychology available in the culture at large. It will be up to the analyst to explain what Lacanian analysis is. If the analysand comes specifically asking for Lacanian analysis, then one can expect that the S.s.K. has already been established in relation to the field of Lacanian psychoanalysis. However, the question still remains whether the particular analyst in question will be regarded by the analysand as a legitimate representative of Lacanian analysis. All these questions will have a direct bearing on the emotional tone that is set at the beginning of the treatment.

The analysand will approach the treatment with either a negative or a positive predisposition (Moncayo, 2008). A negative predisposition is when the ego of the analysand devalues the knowledge of the analyst. A positive predisposition is when the analysand is "willing to acknowledge a certain degree of suffering and inability to help himself/herself on his/her own." Either negative or positive predispositions will hinder or facilitate the development of the therapeutic alliance. In the case of a negative predisposition or a devaluating transference, the analyst has to be careful not to overreact and try to demonstrate what he/she knows. His/her knowing still has to emerge from or be consistent with a place of not knowing. In a case of a positive predisposition, the analyst also has to act from the place of a knowing that does not know that it knows, in order not to be complicit in the development of an idealizing transference (Moncayo, 2008).

Although oedipal phases begin to unfold in phase II of treatment, oedipal phases/themes, clinical symptoms, and the development of analytic symptoms are assessed in the pre-treatment evaluation phase, as discussed above. During the evaluation phase the analyst is utilizing his/her conscious knowledge of the field of psychoanalysis. In other words in this phase the analyst is relying on his/her conscious knowledge rather than on the emerging unconscious knowing of the analysand. Among the things that need to be evaluated, the analyst should be attentive to the analysand's early life history, object-relation patterns, unconscious fantasies, oedipal stories, and vicissitude of the castration complex as well as to the client's subjective structure. The phenomenological questions posed by love, attachment, trust, dependency, self-esteem, and relationship with mother[1] are all assessed. In addition, clients may present with sexual symptoms in a neurotic or perverse manner. Questions related to sexuality, sexual fantasies, sexual orientation, gender identity, and relationship with father[2] are considered together with how the sexual symptoms are presented. Clients manifesting an erotic transference during the evaluation phase (perverse and psychotic clients) are ruled out for short treatment. Clients who brag about their love-making abilities may represent resistance to analysis and/or denial of castration anxiety.

Phase II of treatment and phase I of Oedipus

Formula for phase I of Oedipus $\dfrac{\text{Being with mother}}{\text{Being the maternal imaginary phallus}}$

The second phase of the transference is characterized by the analyst being perceived as a foreground beloved and a background lover. The transference to the analyst may fulfill unconscious wishes of the analyst. The analysand is perceived as a foreground lover (of the analyst) and a background beloved (the pre-conscious gratifications of the transference for the analyst) of the analyst. This is the first structural transformation of the "metaphor of love." Transference love is a metaphor for something about the therapeutic relationship. In this phase of the treatment the analyst has already been established as a S.s.K. in the therapeutic alliance and as an empathic listener of the analysand's pain/suffering. The transference is pre-conscious but the fact that transference is a repetition remains unconscious. It is the analysts' conscious knowledge and their capacity for empathy that turns them into a beloved in transference love. In transference love the analyst is loved for his/her recognition and love of the analysand during the pre-treatment phase. Here transference love simply means the pre-conscious love towards the analyst. The fact that this love is a repetition of phases of Oedipus still remains unconscious and needs to be interpreted and made conscious during phase II of treatment. Oedipal themes will continue to unfold in the remaining phases of treatment.

The beginning of a session and the "instance of the glance"

In terms of logical time, during the second phase of treatment, the "instance of the glance" represents the first encounter with Oedipus. The analyst is perceived as a "beloved," as a mother that triggers oral wishes/privations and revisits the "mirror stage" wherein mother and child mutually recognize each other as partial objects and others. In the "mirror phase" (phase II) of the treatment there is recognition of the beloved but almost immediately there is also a growing recognition that the mother's/analyst's desires are also turned elsewhere. Both the cutting of the session and of speech facilitate the awareness that analysis is a professional/ therapeutic relationship, that the session ends, and that the analyst has a life outside of the session. The imaginary aspect of "seeing" is being transformed under the scansion of speech, and the cutting of the session, by the small "mini-castrations" (Fink, 2007) that gradually introduce the symbolic castration that frees the subject's speech and desire. The "instance of the glance" will be replaced by the "moment of concluding."

As the knowledge of the analyst begins to coincide with the unconscious object of desire of the analysand, the analyst becomes the *objet a*, ideal lover, parent, etc. The quality of knowledge will shift from conscious to unconscious knowledge, or from the analyst being loved for his/her conscious knowledge, to the analyst being loved for his/her knowledge of the unconscious specific to the analysand. It is at this point that transference love needs to be analyzed as a repetition of themes related to the presence and absence of the maternal *objet a* and breast. The client will love and hate the analyst for the analysis of the unconscious. Now transference is established as a result of interpretation and punctuation, whereas in phase I of treatment the working alliance was the product of explanation and empathy (which evoked phase I of Oedipus and led to phase II of treatment).

By maintaining an unconditional desire and interest in all of the analysand's speech, the analyst triggers the "first phase of Oedipus," wherein the boy and girl identify with being the phallus for the mother. In order to be loved by the beloved, the analysand will want to be the analyst's good patient. Common themes analysands present within this phase include: failures of empathy, not feeling loved or recognized, or feeling deprived of the maternal object.

Phases IIIa and IIIb of treatment and phases II and III of Oedipus

During phase III of treatment the analyst is perceived as a foreground beloved/sexual object of desire and background sexual lover, and the analysand is perceived as foreground sexual lover and background sexual beloved. The analyst assumes the symbolic function of the father/analyst in punctuating and cutting the discourse and in representing the phallus and the possibility of phallic *jouissance* (Moncayo, 2008). Even though being with the analyst/mother and feeling like the analyst's/mother's special object led to an experience of feeling loved or recognized, phase II of Oedipus points to a turning towards the father. Although the analyst is established as beloved and the cutting of the session and speech bring on the possibility of more knowledge/*jouissance*, both parties may be in search of different objects of desire that have not yet emerged in the therapeutic relationship. This repeats the phase of Oedipus where the child may perceive that the mother's desire is turned towards a different type of *jouissance* (phallic *jouissance*) and towards an object/signifier that the father is perceived as having.

The analyst should not believe the transference and should pay attention to his/her transference/countertransference when being loved by the analysand. That the analyst does not allow himself/herself to be satisfied by transference love also points in the direction of a different *jouissance*. During this phase of treatment is when the analyst can bring up the sexual themes that emerged in the pre-treatment phase, using any opportunity in the signifying chain to point in this direction, whereas before the analyst may have avoided exploring the same material.

The middle of a session, and the "moment of concluding"

In terms of chronological time the "moment of concluding" can be viewed as the end of a session or of treatment. However, in terms of logical time it corresponds to the middle of a session. The act of cutting a session underscores the fact that the end of each session is intrinsically connected to the end of the treatment. This in turn makes the dimension of concluding operative throughout the treatment. According to Lacan (1945) the moment of concluding comes before the time for understanding. This facilitates the development of understanding and an awareness of the end of the treatment throughout the treatment and not just at the end of treatment. With respect to the point that the "moment of concluding" facilitates understanding, this has two components. First, it refers to the quality or the type of understanding that takes place. Second, the understanding may come faster, and this has an obvious implication with regards to the question of shortening the length of the treatment. It is the variable-length session connected to the "moment of concluding" that has this effect. The scansion of a session itself has two aspects: where it ends and the fact it ends at different times. Both of these dimensions facilitate treatment as well as the termination of treatment in chronological time (the aim and end of treatment).

Phase IIIa of treatment and phase II of Oedipus

In this subphase the No/Name of the Father is introduced by the way the analyst responds to the transference. The third element, the "No of the Father," is hence gradually introduced in the treatment through the cut in the session that produces ruptures. When the analyst cuts the session, he/she is in the place of the father, even from the beginning of the treatment. Since sexuality requires separation and difference, whereas maternal love is predicated on union and sameness, the cut of the session prepares the ground for the analyst to focus on questions of sexuality and sexual difference beginning with phase III of the treatment. The No of the Father constitutes a negation of the mother–child dyad but also constitutes an affirmation of phallic *jouissance*. The oedipal No points to the sexual desire of the parents for each other and to the potential desire of the children when they grow up. Once trust and separation has been established the analysand or analyst can bring up emerging sexual themes that may be uncomfortable to both parties. In this way the cut facilitates the movement through the phases of Oedipus. This is a further dimension of the scansion of a session in addition to the two aforementioned (facilitating understanding and bringing awareness of the end of treatment). The scansion of the session articulates the relationship between the phases of Oedipus and the phases of treatment and facilitates the movement from the a-sexual maternal transference to the analyst being perceived as a sexual being.

Phase II of Oedipus can be read according to the following formula:

$$\frac{\text{Name of the Father}}{\text{Not-being the imaginary maternal phallus}}$$

The "No" of the father addresses the question of not-being for both sexes, and this does not yet represent sexual difference for either sex. In the castration complex the "No" of the father refers to having rather than being. Moreover, unlike the castration complex, the phases of Oedipus do not vary for the sexes (introduction of the "No" to both sexes through the paternal metaphor so that they could separate from the mother).

In phase IIIb of treatment and phase III of Oedipus, sexuality emerges differently for men and women (men – imaginary possession/castration; women – imaginary castration/masquerade/simulacrum). In phase IIIa with the introduction of sexuality and the question of the father, the cut facilitates the transition from phase I of Oedipus to phase II of Oedipus, from the mother to the father. In phase IIIb of the treatment the question of *sexual difference* can emerge in full force.

Phase III of Oedipus (for the girl/woman): $\dfrac{\text{Not Being the Maternal Phallus}}{\text{Not Having the Paternal Phallus}}$

(Notice the double negative for femininity.)

Phase III of Oedipus entails sexual difference proper, which is still in the Imaginary (the boy thinks he has something he does not have, and the girl thinks she does not have something she has). The castration complex varies for the sexes according to the registers and logical types. The girl/woman enters phase III of Oedipus through the castration complex (imaginary castration) in phase IIIb (of treatment). Lacan's notion of the Imaginary includes both fantasy and the perception of visual reality as something independent from the laws of language and culture. In the childhood Imaginary, both sexes perceive the girl's anatomy as lacking the imaginary phallus. A girl/woman enters Oedipus proper through not having the paternal imaginary phallus, but she then exits in phase IV of Oedipus by having the phallus in the Symbolic and by having the imaginary phallus through the Other in sex. The Symbolic represents the Law of culture and education (social laws, and the laws of kinship and language), and the No/Name of the Father.

The boy's having of the paternal phallus in phase III of Oedipus puts him in conflict with the father and hence at risk for losing it.

Phase III of Oedipus (for the boy/man): $\dfrac{\text{Not Being the Maternal Phallus}}{\text{Having the Paternal Phallus}}$

For men and women in phase II of Oedipus sex emerges as an imaginary form of castration of the maternal phallus, which is the central unconscious manifestation of the separation from the mother. The maternal phallus is the imaginary object (baby/phallus) that is used to deny the lack in the mother. In addition, the maternal phallus can either be the imaginary phallus that the mother has taken from her husband/partner and/or the one that she has received from her own father or maternal grandfather (the primal father). In Oedipus the Other separates the mother from her own imaginary phallus. The protestations of the mother with regards to being separated from her child are not only based on the welfare or best interests of the child's objective well-being, but also on her own attachment to the child as her own imaginary object/phallus. In phase III of Oedipus sex can emerge as an imaginary possession of the paternal phallus for men and imaginary castration of the paternal phallus for women. Phase III of Oedipus initiates Oedipus proper for the boy or his love interest for his mother and rivalry with the father. The boy will encounter the castration complex in a second moment when he fears losing the imaginary phallus. It is negotiating the castration complex that leads either to success or failure in Oedipus for a boy. If the boy does not come to terms with the castration complex, he will remain fixated on phase III of Oedipus.

In contrast to this, for the girl the castration complex initiates the girl into Oedipus proper. Grappling with the complex makes sexuality and Oedipus possible for the girl. The girl will look for the imaginary phallus in the Other, but she will also have to find it for herself as a missing signifier in the Symbolic. By complying with the laws of language and culture, the girl will access the positive function of the castration complex. By having paid the ticket of admission at the point of entry to the structure, the girl acquires the privileges granted by the Symbolic. Here the symbolic phallus functions as a missing signifier for the girl that will generate the dimension of metaphoric exchange. Within the Imaginary the phallus will function as an object of the Other in the sexual relation.

As related to the Other sex, not resolving the castration complex in the Imaginary will lead her to become fixated in Oedipus. This fixation signifies that the girl can only "have it" through coupling with an imaginary masculine but that she won't have it as a metaphoric substitute or as the function of metaphor. This is the Lacanian answer to the common feminine critique that under patriarchy a woman has identity or self-esteem only through her relationships with men. However, the reverse side of this problem for men, which is often overlooked, is that men can only be men with a phallic woman by their side.

For the girl during phase III of Oedipus, the castration complex, brought up by the question of possession of the phallus, marks the point of entry to the oedipal phase proper. For girls/women the castration complex does not address how a girl exits Oedipus. This in turn may account for women's rejection of psychoanalysis, since there appears to be no way out of Oedipus from the place of imaginary castration and penis envy. Thus, the question arises as to how do girls or a woman exit Oedipus?

> Whereas in boys the Oedipus complex is destroyed by the castration complex, in girls it is made possible and led up to by the castration complex.
>
> (Freud, 1925: 256)

Renunciation of the penis is not tolerated by the girl without some attempt at compensation. She slips – along the line of a symbolic equation, one might say – from the penis to a baby. Her Oedipus complex culminates in a desire, which is long retained, to receive a baby from her father as a gift – to bear him a child.

(Freud, 1924: 178–9)

But as we now know, having a baby is "not all" for women. Having a baby does not resolve the question of their identity in relationship to the Symbolic and to an economy that requires their labor to an ever-increasing degree. The lack within the Imaginary has a different meaning within the Symbolic. What functions as an impediment to having the phallus for the girl in the Imaginary and in relationship to gender or self-identity becomes strength or facilitation in relationship to language and the symbolic order in general. During latency girls seem to do better than boys in the acquisition of language because they have already paid in advance for the ticket of entry into the Symbolic. The lack within the Symbolic facilitates rather than hinders. It is the Symbolic order that points to the way out of Oedipus for a girl, not the castration complex. This points to the importance of education being a significant aspect of a woman's socioeconomic as well as social standing, as it provides a way out of Oedipus.

Phase IV of Oedipus

Phase IV Oedipus (Boy): $\dfrac{\text{Having the Paternal Phallus}}{\text{Not Having the Paternal Phallus}}$

Phase IV Oedipus (Girl): $\dfrac{\text{Not Having the Paternal Phallus}}{\text{Having the Paternal Phallus}}$

Only by losing it can the boy truly have it. Hence the boy exits Oedipus through the castration complex by losing the imaginary phallus (symbolic castration) in phase IV of Oedipus. The boy has it in the Imaginary and loses it in the Symbolic, and the girl does not have it in the Imaginary and gains it in the Symbolic. Within the Symbolic, having it and not having it amount to the same thing. Within the Symbolic the phallus is the dialectical presence of an absence (signifier of a lack), whereas in the Imaginary the phallus implies a binary/dual/formal disjunction: either masculine presence or feminine absence. However, when sexual difference functions across the registers, dialectical or symbolic logic presides over imaginary formal logic. By losing it in the Symbolic a boy can then use the phallus in the Imaginary as a self-object, whereas the girl uses it in the Imaginary as an object of the Other sex and gains it in the Symbolic as the function of metaphoric substitution.

Phase IV is being suggested as an additional phase in which the resolution of the Oedipus complex occurs for both sexes. This new phase is implicit in Lacan's theory and follows his logic (Lacan's Seminar V and Seminar XX). Moreover, this fourth phase coincides with a newly suggested dimension of time. Logical time is operative within each session, between sessions and between phases of treatment. The end as aim (i.e., the end is the aim, the aim of aims, the aim of an end) is present in all the sessions (as the "moment of concluding") and phases of treatment. The end as aim becomes a fourth phase. Termination still corresponds to chronological time (past–present–future/beginning–middle–end), but a fourth dimension of time or logical time has been introduced: the dimension of the end as an aim within the session and throughout the treatment. As stated earlier, the fourth dimension of time coincides with the space–time continuum of quantum physics. In the fourth dimension, time moves from future to present similarly to turning left or right in the space dimension.

For the boy the castration complex marks the way out of Oedipus. For the boy phase III of Oedipus means having the phallus and the mother to some extent. Therefore, the boy encounters castration in phase IV of Oedipus. Alternatively, in phase III, the boy encounters imaginary having and imaginary castration, and in phase IV the castration complex is resolved via symbolic castration. For the girl, phase III marks the entry to Oedipus via the castration complex and phase IV the exit from Oedipus and the entry to the Symbolic.

The Symbolic is involved in the resolution of Oedipus for both sexes (in phase IV of Oedipus, since phase III is still in the Imaginary): symbolic castration (the gift of the generative lack itself) for the boy and the symbolic phallus for the girl (metaphoric having or the gift of metaphor). Phase III is an imaginary moment of oedipal structure that empowers or gives identity to the boy and castrates the girl (having for the boy and not having for the girl). Phase IV is the reverse. The Symbolic in phase IV of Oedipus castrates the boy and empowers the identity of a girl. In this model castration signifies difference and the Other (sex). Identity or similarity equals having the phallic object, whether imaginary or symbolic.

For a girl the fixation to Oedipus means that she can only be a woman via the recognition of an actual father figure, and to be a woman signifies being plagued by envy and feeling dispossessed of the imaginary phallus. To become unfixated and what helps her exit Oedipus is the lack in the Other. The lack in the Other, in the sense of the lack in the father, will constitute the fourth phase of Oedipus. The girl needs to get past seeing the mother's desire for the father as an indication of an imaginary lack in the mother. The lack is a signifier of desire and as such it is generative rather than the reflection of a deficit. It is possible for the mother to desire the father and also be content with her own lot in life.

In addition, the girl also has to come to terms with the lack in the father. The father is no longer the imaginary father in possession of the imaginary phallus, but becomes a castrated symbolic father that cannot use his own imaginary phallus with his daughter. Due to the prohibition of incest, the father is under the law and renounces the daughter as a sexual object. The father is castrated when it comes to his daughter. With her sense of the lack in the father, who remains a father nonetheless, and her own having of the symbolic phallus because she does not have the imaginary phallus, the father–daughter relationship assumes its full symbolic significance in phase IV of Oedipus. In phase IV a girl/woman has to find a way to come to terms with the lack in a man and have a relationship with a man at the same time.

Phase IV of treatment

Before beginning the discussion of the last phase of treatment we want to re-capitulate the sexual or gender symptoms that people bring to treatment in order to ascertain what could be resolved within and as a result of the treatment.

Men and women may present to treatment with the following phase II and III oedipal dynamics either because they did not exit Oedipus or because they want to revisit the phases and come to a better understanding of their sexual identifications.

In this section, the words man or woman, or masculinity and femininity, as psychic signifiers of sex, will be used as independent categories from biological or anatomical male and female characteristics.

Common masculine complaints:

1   Phallic parade or narcissism is used as a posture to defend against castration anxieties. These men may be good lovers but cannot function in society or within the Symbolic. Phallic parade is the equivalent of simulacrum in women.
2   Sexual impotence with normal or marginal functioning in society. This is the position of the gentleman or the chivalrous man, ready to make any sacrifice for his Lady. These men confuse imaginary and symbolic castration and whether the father said No to sex in general or only with the mother. Symbolic castration is interpreted as an absolute sexual prohibition rather than as facilitating access to phallic *jouissance*.

Common feminine complaints:

1   Lack of sexual satisfaction and desire. This is also known as Mascarade or the hysterical indifference to sexuality and/or the sacrifice and denial of sexu-ality. The Lady continues the beloved/lover position of phase I of Oedipus in an unconsciously seductive manner to deny castration (she has the phallus and therefore does not need it or want it). She is the beloved object of affection that at once entices and frustrates sexual desire.
2   The second category corresponds to women who experience difficulty func-tioning in society because they are either criticized by feminist women for being feminine or mocked by men for the same reasons. These women may equate money with masculinity, and they have to have money like men otherwise they feel worthless. Homemakers, for example, can choose to be feminine and "stay-at-home mothers" and contribute to the economy with

their labor and yet not directly be paid money for their efforts. But only women who do not regard femininity as a deficit/defect will be able to do this without a significant sense of damage to their self-worth.

3   Acting out sexually or confusing love and sex (phase I and II of Oedipus) and/or being confused about how sex relates to Oedipus. This condition is also known as Simulacrum or competing to be as sexual as men. "The woman" represents the phallus in her whole body or alternatively wants to have an imaginary phallus in the form of a dildo or a strap-on penis. Both Mascarade and Simulacrum represent forms of hyper-femininity in different ways. Simulacrum is a form of hyper-masculinity within femininity, whereas Mascarade is a form of hyper-femininity and denial of phallic sexuality.

The difference between the third and fourth phases of treatment represents the difference between when treatment ends versus termination, as it relates to the crossing of the phantasm and acquiring a new relationship to the symptom in the form of identification with the *sinthome*. Only analysis proper (not brief analysis) would arrive at the logical end of the treatment.

It is interesting to note that the concept and practice of brief analyses has helped clarify the ingredients and practice of psychoanalysis in such a way that the two can be distinguished and the aim and scope of both may be more precisely determined.

Termination as a fourth phase of treatment would also be related to the fourth phase of Oedipus discussed above. For analysis proper to end, the analyst has to move past the beloved mother of the first phase of Oedipus and past the beloved father of phase II and III of Oedipus. The analyst needs to occupy the place of the lack in the Other and of the symbolic father and mother, both of which are characteristic of the fourth phase of Oedipus.

In phase II of Oedipus and phase IIIa of treatment, the father/analyst represents the possibility of separation from the mother, but this issue is dealt with entirely from a non-sexual perspective in the transference. The analyst is the beloved who helps the client separate from the mother. In phase III of Oedipus and phase IIIb of treatment, the analyst is the sexual beloved who helps separate from the mother and the father but remains as an ideal impossible or forbidden sexual beloved. The client leaves the treatment accepting the therapist as an impossible lover, but the therapist remains idealized (or hated/devalued) and the transference, therefore, is not resolved. In phase IV of treatment the analyst surrenders the beloved position but remains as lover of lack. The analyst is not a good object but remains as the possibility of pure desire. The analysand is a beloved, but no longer the lover of the analyst. The analyst as lover of lack supports the desire of the analysand for someone else not the analyst by no longer being the ideal sexual beloved.

The distinction between the third and fourth phases of treatment, or between the ends of treatment versus the termination of analysis, also allows one to think about the differences between analysis proper, the conditions of a brief analysis, brief therapy, and psychotherapy.

Within the psychoanalytic field it is common for people to think that once a week is counseling or supportive psychotherapy, twice a week is insight psychotherapy, and three or four times a week is analysis proper. With the framework under consideration in this chapter, these distinctions can be reformulated in qualitative terms. Supportive psychotherapy works mostly within the first phase of Oedipus, insight psychotherapy works within phase II and III of Oedipus, and analysis proper works within phase III and IV of Oedipus. Lacanian analysis has an explicit framework to work through a fourth phase of Oedipus that up to now was implicit within Lacanian theory and practice but remained entirely unformulated within Freudian psychoanalysis prior to Lacan.

Within the qualitative model being proposed, the phases of Oedipus can be thought of as phases of a single treatment, but can also be used to determine the range and depth of a treatment despite its frequency or length. There can be four-times-a-week analyses that remain within phase I of Oedipus, and there can be once-a-week analyses that engage the entire spectrum of oedipal structure. However, with regards to the length of treatment, it is unlikely that the fourth phase of Oedipus can be reached, let alone resolved, in a brief analysis even if done by analysts. An exception to this would be the case of someone who has already gone through a previous course of analysis. In this instance a brief analysis could perhaps take a person from phase III to phase IV of treatment and therefore allow them to exit Oedipus and resolve the transference neurosis. In this case the ending of treatment and resolution of the transference neurosis becomes one and the same thing.

What could be hoped for and the possible resolution of presenting symptoms

If brief analysis may only go to phase III of Oedipus, this raises the question of what this phase may mean to the different sexes. If treatment ends at phase III of Oedipus, this raises the question of whether both sexes remain fixated at a particular phase of Oedipus. The phases of treatment cannot be identical to the phases of Oedipus, for the simple reason that time cannot be rolled back and that everything that comes after redefines what came before. This means that although phase III of treatment shares a structural similarity with phase III of Oedipus, a man, for example, has already encountered at least imaginary castration before he has entered treatment. The difference is that in brief analysis the imaginary castration can be transformed into symbolic castration. However, the source of castration is the lack in the Other, and the symbolic father/mother is only addressed in analysis proper in the transference relationship to the analyst.

Having completed a brief analysis, a man may have addressed symbolic castration and therefore leave with a legitimate sense of having the phallus. But, by not having worked through the lack in the Other, he remains vulnerable to a return of symptomatology and imaginary castration fears. In addition, even if the treatment is regulated by the desire of the analyst (not to remain in the position of the beloved), due to not having worked through the lack in the Other, and the transference neurosis therefore, the analyst may still remain in the transference position of the subject supposed or de-supposed to know. A woman may have recuperated an ability to enjoy phallic *jouissance* and to access a symbolic form of identity, but this symbolic identity, without having resolved the question of the lack in the Other, remains prone to regress to imaginary forms of having the phallus in masculinity.

The treatment may end with some intimations of phase IV even though these intimations do not by any means imply resolutions. As already stated, and for the most part, there is no resolution of the transference neurosis in brief analysis. A character transformation will not take place, and clinical rather than existential symptoms and themes will be addressed and alleviated. In contrast to this, analysis proper can inoculate a subject against existential issues and not only clinical symptoms.

Case example

The following case vignette further illustrates the model under consideration. This case vignette was previously published (Moncayo, 2008) but is presented here in modified fashion to suit the purposes of this chapter.

A client, whose first and last name can be translated into "the one who sees into the loss of being," came into treatment complaining of depression. She met the DSM–IV criteria for dysthymic disorder. When asked about her depression she complained of the experience of always being abandoned or left by others. Through the permutation of her name, her problem/symptom (being abandoned) can be translated into "the other has caused a loss of being in me."

Based on the relationship between the symbolic meaning of the proper name and the patronymic, in contrast to the manifest meaning of the presenting symptom, the analyst observed an inverse unconscious relation between the name and the symptom. The ego defenses of the analysand transformed active into passive: from an active act of seeing into the lack in the other into a passive act of being left by the other (due to her own shortcomings or defects). The client herself at a different time stated that she "sees things in the other." However, by this she meant to express pride in her abilities as a "seer" rather than recognition of a character flaw of always looking for defects and devaluing the other.

The focus on the meaning of her name and her description of herself as a seer, as well as the focus on the suffering embodied in her depression, represent imaginary forms of empathy both with the suffering or *jouissance* of the patient and her ego defenses. Imaginary empathy goes from the known to the known, but by facilitating new symbolic relations between what she already knows, the Imaginary now turned Symbolic can also help the subject go from the known to the unknown, and hopefully eventually from the symbolic unknown to the unknown of the Real.

By redefining her symptom as a loss of self or being when the other leaves her (pointing to the narcissistic dimension of an object), and bringing the symptom into relation to an ego-syntonic character trait, an enigma is evoked wherein her perceived strengths are intrinsically bound up with her downfalls or weaknesses.

Initially the analyst accepted the analysand's view of herself and expressed interest in her story. The analyst is the lover and she is the beloved. Since the analyst did not challenge the client's view of herself and expressed interest in her, this laid the ground for the analyst becoming the beloved that shared her qualities of a seer. She extends her own perceived attributes to the analyst.

In the pre-treatment phase the analyst became the S.s.K. The analyst supports her defenses by mirroring her views of herself and finding support for these views in the significations embedded in her name. However, and at the same time, such significations begin to reveal that the positive quality of being a seer could have a negative/destructive (to both self and other) side of fault finding. At this juncture imaginary empathy begins to slide into symbolic empathy thanks to the intervention of the signifier. Symbolic empathy begins to question the meaning of ego-defenses but without judging or criticizing the client.

The analysand complained that her husband left her and how could he dare to do this, since after all he was the needy and weak one of the two. She was surprised and devastated when he left. He had been the one to adore and idealize her. He admired her way with words and her ability to communicate. She instead perceived him as incompetent and lacking in the use of language, although she recognized that he was a good provider and that she very much enjoyed how well he treated her, especially financially.

Having said this, she said that she brought a basket of communication to the marriage but that he brought nothing instead. The client was not aware when she said this that a food basket usually refers to the ability to provide for basic needs. She accused him of not bringing a basket when she herself recognized that he was a good provider and he in turn recognized her ability to communicate. Despite the little respect she had for him at the beginning and especially after he left her, she continued to use his last name (the name that means loss of being). She felt more secure using his name. His name served as a stopgap for her own lack, and at the same time the name and her husband signified the lack of being and of the Other.

In the next phase of treatment the analyst listened to the analysand's abandoning history/story/script. Once the analysand saw the analyst as S.s.K. or as a seer like her, then she could share her abandonment story. This led the way to themes from the first phase of Oedipus. The client liked to think of her theme of abandonment by others as repeating a prior abandonment by her mother and father. This much had been told to her by her previous therapists. However, her relationship to her parents had the same kind of features as her relationship to her husband. The analysand stated that her mother did not love her and that she preferred her sister. But the next moment she proceeded to say that her mother thought she, the client, was the most beautiful of the girls and that her sister was not very attractive and was in fact very sickly throughout childhood. She, of course, does not say how much she challenged her mother or that her mother was not very attractive either, or that her father was very handsome and that she was her father's beautiful girl. All this came out later in the course of the analysis and led to a reformulation/rectification of her symptom of being abandoned.

The reformulation of the patient's symptom of abandonment established by prior psychotherapy is consistent with what Svolos (2004) called, following Lacan, a rectification of the subject's relation to the symptom. Only by co-construction of a new psychoanalytic symptom or object (as Bion would call it), with the participation of both analyst and analysand, can the analysis proceed to a second phase of recognizing fundamental fantasies, and then to termination under the co-direction of the unconscious and the desire of the analyst, in the strict Lacanian sense of the term.

In the case of this analysand, the fears or feelings of abandonment are part of a fantasy of abandonment by her father. The alleged abandonment constitutes an actual oedipal rejection. Because of the incest prohibition she could not have the father. Despite the client's own oedipal challenges, it is the mother who receives the paternal phallus and not the daughter. If anything the client succeeded too much in Oedipus and then spent her life working to lose. The client thus presents the problem as being associated with phase I of Oedipus, but the analyst, by asking more questions about her abandonment story, gets to themes of phase II and III of Oedipus.

Moreover, the analysis of dreams begins in phase II of treatment, and the dreams aid the analyst in determining whether the fixation or problem originated in phase I, II, or III of Oedipus. A memory and a dream reported by the client assisted in making conscious her oedipal themes. Her sister once dressed her up in one of her mother's beautiful dresses and had her show up at the door of their house. The client looked so much like a beautiful grown-up woman that her mother mistook her for her father's alleged "other woman." The client reported this memory in a naïve and innocent way, but without comprehending its meaning. In contrast to this, in other instances the client was very willing, able, and ready to interpret her experience and her dreams in terms of her abandonment script.

During the "instance of the glance" the analyst has to see the manifestation of the unconscious, not as a flaw, but as foolish knowing and knowledge, in the analysand and the analyst. For example, the analysand said that her mother did not love her but then said that her mother thought she was the most beautiful of the children. One could say, with Karen Horney (1939), for example, that this is a contradiction the analyst is pointing out to the analysand (her mother does not love her/her mother loves her), or that this is a manifestation of unconscious knowing that the analysand does not know or does not want to know that she knows. Since she does not want to see (here she is blind) how her mother loves her, or wants to deny it, this knowledge is unconsciously held.

The analyst sees the unconscious as knowing and not as flaw or defect. Both forms of knowledge are correct but need to be re-interpreted or re-framed. This leads to a therapeutic alliance between the positive idealizing transference to the analyst supposed to know, wherein the analyst is perceived as a Carlos Castaneda type of figure, or as a "seer" or "witch doctor," and the unconscious knowing of the analysand. Moreover, the pointing out of the contradiction represents moving from themes of phase I, where the theme with the mother prevails, to phase II of

Oedipus, where the intervention of the father and sexuality begins. One could say that the fact that this client had already worked on the abandonment theme before made it possible to move quickly to reframe the problem as related to phase II of Oedipus.

Under symbolic function the analyst gives the analysand from his/her own lack of the symbolic phallus rather than the deception of giving an object that does not exist. This analysand wanted her analyst to either be the *objet a* of her fantasy, to love her and lack her as his *objet a*, which is perhaps what she succeeded to get from her mother, and for the analyst to give her the imaginary phallus that she wanted to receive from her father. By showing the analysand that the analyst accepted the lack within desire, that he was and was not Carlos Castaneda (the famous 1970s Mexican-American anthropologist and Toltec sorcerer), or that he had and not had what she perceived him as having, this facilitated a regression from Carlos Castaneda, as a signifier of the analysand's desire, to a signifier of a desire for her own father.

In this way, the unconscious knowing of the analysand replaced the knowledge of the analyst. Following the transference to the subject supposed to know, the analyst takes his/her position of lover of the unconscious knowing of the analysand. It is the analysand being in the position of the beloved that will support the analysand in the unpleasant task of recognizing unconscious knowing and the experience of lack in privation, frustration, and castration. The analysand recognized that she was not abandoned by her mother or father and instead found the signifiers of her own unfulfilled desire. These meant that she was loved and desired but that what she wanted was not something that could be given to her.

These discoveries or truths of desire do not in any way diminish or conceal the shortcomings or flaws of her parents. They become, however, an accepted aspect of the lack and inconsistencies of the Other. Had the analyst joined the analysand in her praising of him and proceeded to love her back by pointing out her good qualities and the shortcomings of her parents, and supported her in her grievances against parents and lovers, the analyst and the analysand would have joined in a narcissistic collusion, of mutual imaginary admiration, and had a wonderful love fest and romantic first phase of analysis. However, the analyst and analysand would have effectively aborted any possibility of real future treatment.

This example shows how much a pre-oedipal interpretation of subjectivity fits well with the ego's conscious level of comprehension. The ego wants to know and receive from the other what their defenses know all too well. The analyst has to ignore both the knowledge of the patient's ego as well as his/her own common-sense understanding. Instead, the analyst listens for the words of the Other that the patient seems to ignore. With pre-packaged knowledge the analyst can only give back to the analysand what she already knows. But what she already knows is equivocal. What her ego knows only seems to make matters worse: it reinforces her abandonment destiny. In truth the analyst can only give her back what she already knows (unconscious knowing) but does not know that she knows.

Limitations of the brief Lacanian analysis model

A variable-length Lacanian analysis is a second-best practice to an entire course of Lacanian analysis, and thus it is not an optimal method of treatment. It is a response to institutional requirements, lack of financial resources, lack of time, and lack of desire to engage in a long-term course of treatment. It can also be used as an institutional/academic tool for empirical outcome research. It is distinguished from analytic brief therapies by its thematic focus on unconscious fantasy and by the requirement that the therapist/analyst must have undergone an analysis of long duration. The difference between a short analysis and analysis proper is that in the former there is no resolution of the transference neurosis and the question of traversing the fantasy – crossing of the phantasm – is not entirely worked through. In addition, in brief analysis there is an agreed-upon ending point and the analysand does not get a chance to leave or to be "weaned" out of the treatment. Given the time limitation there is a limit to how much effectiveness can be packed into this model. However, by identifying and incorporating the distinct phases of Oedipus into the treatment, effectiveness may be enhanced and maximized.

Notes

1 Whoever assumes Maternal Desire in the family.
2 Whoever assumes the Paternal Function in the family.

References

Evans, D. (1996). *An Introductory Dictionary of Lacanian Psychoanalysis*. London and New York: Routledge.
Fink, B. (2007). *Fundamentals of Psychoanalytic Technique: A Lacanian Approach for Practitioners*. New York: W.W. Norton.
Flegenheimer, W.V. (1982). *Techniques of Brief Psychotherapy*. New York: Aronson.
Freud, S. (1915a). A case of paranoia running counter to the psycho-analytic theory of the disease. *GW*, X: 242; *SE*, XIV: 269.
Freud, S. (1915b). The unconscious. *GW*, X: 277; *SE*, XIV: 178.
Freud, S. (1916–17). *Introductory Lectures on Psycho-Analysis*. *GW*, XI, 386; *SE*, XVI: 371.
Freud, S. (1924). The dissolution of the Oedipus complex. *GW*, XIII: 401; *SE*, XIX: 178–9.
Freud, S. (1925). Some psychical consequences of the anatomical distinction between the sexes. *GW*, XIV: 28; *SE*, XIX: 256.
Freud, S. and Breuer, J. (1893–5). *Studies on Hysteria*. New York: Avon Books, 1966.
Horney, K. (1939). *New Ways in Psychoanalysis*. New York: W.W. Norton.
Lacan, J. (1945). Le temps logique. In J. Lacan, *Ecrits*. Paris: Seuil, 1966, pp. 197–213.
Lacan, J. (1953a). *Ecrits* (B. Fink trans.). New York: W.W. Norton, 2002.
Lacan, J. (1953b). The function and field of speech and language in psychoanalysis. In J. Lacan, *Ecrits: A Selection* (Alan Sheridan trans.). London: Tavistock, 1977.
Lacan, J. (1954). Introduction to Jean Hyppolite's Commentary on Freud's "Verneinung" (p. 317). *Ecrits. The First Complete Edition in English* (Bruce Fink trans.). New York: W.W. Norton, 2006.

Lacan, J. (1954–5). *The Seminar. Book II. The Ego in Freud's Theory and in the Technique of Psychoanalysis* (Sylvana Tomaselli trans., notes by John Forrester). New York: W.W. Norton; Cambridge: Cambridge University Press, 1988.

Lacan, J. (1956–7). *Le seminaire. Livre IV. La relation d'object* (J.-A. Miller ed.). Paris: Seuil, 1994, pp. 119–20.

Lacan, J. (1957–8). *El seminario Libro 5: Las Formaciones del Inconsciente*. Buenos Aires Nueva Visión 1979.

Lacan, J. (1964). *The Seminar. Book XI. The Four Fundamental Concepts of Psychoanalysis* (Alan Sheridan trans.). London: Hogarth Press and Institute of Psycho-Analysis, 1977, p. 212.

Lacan, J. (1966). *Ecrits*. Paris: Seuil, p. 349.

Laplanche, J. and Pontalis, J.-B. (1968). Fantasy and the origins of sexuality. *International Journal of Psycho-Analysis*, 49: 1–18.

Laplanche, J. and Pontalis, J.-B. (1973). *The Language of Psychoanalysis*. London: Karnac, p. 318.

Levenson, H. (1995). *Time-Limited Dynamic Psychotherapy: A Guide to Clinical Practice*. New York: Basic Books.

Moncayo, R. (2008). *Evolving Lacanian Perspectives for Clinical Psychoanalysis: On Narcissism, Sexuation, and the Phases of Analysis in Contemporary Culture*. London: Karnac.

Nobus, D. (2000). *Jacques Lacan and the Freudian Practice of Psychoanalysis*. London: Routledge.

Racker, H. (1960). *Transference and Countertransference*. New York: International Universities Press.

Svolos, T. (2004). Fundamental fantasy as the axiom of the unconscious. *Journal for Lacanian Studies*, 2: 4–17.

Chapter 5

Postmodern theory and culture and Lacanian psychoanalysis

Postmodernism, poststructuralism, and psychoanalysis

In this chapter I will address the meaning of the term postmodernism, and whether postmodernism, as a theory or cultural form, represents a development beyond the reach of Freudian psychoanalysis and whether Lacanian psychoanalysis is a postmodern form of Freudian psychoanalysis needed to address and explain the postmodern condition. At stake is the question of the varied meanings and definitions of both postmodernism and psychoanalysis currently available within the fields of philosophy, psychology, and the social sciences or humanities in general. In other words, postmodernism and psychoanalysis mean different things to different people.

Because the term postmodern may mean different things to different theorists, a particular reader could raise the objection that the definition of postmodernism that I am advancing or critiquing is not representative of his or her definition of postmodernism. In a way, the fact that so many definitions abound for the same thing for some may represent evidence enough for the existence of a postmodern phenomenon. As a paradigm, postmodernism favors pluralism and difference rather than a central and all encompassing master or meta-narrative. Since according to postmodernism the completeness and consistency of any school of knowledge remains indeterminate, the only legitimate gesture is to celebrate diversity and a pluralism of points of view. This is the equivalent of multiculturalism in the larger culture. In the analytic field one finds different schools of psychoanalysis that can be clearly identified and discussed, whereas the same may or may not be true of postmodernism. I will distinguish between a postmodernism that simply mirrors the state of postmodern culture from one that can be used to critique the latter while at the same time remaining distinct from the ideas associated with modernity.

I will straightforwardly identify my sources for the discussion on postmodernism. Two of the basic reference texts for this chapter are Lyotard's *The Postmodern Condition* (1979), and Best and Kellner's *Postmodern Theory* (1991). Although I have been a reader of Foucault, and a student of Deleuze and

Guattari, a very close examination of their poststructuralist thought would lead me too far astray from the purpose at hand. For the application of postmodernism to psychotherapy and psychoanalysis, I will rely on Frie and Orange's *Beyond Postmodernism: New Dimensions in Clinical Theory and Practice* (2009). This text uses postmodern and poststructuralist ideas almost interchangeably, although the two schools of thought can also be differentiated.

Both give primacy to discourse and share a critique of modernity but go about it in different ways. Although postmodern ideas have more diffuse origins (see Best and Kellner, 1991; Smith, 1989), I consider postmodernism principally related to the work of Lyotard and Baudrillard. Although Lyotard was another French theorist who was part and parcel of an impressive array of French thinkers that emerged in the past century, his thought differs from the poststructuralism of Deleuze and Guattari, Foucault, or Derrida. The two North American schools that have used postmodern ideas the most are the intersubjective and relational schools of psychoanalysis. Finally, for a more general context, and particularly for the spiritual aspects of postmodernism, it is also worth noting Huston Smith's *Beyond the Post-Modern Mind* (1989).

Overall postmodernism seems to designate a term used to express a desire for paradigm change and epistemological breakthroughs needed to understand a new cultural era. Whether postmodernism accomplished a break with previous knowledge or not, and whether the cultural changes in question represent progress or regression is precisely what is at stake in this chapter. Most authors identify modernity with the Enlightenment, and postmodernism with the current state of Western culture and a particular theoretical orientation. However, from a cultural point of view, there is disagreement as to the differences or similarities between advanced modernity or "ultra-modernism" and postmodernism. In addition, as Best and Kellner (1991) point out "By the 1980s, the postmodern discourses were split into cultural conservatives decrying the new developments and avant-gardists celebrating them" (p. 15).

Habermas (1987) has critiqued postmodernism as a conservative ideology developed to undermine modern values. Emancipation, for example, is as a key modern concept/value championed by modernity, critical theory, and Habermas himself. Overall, postmodern theory identifies modernity with attempts at establishing totalizing social projects or visions of a great society, and reason and notions of causality are tools or means to realize them. The concept of emancipation and liberation (of the working classes, women, sexuality, etc.), for example, was central to these efforts. Postmodernism instead privileges pluralism and difference, the part over the totality, and the principle of indeterminacy within and between different points of view, political or otherwise. Guattari, for example, usually considered a poststructuralist, criticized postmodernism for abandoning the concept of social emancipation. In this example, it is easy to see how the lines between the modern and the postmodern can be blurred.

Nevertheless, poststructuralist theorists parted ways with totalitarian Marxism, communist parties, and the like and, instead, were drawn to local or micro-political or molecular change movements such as feminism, minority and patient rights, the struggle for ethnic and racial identity, and gay and lesbian rights. The value and importance given to the fight against oppression and the struggle for liberation remained the same except that it became divested of its totalitarian implications.

> Women fleeing the patriarchal family, homosexuals throwing off the straight-jackets of heterosexual conformity, and people of color attacking racist ideologies are further examples of lines of flight from molar lines and a process of becoming "minority."
>
> (Best and Kellner, 1991, p. 102)

The historical examples provided by totalitarian Marxist societies were used to reject ("modern") Marxism once it became clear that rather than solving the problem of oppression and domination, the dictatorship of the proletariat had replaced one type of oppression for another more lethal one. Under the dictatorship of the proletariat, the "tortilla" had been flipped over and now it was the turn of the wealthy class to "eat shit" instead of the poor (a translation of a common slogan chanted in street demonstrations in Latin America).

But although postmodern theory no longer seeks to seize state power via armed revolution, the question still remains as to whether the struggles for emancipation solve the problem of domination or simply reverse the roles and make the servant the master and the master the servant. Perhaps both things are true at the same time. The challenge to the existing order brings some changes and also some unintended or unconscious consequences. The order is challenged and preserved at the same time. It is changed because now the servant is in the place of the master, but is preserved because the master–servant relationship continues albeit in modified fashion. In my opinion, and as I argued in chapter 1, on identity and identification, only a logic of contradiction can begin to disentangle such a complex knot of contradictory strands.

There are many examples of this state of affairs in postmodern culture. I leave open the possibility that these phenomena could be seen as unintended consequences of otherwise necessary cultural developments. As Lacan has said, what you gain on one side, you lose on the other. In addition, the notion of unintended consequences needs to be examined from the point of view of the unconscious in psychoanalysis. The fact that things happen together or in co-relation does not mean that one is the cause of the other. There may be a third mediating cause such as the Freudian unconscious.

Furthermore, the fear of domination by the oppressed is a common thread of both conservative and reactionary right-wing thought. A clear example of the latter is provided by the election of the first African-American president of the United States. Barack Obama embodies Martin Luther King's famous statement that a person should be judged by their character rather than by the color of their skin. President Obama is civil, articulate, and gentle to the point where some could even accuse him of being ineffectual and certainly not as tough and decisive as white Republican presidents claimed to be. Yet right-wing extremists are busy denouncing Obama as the new Hitler.

At the same time, middle-class white European Americans, as well as other ethnicities, are afraid of the image of the angry black male stereotype. Fanon (1952) already used psychoanalysis and Lacan to understand this phenomenon. Black masculinity represents the repressed phallic principle, the repressed desires that whites fear, and secretly envy. At the same time, I argue, "black" unconsciously represents the rejected "lack." Since whites and the master reject lack and project it into blackness/"lackness," African-Americans are faced with the dilemma of owning symbolic castration for both races, or disowning castration altogether. Since the white master disowns symbolic castration and lives under the illusion of phallic supremacy, he/she fears castration by African masculinity.

By the same token, since African-Americans can be faced with the burden of symbolic and imaginary castration for both races, they can also easily fall into the counterpart illusion of a life without symbolic debt and end up alienated from the Law and caught up in the criminal justice system. Fortunately many African-Americans passed through the double jeopardy (of normal repression/ symbolic castration and unnecessary oppression/holding castration for both races) and made it into the middle class alongside whites. Like Martin Luther King and President Obama, they provide an alternative model for the rest of their community.

The fact that white people can accept being led and taught by African-American leaders sends a message that whites are finally owning their lack and their symbolic debt to African-Americans and the black race. Again, by the same token, now African-Americans have to live under the same laws and social rules as the rest of society. To the extent that whites resent legitimate African-American leadership, they still live under the illusion of imaginary and unbarred phallic supremacy, and the conflict between the races continues unabated. In this instance, whites lose the legitimacy to scrutinize or critique the actions of African-Americans or other ethnic minorities.

Although it is legitimate to scrutinize character and violent or antisocial actions, most non-African-Americans, who are not overtly racist, act in politically correct ways, and are afraid of engaging in criticism or confrontation of problematic behavior on the part of African-Americans. Whether it is gun violence, the drug trades, out-of-wedlock pregnancies, children being raised by grandmothers, rude behavior, or the excesses of rap culture, non-African-Americans have to be very careful not to critique these actions and attitudes for fear of being attacked or accused of racism. Liberals and African-Americans tend to tolerate or justify violent actions on the basis of the history of slavery and centuries of racism and discrimination.

A second example from late modernity is the generational or baby-boomer shift from authoritarian to permissive childrearing. Many examples of parental permissiveness or decline are available within popular culture. Whether the television shows the Nanny and Brat Camp, or the proliferation of therapeutic boarding schools for out-of-control teens, the high-school drop-out rates (three out of ten students drop out of school and seven out of ten don't finish college), or the overt disrespect for parental or paternal authority, all point in the direction of parents being on the defensive when it comes to children and childrearing. Many Latino parents in the United States, for example, who still use physical discipline, report that their children threaten them with calling the police in response to parental attempts to discipline them, and not only when parents want to use corporal punishment. On the other hand, despite what I have just stated, I am not arguing that these excesses are sufficient reason to question the merits and protections of modern child abuse reporting laws, for example. The problem is more complex than this.

In addition, is this critique identical to the well-known Lacanian argument regarding the decline of the paternal function? Am I simply providing further evidence and argument to this effect or in the same direction? Lacanians typically associate the postmodern with the decline of the paternal function, and in many ways this association is justified. On the other hand, in this chapter I am also proposing the idea that Lacanian psychoanalysis can be considered a postmodern reading of Freud that can be used to critique postmodern culture. So what, then, is a postmodern reading not only of Freud but also of Lacan? I argue that it is the later Lacan that can be considered postmodern and poststructuralist, as represented by the evolution of his ideas about Oedipus and the Symbolic. In fact, the later Lacan may have also been influenced by postmodernism and poststructuralism.

According to evolved Lacanian theory, it is not simply a question of going back to the good old times when the father in the family reigned supreme and abuses of paternal authority went unquestioned. This fantasized nostalgia for a primal father is also predicted by psychoanalytic theory. Human beings are plagued by two basic and contradictory myths: the wish to kill the father, the parents, the authority, and the opposite wish of the father, the parent, and the master to kill the children, subordinates (including women), and servants. The first is known as the Oedipus myth, and the second Freud invented under the name of the myth of the primal horde. However, the idea that the father wants to kill/abuse his children is not only a vestige of barbaric societies since it also runs through the Bible. At different points Abraham and Moses have to dissuade God from wanting to destroy his offspring and creation. In the case of Jesus, God the father does end up killing/ sacrificing his own son. We also know that in Muslim societies fathers may kill their daughters if they suspect them of sexual misconduct in the eyes of Muslim law.

Nobus (2002) has already noted that a fear of fatherlessness is nothing new. The notion of God the father as the legitimate power behind the power of the father in the family goes all the way back to the structuring power of the church within Medieval society. In that view, social harmony and order are held together by a double-parallel submission: of the father to God and of the mother and children to the father. This idea runs through the three forms of monotheism and is the premise that most forms of religious fundamentalism want to return to. The difference between traditional religious fundamentalism and a modern view of the family seems to lie simply in the secularization of the religious principle that otherwise remains unchanged. The idea of God is replaced by a notion of a symbolic order held together by the paternal metaphor. Nobus also mentions that Durkheim, the noted 19th-century sociologist, also had concerns regarding the decline of paternal authority and the consequence of this for the moral development of the child and, therefore, of future generations.

However, the difference between this argument and the one I am advancing is equivalent to that between the early and later Lacan. The nostalgia for the primal father does not have a happy ending, since it simply replaces one problem for another. The order of the father also produces the abuses of the father, whereas the curbing of patriarchal authoritarianism leads to the disorders of postmodernism. What I am proposing is that the nostalgia for an ideal father is a defense against emptiness, and it is emptiness, correctly understood, that underpins the symbolic order without producing the excesses of the father figure or of the master. I submit that emptiness organizes the symbolic order without representing an affront or rejection of democratic values. In fact, emptiness is the guarantee that democratic values may actually work in the absence of authoritarian figures. Emptiness at the level of the subject ($ or 8), rather than the Other (Ø), is what causes the subject to be civil qua signifying subject within a democratic system of signifiers. Civil here means three things: equanimity, reasonableness in the sense of the recognition of the rules of the order (each signifier is different yet related to other signifiers), and the capability for love on the basis of the emptiness that all subjects and signifiers share (similitude rather than similarity).

A third example of a traditional and modern predicament that was transformed into a postmodern condition is the case of patients' rights. At this point the excesses and limitations of the traditional psychiatric order have been amply documented and written about by a whole generation of scholars and practitioners (Laing, Guattari, Szasz, Castel, Foucault, Battaglia, to name only a few). In addition, the media and Hollywood have amply documented the excesses of the psychiatric establishment (*One Flew Over the Cuckoo's Nest*, *Changeling*, etc.). In response to the critique and the limitations of hospital-based psychiatry, the community mental health system was established, and strong legal limits were set on the capacity of the psychiatric system to generate involuntary commitments. The problem remains, however, that patients at this point can refuse treatment, and be as homeless and delusional or addicted as they want to be, so long as they are not a danger to self or to others. The society of citizens and taxpayers is still responsible for their hospital bills and social services, but they cannot be compelled into treatment.

What often happens is that these patients/clients keep going in and out of the hospital at huge expense to the system, and the problem is only addressed when these difficult and often homeless patients/citizens threaten businesses or the tourism industry. When this happens, the system sends social agents of control, known as "case managers," to walk the streets trying to engage clients who don't want to engage and are treatment-resistant. Such case managers are viewed by the system as social welfare agents rather than as health or clinical providers. The blame and responsibility for the failure to engage is placed on the clinicians rather than on the individuals who are refusing to enter treatment of any kind (not just medication).

A fourth and final example is the relation between the sexes. Symbolic of a postmodern state of affairs is a new character that has emerged in the sex industry: the dungeon "Mistress" or "Dominatrix." Men pay for a dominant woman dressed in leather to whip them into submission. In addition, the fantasy of a woman with phallus is a recurrent and emerging theme (anecdotal, some would say) in the psychoanalysis of young men in their thirties. This would be another example of how the relation of domination between the sexes has simply been reversed while the relation to the phallus remains a constant for both sexes, despite feminism and postmodernism.

The solution to this dilemma, of course, is not to go back to the traditional patriarchal order but rather to examine the unconscious desires of both sexes that manifest in new forms of domination even when the old social forms are no longer operative. This critique still leaves standing and operative the critique of masculine domination or supremacy, with the caveat that either males or females can participate in and perpetrate such version of masculinity. Conversely, the postmodern version of Lacanian psychoanalysis that I am articulating can also be used in a positive direction. So long as the paternal/parental metaphor and sexual difference is preserved, both males and females can occupy the place of masculinity or femininity, of the mother's desire or the paternal No/Name of the Father. A gay or lesbian family could in fact function as a family, as they often do, so long as these differences and functions are preserved/contained within the family. In such cases the normal exception confirms the norm or the rule.

Foucault and Lacan both wrote about how the law or the repression of sexuality produces desire more than represses it. What appears to be a repression is what generates desire or the anti-repressive impulse. Conversely, what appears to be a fight of desire against repression turns out to be a new way of repressing.

From this perspective, the relationship to authority and the law can be regarded as regulated by a principle of contradiction. The problem with patriarchal authoritarianism is that it is plagued by the same problem it criticizes in the other. For example, the Nazis believed in the historical, intellectual, and racial superiority of the German nation while murdering Jews for believing in their own racial and spiritual "chosenness." Authoritarianism is self-contradictory without recognizing the contradiction.

On the other hand, the problem with rebellion against authority is that it is plagued by the same problems that the rebellion criticizes in the authority. For example, the Sandinista functionaries or government officials that replaced the Somoza government in Nicaragua, under the Sandinista revolution began using government funds to give themselves the same privileges that the previous government had and that the Sandinistas had ardently condemned and fought against. This of course is not to deny or apologize for the abuses of the Somoza government, or for the fact that the United States supported violence (the *contras*) against the Sandinistas, but simply to point out that rebellion is also plagued by self-contradiction and identification with the aggressor. Rebellions often don't consider envy as an unconscious wish or motivation. Instead they believe that criticism is guided by purely rational, altruistic, and objective considerations.

Freud believed that Marxism had an incorrect understanding of human nature. For Communism, egoism, narcissism, or individualism represented a capitalist corruption of human nature. Left to its own devices, human nature in a communist society would be revealed as altruistically inclined and spontaneously socialistic. Freud considered that altruism fails to recognize the egoism lurking within altruism. Conversely, however, Freud also did not recognize the other-centered nature of narcissism. With Lacan's theory of the mirror stage, narcissism can be defined on the basis of identification with the Other or with the Other's desire. Narcissism is Other-centered, and altruism is narcissistic. The One is the Other, and the Other is the One.

Finally, emancipation or liberation is not only a modern value. I submit that with modernity only the purpose/object of emancipation changes from the id to the super-ego. Traditional culture used the super-ego to achieve emancipation from passion and from nature (id), whereas modernity seeks emancipation from the same super-ego that was the agent of emancipation for traditional culture.

Ego identity politics

In a similar way to how the unconscious super-ego was a target of psychoanalytic therapeutic interventions, modern values challenged the traditional rigid distinctions and prejudices surrounding class, gender, sexual orientation, race, religious, and ethnic identities. However, in challenging traditional identities and values, advanced modernity may have inadvertently established some fresh new prejudices of its own. These have become an integral part of what is now being called identity politics. Oppressed groups wear their minority status as a badge of honor, a title, and instead of targeting domination itself, or the nature of the super-ego (as it is done in psychoanalysis), they sometimes become the new forms and faces of the super-ego and domination, or a caricature version of the oppressor. Within psychoanalysis this is known as identification with the oppressor or the enemy. For example, instead of forbidding sexual deviation from the norm, sexual pleasure, or rebellion, the super-ego now demands pleasure and rebellion and censors the open exploration and discussion of the nature of perversions.

This phenomenon has also been recognized in the field of postcolonial studies.

> The danger for anti-colonial resistance comes when the binary opposition is simply reversed, so that "black", for instance, or the "the colonized" become the dominant terms.
>
> (Ashcroft, Griffiths and Tiffin, 2000: 26)

Ashcroft points out that Homi Bhabha, the noted postcolonial theorist, redeployed the psychoanalytic concept of ambivalence to describe the love–hate relationship between colonizers and colonized, oppressor and oppressed. Oppositions to authority often contain contradictory processes of identification. Although oppressed groups can identify the source of their social oppression, to a significant extent they may still remain unconsciously identified with the oppressor/ aggressor in their fight against oppression.

Within North American ego psychology, the standard of normality was the degree of adjustment or assimilation to normative society (ego identity). In the example of North American culture, this translated into assimilation to the melting pot. However, the content of the pot was defined primarily by white Anglo-American culture. African-Americans, Asian-Americans, or Latino-Americans, by virtue of the color of their skin, their facial features, or their status of not being native English speakers, represent a negation of the particular national and linguistic ego identity or unary trait of white Anglo-Americans. Minorities represent the identity of not-being white and Anglo-American. In this sense, ego identity and identity politics are two sides of the same coin. As explained in chapter 1, the unary trait is a narcissistic form of ego identity (ego-ideal) through which a particular group takes pride in belonging to a particular class or group defined by the trait.

Minorities were faced with the choice of either identifying with the majority despite the ambivalence (being secretly rejected and secretly rejecting themselves), or rejecting the majority identity or ego-ideal. In response to this dilemma, in the United States, for example, minorities appropriated their differential status by making it explicit that they were hyphenated Americans, yet Americans nonetheless. In other words, the hyphenated compound or bicultural identity represents a negation of the appearance of a melting pot, or of an "All-American" ego identity. At the same time it redefines American as a multifaceted or continental identity.

For white Anglo-Americans, minorities represent a formal (dual or binary) rather than a dialectical negation. In addition, minorities may make this negation explicit by rejecting the dominant signifiers of white Anglo-American identity. This state of affairs amounts to an impasse: one formal negation reflects or mirrors another formal negation. For example, Arthur Schlesinger (1998) wrote his bestselling book *The Disuniting of America*, where he argued that identity-based multiculturalism threatened the integrity of the (white Anglo-American) nation. However, Schlesinger only recognizes the negation of the dominant white Anglo-American melting-pot ideal. His conservative argument fails to recognize the formal and non-dialectical negation of minority identity by the majority culture.

Both sides suffer from being unable to turn the psyche towards non-identification. **Non** is a dialectical prefix that can be differentiated from **not** as an adverb that represents a formal rather than a dialectical negation. Non-identification represents the potential "unariness" of the One within multiplicity, as distinct from the imaginary unity of the oneness of a national identity and as distinct from a multiplicity without the function of the zero in each of its parts or numerical components. The first is a unary trace, the second a unary trait. Multiculturalism represents a dispersion or migration without any glue or Third to hold it together.

Non-identification represents a negative dialectic and not a synthesis between identity and the negation of identity. Biculturalism precisely represents such a synthesis: I am both Latino and American. But Latino and American still stand as categories or unary traits opposed to one another, or to other possible cultural configurations. Non-identification differs from both identity and the formal nega-tion of a particular identity. By being empty of designation, non-identification over-includes identity and the negation of identity.

Negating and affirming national and ethnic identity are equally acceptable. Because I don't have to feel special to be Latino, then I can truly be Latino. Because I don't have to feel special or number One to be American, or North American, then I can truly embody the quality of being American. Non-identification is a unary trace rather than the unary trait of being special for this or that reason. The unary trace builds continuity and coherence in identity without constructing ego-based identities. The concept of the unary trace was developed in chapter 1 on identification.

The super-ego in Freud is not only a reflection of the oppressor in the form of an internalized form of oppression. The super-ego is fueled by unconscious wishes and their corresponding affects. For example, while internalizing the will of the parents, the super-ego takes up the anger towards the parents and turns it against the id-aspects of the self. Just like the parent says bad boy/girl to the child, the child says the same thing to himself/herself.

The anger of the child is and is not a reflection (fear) of the parent. In conditions of normal repression/discipline, the anger of the child is not a reflection of the parent. The individual cannot place the entire blame for the super-ego, or for unconscious repression, on the parent or on society. But once the identification with the parent is consolidated (in the ego-ideal) and the child takes pride in a shared unary trait, the ambivalence is transferred from the super-ego to the id, and from the parents to the social Other (represented by minority groups). The social Other becomes the target of the anger that the child had towards the parents.

But this alleged solution is not possible when there is persistent ambivalence and an inordinate amount of anger on the part of the parent. In this second example, the anger of the parent grows exponentially in the mind of the child. In the case of angry and cruel discipline on the part of the parent, the anger of the child will be redoubled as an effect of the anger of the parent. This is turn can lead to failure or distortion in the formation of the super-ego. Instead of the super-ego yoking the anger and turning it against itself, the anger will be turned against the content of the super-ego itself. The id will become the standard of the super-ego instead of the ego-ideal being the standard of the drives.

This set of conditions with regards to the formation of the super-ego can be directly affected by the conflicts between the parents and the sexes. If the parents' arguing has reached a certain threshold where they undermine each other's authority, this will create a situation where the parental/paternal metaphor will become discredited. The discrediting of the parental metaphor compromises and distorts the development of the ego-ideal in the children.

In this way postmodern children face a similar predicament to the formation of the super-ego in minority groups when the ego-ideal represents standards of the dominant group rejected by minority groups. Often minority youth come to reject both the standards of the white majority and the standards of their traditional ethnic culture. What fills the gap is the reversal of values by which the id frames the super-ego rather than the other way around. An example of this is the code of conduct often associated with gangs, whether African-American, Asian-American, Latino-American, the Hells Angels, white supremacists, etc.

These examples can be used to understand liberal and conservative approaches to the relationship between majority and minority cultures. It is as if conservatives regard the white majority culture as a benevolent super-ego and don't understand why minorities reject such a super-ego, to the detriment of the society. Minorities, and liberals in turn, view the majority super-ego as primarily malevolent and regard the anger and rebellion of minority groups as legitimate and justified. Liberal politicians often don't have a category by which to think of aggressive-ness or narcissism as not simply a mere reflection of the social environment.

Psychoanalysis, as a theory, combines conservative and liberal strands. There is a conservative strand contained within psychoanalysis where it places respon-sibility on the individual rather than on society. On the other hand, psychoanalysis also has a radical bent because it seeks to undo the social repression of desire and to help the individual find his/her own desire independently from the desire of the Other. However, the Freud of the second topography, and of ego psychology, also partook of the illusions of bourgeois individualism. In this respect Lacanian psychoanalysis has succeeded in establishing a new foundation (that is actually no foundation: Ø) for psychoanalysis on the basis of the unconscious and the theory of the subject. Lacanian theory only uses the ego concept to explain an inevitable imaginary or narcissistic dimension of subjectivity.

I realize that identity politics is an aspect of postmodern culture but not neces-sarily of postmodern theory. Much postmodern theory rejects identity politics. However, I am also linking identity politics to postmodern theory where the latter advocates for local or micro-political fights against oppression instead of the totalitarian tendencies of the Marxism associated with modernity.

In this sense, postmodernism can be seen as a logical corollary of modernity or a form of ultra-modernism rather than as an anti-modern form of ideology. Modernity produced a symptom of excess to the extent that it failed to recognize key authentic properties of traditional culture, and how certain oppressions/alienations of traditional culture were unconsciously transmitted to modern consciousness via oppositional type of identifications.

The ego wants to be the master of his/her own house and, therefore, retains an aspect of identification with and idealization of the master or the master's discourse. Identity politics becomes a form of ego identity if it is used to cancel the self-cancellation necessary for a symbolic identity. If identity politics fails to theorize a necessary negative moment in relationship to culture, because all negativity is reduced to oppression, then the view of ethnic, racial, or gender identity in relationship to the dominant culture turns out to be purely imaginary or idealized. Deleuze declared that he detested the work of the negative associated with Hegelian philosophy. Idealized minority ego identity (becoming minority) is used as a way of closing or suturing the positive lack or emptiness within the subject.

Although Habermas claims to be the living heir of the Frankfurt school, the latter (Marcuse, Adorno, etc.) also contained a deep critique of modernity. Critical theory understood modernity as containing masked forms of oppression and domination under the veils of instrumental reason and scientific objectivity. Modernity contains both a belief in science but also a critique of instrumental reason or of the logic of empiricism within the social sciences. Modernity, in fact, contains different forms of reason, and dialectical reason can and has been used for a critique of modernity and scientific objectivity.

This theme is obviously continued in postmodernism, although the status of dialectical reason is somewhat ambivalent and unclear within postmodern thought. Postmodern or poststructuralist thinkers criticize totalizing/synthesizing dialectical thought as well as binary thinking or logic. However, binary thinking is more characteristic of formal logic than dialectical logic, and the pluralism that postmodern thought champions often contains larger assemblages and combinations of many binary pairs. In addition, postmodern culture, in contrast to postmodern theory, still contains many examples of binary logic as seen in the genetic code and in digital computer logic. The computer-based information age that is often seen as a quintessential postmodern social formation is still organized on the basis of binary digital computer logic.

Rather than rejecting formal or dialectical logic, it may be more important to recognize not a hierarchy between them, but their functioning within a multimodal or multidimensional ensemble or assemblage. For an account of postmodern phenomena, postmodern or poststructuralist theory may need to go back a decade and redeploy the post-Hegelian negative dialectic of critical theorist Theodor Adorno. Adorno (1966) proposed a negative dialectic whereby every synthesis or synthetic judgment can be negated: neither this nor that nor a synthesis of both this and that. In Lacanian terms, the All requires the logic of the not-All, or the Symbolic always points to the void of the Real at the same time that the Real is circumscribed by the Symbolic.

I mentioned above that outside French theory, Best and Kellner have identified conservative strands within postmodern theory that decry the developments within postmodern culture. This is one example of how postmodern theory can also be used to critique postmodern culture and other forms of postmodernism. Lacanian psychoanalysis can be viewed as a postmodern form of Freudian psychoanalysis that can be used to critique postmodern culture and poststructuralism. As already stated above, Lacanian thought, as well as psychoanalysis in general, has both traditional and radical or emancipatory strands.

Postmodern culture is also associated with negative qualities: fragmentation, the breakdown of the (bourgeois) nuclear family and the social-familial order, and the unleashing of imaginary drives and impulses. "The postmodern is associated with the pagan, with the absence of rules, criteria, and principles, and with the need for experimentation" (Best and Kellner, 1991, p. 164). Postmodern culture becomes intrinsically associated with the borderline and narcissistic character disorders and an inability to postpone gratification and tolerate frustration. Lasch (1979) had already indirectly recognized the negative characteristic of the post-modern in his book *The Culture of Narcissism*. However, Lasch, or the object-relations approach to the borderline condition, did not associate the borderline condition with a decline in the paternal function. If anything, it was the mother and the lack of secure attachment or good-enough mothering that was responsible for the condition.

The rejection and disavowal of the necessary function of the father, due to a misapprehension and confusion between the imaginary and symbolic fathers, led to a problem with recognizing lack, limits, and boundaries widely spread across postmodern culture and the baby-boom generation. Just as early modernity and the Protestant ethic suffered from neurotic forms of inhibition and avowals of the law of the imaginary father, and rejections and fears of the feminine, and of homo-sexuality, the postmodern condition suffers from the disavowal of the symbolic father and avowals of the desires of the imaginary mother.

Emancipation is a central theme running through traditional, modern, and post-modern culture. People often identify emancipatory interests with critical reason and modernity itself. The modern state is organized around the protection of civil rights, and the rights of a minority over the tyranny of the majority. Marxism sought to liberate the working classes from the oppression of the ruling classes, and women proclaimed their liberation from subordination under a patriarchal social order. This theme has only been continued and generalized to include the rights of children and other protected social (patient's rights, disabilities, etc.) and sexual minority groups.

Emancipation is also a classical and traditional theme. Traditional religious culture observes in the nihilism and anomie of postmodern culture the conse-quences of modernity's rejection and critique of traditional morality. Modernity critiqued the super-ego and inverted the relationship between desire and morality. Instead of desire being the cause of suffering, the super-ego became part of the problem rather than the solution to the problem of suffering and desire. Traditional culture had invented a super-ego to control the problems caused by desire and the drives within the individual and society. Modernity and Freud diagnose religion and traditional morality and repression as the cause of much neurotic psychopa-thology. Modernity erects the rational ego as an ego-ideal that reconciles the conflict between the super-ego and the id. In opposing the id, the super-ego had acquired the passion of the id and turned it against the id.

However, the ego or the ego-ideal is a differentiation within the super-ego, and the antithesis always preserves characteristics of what it replaces. The ego identifies with the oppressive super-ego, and social empirical science, for example, continues some of the dogmas and rigidities of traditional religious culture. Therefore, the Western enlightenment also contains strands that turn reason against itself. Critical reason critiqued scientific thought (within the social sciences) and preserved the insights of spiritual thought. The work of Erich Fromm (1950, 1960) would be an example of the latter coming from a member of the Frankfurt school that although incorporating Marxist and Freudian modern ideals also absorbed and championed traditional spiritual ideals. I believe that Fromm represents an aspect of modernity that is continued into the spiritual strands of postmodernism. From this perspective the intent of the Enlightenment was not only to eliminate religion and replace it with science, but also to produce a religion or spirituality compatible with science.

There are conservative strands of postmodernism that preserve aspects of traditional culture. This is also seen in the work of Lyotard, since in his work science becomes one more form of discourse alongside other traditional discourses. In addition, the work of Baudrillard also privileges the significance of traditional rituals that temporarily suspend the utilitarian imperatives of instrumental reason.

In contrast to this, poststructuralist French thought learned from the mistakes of the French and Marxist revolutions and continued the atheistic strands of modernity to their logical consequences. Poststructuralist thought is a form of ultra-modernism that includes and even champions the chaotic impulses of mental and social disorders. The French avant-garde celebrated new developments beyond enlightened modernity, as seen in the examples of the Marquis de Sade and Artaud who were considered to be precursors of postmodern thought. Deleuze (1967) wrote "Coldness and Cruelty," and in *Anti-Oedipus*, Deleuze and Guattari (1972) used Artaud's example to develop their notion of schizo-subjects and schizo-analysis. For Deleuze it is a masochist who is rendered free for a new life in which the father and the signifier play no role. The masochist is bent on empowering the Venus in furs or the phallic mother.

Deleuze and Guattari (1972) followed Reich in appropriating the positive revolutionary aspects of desire and of psychopathology in the same way that Foucault defined psychiatry as a form of social control and a modern form of domination. For these authors excess is plenitude rather than suffering or *jouissance*, as Lacan (1968, 1969–70) defined it. Desire is a cybernetic machine. However, Deleuze and Guattari miss the links between consumer capitalism and the illusions of the computer age with all its addictions to computer games and extreme forms of online pornography. They claim that psychoanalysis colonizes the id and desire by defining desire as lack within a conservative social-symbolic order. However, far from thinking of Oedipus as an objective structure, Lacan came to understand Oedipus as a mythic defense and as a construction erected against the void and what he came to call the lack in the Other.

Capitalism is driven by the master's discourse, not by the discourse of the analyst or psychoanalysis. The symbolic function of castration undermines the master's discourse, because symbolization requires the scansion of the imaginary phallus as a master signifier. Within psychoanalysis, the phallus is a lack, not a victorious emblem or flag of masculine supremacy. Psychoanalysis as an ethics of desire is a basis for a critique of conformity, hypocrisy, and traditional morality while at the same time understanding and theorizing the fundamental ethical structures that organize both society and desire: the prohibition of incest and the differences between the sexes.

Lacanian psychoanalysis is also postmodern in that it seeks to organize itself within non-hierarchical organizations that emphasize self-organization and responsibility culminating in the self-authorization of the analyst within the context of a psychoanalytic community.

Lacan differentiated between malevolent and benevolent forms of depersonalization and ego loss. The necessary sense of the loss of the ego is a development beyond modern Freudian psychoanalysis. However, although the ego and the super-ego are deconstructed at the end of analysis, the symbolic subject and the subject of the Real are not eliminated and remain as non-substantial and non-reified categories. Not being substantial entities, the latter cannot function as supports for individualism or for forms of narcissistic or nihilistic self-destruction. Analytic discourse is ordered while being non-hierarchical. Lacanian theory provides tools to be able to understand and differentiate the creative versus the destructive aspects of the death drive.

Within the logic of what Lacan called *sexuation*, sexual difference supports the loss and renunciation of the imaginary phallus that needs to take place in order for humans to enter the social symbolic order as sexed beings. The sexes are equal because they are different or because they have different ways of paying their dues to the culture. The postmodern egalitarian discourse about the sexes, rather than promoting diversity, erases the differences between the sexes and subsumes both sexes under a masculine, individualistic, and competitive ethos.

Under the ideal of everyone being the same, or the rejection/disavowal of the norm that distributes differences, the difference that is disavowed does not disappear but merely goes underground as a secret form of enjoyment. There are no fathers, and no fathers and sons, but the daddy–son, top–bottom relationship reappears, for example, in sadomasochistic forms of enjoyment. Forms of imaginary masculinity are rejected but then reappear in the discourse and imaginary of certain forms of lesbianism. It becomes clear that what is being rejected is not masculinity per se but only masculinity in males. Masculinity, domination, and the imaginary phallus are alive and well between women and between masculine females and feminine men. Stereotypically feminine behavior is rejected in females only to be enacted by feminine men that are more feminine than females. The point is not to criticize masculine females or feminine males but rather to recognize the ubiquity of sexual difference.

Without a Freudian–Lacanian American understanding of sexuality, Anglo-American gender theory and culture either reduce sexuality to being an imaginary sociological effect of social-power relations, or sexuality becomes a purely biological and genetic phenomenon. Psychoanalysis is reduced to being a tool to produce normative heterosexuality, and sexual diversity and perversion become sites of social dissidence and involution. Alternatively, the entire field is turned over to brain research to empirically and conclusively prove that the difference between the sexes, and sexual orientation, have nothing to do with the father and are genetically determined. Simply to state that sexual orientation could have something to do with Oedipal structure is enough to trigger a political investigation/censorship by the powers that be. This is another example of how identity politics as a form ideology can coexist and be complicit with university discourse and even the most blatant forms of anti-theoretical empiricism.

Postmodern theory and relational psychoanalysis

Relational postmodern thought sometimes has a way of mistaking the difference between Lacanian and Freudian ideas. The distinction between fantasy and reality offers a clear example of this.

> To the extent that Lacan's ideas are a direct extension of Freud's, it can be argued that his work is not yet fully representative of the postmodern turn. The emphasis on distinguishing between fantasy and reality in the imaginary, in order to make objective interpretations of the unconscious is still characteristic of Enlightenment reasoning about reality and objectivity.
>
> (Frie and Orange, 2009, p. 12)

This should come as no surprise, given the tendency of the different trends within psychoanalysis to completely ignore each other's literature. As stated in chapter 2, Lacan (1962–3) argued that truth has the structure of fiction, and in the seminar on anxiety (1962–3) he distinguished between objectivity and *objectality*. *Objectality* points to the fact that reality is always constructed via the Imaginary and the imagination.

Lacanian ideas about language and logic provide a non-dual alternative beyond objectivity and subjectivity, self and other. Classically or within modernity, objectivity was construed as rational and non-subjective, whereas subjectivity was construed as having to do with fantasy, prejudice, and emotional experience. But already after Kant there is no object without the a priori categories of reason, and reason is a function of the social subject given that reason proper does not exist in nature by itself without a subject. In addition, there is no subject that is not first an object of the social Other, and a subject of the Unconscious. Therefore subject and object co-arise or mutually interpenetrate one another.

The relational, intersubjective, and narrative ideas running through postmodern thought in the English-speaking world seem to misconstrue what Lyotard had to say about narrative truths. Discourse and narration or enunciation is not a world co-created or co-constructed by the conscious egos of those having a conversation. Lyotard does not "reject the universals of ancient myths and the possibility of meaning" (Teicholz, 2009: 70). For the most part myths represent a form of ancestral knowledge rather than a product of modernity and do not constitute grand and totalizing narratives. Lyotard's critique was aimed at metaphysical philosophy but not at the traditional mythical mentality. Myths are aphoristic knowledge fragments that, like the unconscious, represent a bridge between the Symbolic and the Real, the visible and the invisible.

Lacan himself is not a great modern hero devoid of lack or limitation. Lacan paid with his person and suffered subjective destitution and even humiliation more than once. The point is not the man but the power of the historical text, the practice, and the ideas.

The narrative approach, as represented in the field of psychology or psycho-analysis, typically defines a narrative without ancient and classical references, or any historical perspective. As such, it represents a renewed version of a marriage between idealism and empiricism. Within this form of epistemology the world is being created in the here and now by the conscious intentions of the speakers as they define them. The unconscious historical dimension of a lineage or of the arrow of time is lost to the narrative perspective.

From this perspective, it is possible to argue that the narrative approach, thus defined, represents an imaginary version of language and a new form of social Cartesianism: "We are the authors of our own thoughts." The relational school goes from the one-person psychology of "I think therefore I am," to the two-person psychology of "We think therefore we are." What is missing here is the dimension of the Lacanian third of the Symbolic. A one- or two-person psychology would be the equivalent of me saying that all of the ideas presented in this book were entirely fabricated by me (which is also true but on an entirely different logical level). This is an aspect of individualism and of the age of narcissism manifested within theoretical discourse itself. The ego rejects all the theoretical work of those who came before and only accepts the theory that is co-constructed by current individuals in the here and now.

The intersubjective or relational forms of psychoanalysis interpret the anti-metaphysical bent of postmodern philosophy as a rejection of theory altogether. This is also a meeting point between phenomenology, existentialism, and post-modern thought (Thompson, 2004). Metaphysics is rejected for its association with absolute theories or abstract reason. Within metaphysical philosophy the unknown or unknowable is reduced to abstract ideas existing in a theoretical world behind appearances and divorced from direct experience. In contrast to this, Lacan's theory recognizes the materiality of the signifier (language is a concrete idea that determines perception and the characteristics of appearances or images), and at the same time Lacan theorizes a dimension of <u>experience</u> beyond language and ordinary logic (the Real).

Although it is important to conceive a dimension of experience beyond theory, the problem with the anti-theoretical bent of phenomenology or relational psycho-analysis is that by rejecting robust theories, such as that of Freud, one may end up replacing strong theories with theories of lesser range and depth. When the method replaces the theory, instead of replacing theory with no-theory, an elaborate theory is exchanged for a less elaborate and simplistic construct, but a theory nonetheless.

The theory itself, just like language, is empty and does not leave any traces, for only people do. Once words are written or spoken they vanish into thin air until someone reads them or utters them once again. Via the imaginary ego (ideal ego and ego-ideal) people attach their non-self to words and concepts and become entangled and hindered by them. What is needed, therefore, is not a minimally theoretical psychoanalysis, as empiricism advocates, but a practice of non-knowing or unknown-knowing that, instead of clinging to concepts, remains open to the signifiers, affects, and the overall experience of the analysand.

At the same time, concepts and understanding need to be used, not for analysts to be loved or admired by their analysands but to listen to their desire and cut and tear into the walls and defenses that are perpetuating their suffering. It is the type of defense that distinguishes the different forms of psychopathology and clinical suffering. It is very important for the analysand that the analyst understands this very clearly. The theory itself needs to be as rigorous, specific, and widely applicable as possible, but without ever becoming a rigid closed system or a top-heavy structure that can be easily tipped over.

Death of the ego and subjective destitution

Another key concern within the modern–postmodern debate is the alleged death of the subject proclaimed by postmodernism and the question of how to reconcile this with a sense of agency, independence, continuity, and coherence within self-experience. This is another aspect within which Lacanian ideas may be useful.

First of all, only the ego died (not the subject), because it was an imaginary construction to begin with. But without the ego what gives unity and stability to the experience of the subject? Roland Barthes (1984) articulated ideas that are similar to Lacan's, despite not being a psychoanalyst. The subject of the sentence holds together both language and subject alike. The subject is a metaphor (not an entity) that is constantly changing while remaining stable at the same time. However, for Lacan, the signifier/subject, as a signifier of desire, helps regulate *jouissance* and is itself regulated by transformations within *jouissance*. It is the quality or modality of affective experience and *jouissance* that helps bind the subject together. The subject of *jouissance* is the Lacanian subject of the Real, which is empty of definitions within language. As soon as one tries to define the agency of a Real subject within language, an empirical ego becomes reified or falsely constructed. Freud (1919) points to this when he refers to "the greater unity which we call his ego. . .":

> In actual fact, indeed, the neurotic patient presents us with a torn mind divided by resistances. As we analyze it and remove the resistances, it grows together; the greater unity which we call his ego fits into itself all the instinctual impulses which before had been split off and held apart from it.
>
> (p. 161)

Strictly speaking, the ego is simply a name within language that points to some-thing (the greater unity) beyond language. What Lacan calls the One in the Real beyond language incorporates "into itself all the drives which before had been split off and held apart from it" (Freud 1919, p. 161).

Between the Real and the Symbolic, the subject is a *unary* trace that does not leave any traces and therefore is not susceptible to reification. The unary trace is simply an *instance*, not in the sense of agency, but in the sense of a vanishing point instant. As I mentioned in the first chapter, on identification, there are two important unary traces for the subject: the specular image of the body, and the name or names of the subject. Both of these unary traces locate the subject within imaginary and cultural–linguistic–symbolic coordinates and provide continuity across time and space. Now someone could ask: "What about the intimacy of personal experience and the uniqueness of each individual subject? I argued that according to Lacan, uniqueness and autonomy is an illusory experience within the Imaginary. Subjects appropriate for themselves traits that arise elsewhere within the Other while thinking that the experience is original to them.

The mature or adverted subject is the subject that can recognize the influence of the desire of the Other as well as his or her own unconscious desire for recognition and come to an informed choice as to what of the Other he or she will keep for himself/herself. The subject comes to speak the words of the Other in his or her own voice and name (which also came from the Other). This way Lacanian theory is consistent with Heidegger's concepts of appropriation and authenticity, and with the Freudian and modern interest in emancipation from the traditional enslavement to the super-ego and the realm of hypocritical morality and imaginary social appearances (Thompson, 2004).

Subjective authenticity in Heidegger implies facing up to psychic reality rather than repressing it under the weight of social normative expectations. In order to stand up for what he believed in, Freud was willing to undergo a significant amount of rejection and social criticism. At the same time Lacan's thought differs from a notion of authenticity if the latter is based on a naïve and dualistic distinc-tion between genuine and deceptive experience/expression. For Lacan truth has the structure of fiction, and the only way not to deceive is to acknowledge a struc-tural deception built into language (I am lying).

Lacan taught that the core of the subject is *extimate* to the ego, although inti-mate to the subject qua nothing (of the Real). The core of being cannot be the Other because the Other cannot complete the subject or give subjects their own being. On the other hand, the core of being is not a strong personal ego either, because the ego is an unconscious formation rather than the essence of a human being. I argue that the being of the subject has to be found in non-being and beyond being and not being.

In non-being or beyond being and not being, the ego and the object are both taken away and preserved, at different times, in different ways. When the ego is taken away, what remains of the object is the object not as *sache* (object in German) but as both a signifier and *das Ding* (the no-thing). When the object is taken away, what remains of the subject is not the self-consciousness of the ego, but the subject as the positive signifying realization (a markless mark) of all things being without inherent nature. This is the Hegelian absolute subject or the substance (matter and form) conceived as subject. When the substance is conceived as subject, then the substance is empty and the essence is emptiness (the moon is the subject/mind, and mind includes the luminosity of being). The object or transcendent reality, and the transcendental concepts or ideas, are both empty because an absolutely empty subject is presupposing them.

The negation proceeding from and equally canceling the Other and the subject has to be first accepted and then denied. The individual subject is most himself/herself not in the social Imaginary, nor in the interior landscape of desire, nor in the mask or the false self that the individual wears in public. The subject may not even be most himself/herself when operating within the symbolic rules (of grammar, kinship, or logic) that determine the meaning of language and communication. No, the individual is most himself/herself, his/her true self, in the wondrous emptiness of Being rather than in the personal ego, the Other or the totality. The individual is most himself/herself when and where he/she is unrepresentable as a form of *jouissance* (pain/pleasure). The subject can either vanish (the object of the drive takes the place of the ego) under a perverse form of *jouissance* (the delusive *jouissance* of the Other) or realize itself as an Other *jouissance* (This) beyond representation.

Common social objectives and purposes are means for the ego to attain an imaginary unity by using objects of social utility to close the gap of being within the subject. However, the individual acquires his or her inherent rights as a human being not through purposes, objects, or aims, but by realizing the being and vacuity of the subject as an end in itself. When the ego disappears under the signifier, the subject of the Real reappears or is produced as an empty place or an Other *jouissance* within discourse or speech that facilitates and sustains the flow and structure of signification.

Structuralism and poststructuralism in Lacanian psychoanalysis

Another important question tied to the difference between postmodernism and structuralism is whether Lacan was a structuralist when it came to questions of meaning and signification. It is well known by now that Freud's thought combined both positivistic and hermeneutic strands. In Freud the theory or text is supposed to be describing an objective reality/truth with regards to psychical structure that remains outside and independent from the text. Within hermeneutics and postmodern thought, however, the object as such can only be defined within the text itself. The object does not have existence outside the text. To exist within the Symbolic is to already be outside and external to the Real.

According to Lacanian theory, reality is defined along Imaginary and Symbolic dimensions. However, Lacan not only differs from Freud, but also differs from hermeneutics for the same reason that he differs from the slogan attributed to Derrida (1976): "there is nothing outside the text." The register/dimension of the Real and of *jouissance* is in fact outside of the text, although it is also defined in reference to a text. The beyond a text or the Symbolic is also defined in interaction or relationship to a symbolic form, although it is not reducible to the symbolic form.

In this regard Lacan (1974) is postmodern because he retains a dimension of intensity within *jouissance* that remains distinct from the signifier. In addition, although signification is always sliding under the metonymy of the signifier, and the object of desire is forever changing and infinite to one degree or another, Lacan emphasizes that nevertheless the object always remains the same. It is always a question of either the phallus or the *objet a* as cause of desire. Although Lacan has been accused of phallocentrism and logocentrism, I am arguing that these two charges do not really apply. The phallus turns out not to be a master signifier since it simply points to a lack that ultimately does not have any inherent meaning or is actually senseless. In fact his notions of *lituraterre*, of the *objet a*, and of the senseless signifier are very close to Derrida's notions of *differance*. When people criticize Lacan, they often refer to the early Lacan rather than to a corpus that continued evolving throughout the author's life.

The ability to differ, and to provide new interpretations, or new combinations between the signifier and the signified, which constitute the hallmark of a creative, inventive, and independent mind, precisely refers to this empty Utopian no-place within a subject. A subject allows himself/herself to be cancelled by the Other of language and knowledge, among other things, only to use this self-cancellation as the platform from which to permutate and transform the larger symbolic structure.

The symbolic inheritance of humanity, which was laid down by the innumerable efforts of those who came before, is under perpetual reconstruction and combination. The choice of words and actions, that is always taking place within a subject of discourse, is made within a context that determines the range of possible outcomes. Choice is a forced choice between larger assemblages of this or that, now or later, here or there. Whichever side is chosen, the other side is never completely eliminated. What we gain on one side, we lose on the other.

The influence of Heidegger on North American relational psychoanalysis relies on Heidegger's (1927) notion of Being and ignores to what extent Lacan had already incorporated Heidegger's thought into psychoanalysis. For Lacan (1972) the *objet a* provides a semblance of Being and Being remains Real in the sense that it lies beyond representation. Relational and poststructuralists seem to dislike and reject the concept of representation because it seems to leave out the Being of the subject or the Becoming of desire. But by rejecting the concept of representation, they inadvertently create a dichotomy between Being and language, the pre-verbal and the verbal, mind and body, the Symbolic and the Real. What is needed in the analytic field is a multidimensional perspective that will distinguish dimensions while bringing them into relationship with one another.

At times this multidimensional perspective can also be found within intersubjective theory. Storolow (2009), for example, inadvertently brings Heidegger and Lacan close to one another. He follows Heidegger in saying that representation is not opposed to Being because it is "constitutive for our being with one another" (2009: 149). Metaphor is the substitution of the being of one subject for the being of another. As discussed in the next section, the relationship between S_1–S_2 represents both a linguistic/mathematical relation and the symbolic relationship between two human beings.

A symbolic structure is operative within our experience, although we may not have any conscious notion of such a structure when we are speaking or addressing one another. The structure is unconscious in a descriptive sense. However, a theory is required to apprehend its determinations and conditions within our experience. A primordial structure of being does not pre-exist language, the existence of subjects or subjectivity. There is no being separate from speaking beings. In the Borromean knot there are relationships between independent dimensions that circumscribe one another. The existence of speaking beings points to a dimension of being beyond language (the Real or the mysterious dimension of Being according to Heidegger) and the dimension of being beyond language is only known through the experience of specific speaking beings. Without the notion of the signifier or of a subject, Being could not be particular or relative to a specific situation. There would be bodies without differences, and individuals without names or distinctions.

Affects in psychoanalysis

Since according to Lacan human beings are speaking beings, following Lacan it is possible to say that the relationship between signifiers is also a relationship between subjects, and the relationship between subjects is also between speaking beings.

Although the signifier is what represents a subject for another signifier, is there something of being and of the subject that is outside the dimension of the signifier? When speaking of the transference, Lacan speaks of the metaphor of love with respect to the reciprocal substitution and interchangeability between the positions of lover and beloved. Clearly lover and beloved are two signifiers that are in a relationship of reciprocal implication. So if you say lover, then lover is a signifier that represents a subject for another signifier, that is to say, the beloved. Yet love is an affect and a passion central to the phenomenon known as transference. Transference involves an affect and every affect could involve transference or, in other words, a signification/substitution.

But what aspect of an affect is not simply reducible to a word or a signifier? Again back to the same question, what of the subject or of being is lacking/languishing within the signifier?

In the metaphor of love, metaphor is the substitution of the being of one subject (the lover) for the being of another (the beloved). If instead of saying "You are a beautiful flower," a subject says "You are like a flower to me," not only is there a singular metaphor of love implied, but a flower is representing the beloved, and "You" is representing the being of the subject as a lover. Or if instead the subject says "You represent everything that I hate," not only does the other represent the hate of the subject, but the other may also represent a norm that regulates the process of substitution and representation (the big Other cannot give you your being).

Lacan links love not only to the signifier but also to unknown-knowing (or the unknown that knows). Analysands love their own unconscious knowing, or their lack, via the mediation or alienation in the analyst (the Other). Here the analyst holds the illusory promise of restoring the analysand to his or her own being or lack-of-being. The examples of love and hate represent how the two basic affects of love and hate are related to the presence or absence of knowledge in the Other.

In addition, a flower also represents the maturity and fruition of a passion for knowing or realization, also known in Lacanian theory as the beautiful being of the *agalma*. Hate in turn represents a passion for ignorance or an attachment to **not**-knowing or ignoring someone or something about desire or about the law or the laws that organize experience. The *agalma* is reached via **non**-knowing or unknown knowing as a way of knowing beyond knowledge. Non-knowing is not the same as not knowing or ignorance. The prefix "non" represents a negative dialectic, whereas the adverb "not" represents a formal or dual form of negation. Non-knowing is tied to love and is a form of doctoral ignorance (Love is the unknown that knows about lack or emptiness – the One mistake of being [Lacan, 1976]).

> *Inscitia* is brute ignorance, whereas *inscientia* is non-knowing as such, as empty, and as call from the void at the center of knowledge.
>
> (Lacan, 1960–1; English translation is mine)

The question of affect is a phenomenon that is given significant attention within postmodern discourse. In psychoanalysis, and psychiatry in general, affect is associated with the body or physiological states. According to Freud, affects represent the body and the source of drives in the body. Freud often spoke of a quota of affect or of excitation. This is the equivalent of the postmodern interest in the pre-representational.

> In the "Logic of sense" . . . Deleuze's focus is on criticizing identity logic and privileging the pre-representational realms of bodies and their intensities over representational schemas of meaning.
>
> (Best and Kellner, 1991, p. 84)

Freud's shift from the catharsis of affect to insight and interpretation, and from the import of trauma to that of fantasy, have been fully reversed by certain postmodern forms of psychoanalysis. This also converges with other trends in contemporary psychoanalysis that challenge the role of insight as a curative factor in psychoanalysis. Corrective emotional experiences and emotional working through are considered more therapeutically effective than insight. Aside from the fact that Lacan argued for a different understanding of the practice of interpretation, Lacan responded to this tendency in his usual provocative fashion by stating that affects don't pre-exist the words that we have for them.

Nevertheless, although Lacan gives primacy to the signifier over affect, he also postulates a dimension of *jouissance* beyond language. Probably for this reason he stated that anxiety is the only affect (that does not deceive under the signifier). *Jouissance* is not an affect but bears a relationship to the organism and to the Real, and the connections between affect and the body in Freud have already been mentioned. *Jouissance* is on the next metalevel before and after affects. *Jouissance* exists or not at that place where the drives implicate one another: unions that lead to separations and separations that lead to unions. Within Lacanian theory, this place or point beyond knowledge can also be identified with the death drive.

Symbols and signifiers determine affects, yet the latter also bear a relationship to *jouissance* in terms of where they fall in a continuum between pleasant and unpleasant feelings and neither pleasant nor unpleasant. A feeling of neutrality or equanimity is an example of a feeling that is neither pleasurable nor painful or is a feeling that is not a feeling. Within Zen teaching, equanimity is the function of essential emptiness or the emptiness of essence that represents a dimension of the death drive and the desire of the analyst linked to the Real and to sublimation (a dignified void at the center of the Real, according to Lacan in Seminar VII; 1959–60).

In his writings, Bion (1992) carved out a place for a primary form of unknown emotion that according to him is not predetermined by any form of signification. The signification has yet to evolve that could process such form of primary emotion. Within the Lacanian framework both the unknown and an organismic experience could point to the dimension of the Real that is outside signification. The evolution of signification represents permutations within the Other or within the lack in the Other that open the Other to *jouissance* and its transformations.

According to Lacan, anxiety is the affect or emotion that does not deceive with respect to the presence of the *objet a* as the semblance of being. At the same time, Lacan says that anxiety as an affect is an effect of the desire of the Other. The Other wants the *objet a* as their lost object and the subject is occupying the place of this object for the Other.

Now in Freud anxiety is about the absence rather than the presence of the object. When a representation is repressed, the affective component of a drive, according to Freud, is suppressed (inhibited in its development) and then transformed and released in the form of anxiety. It is in this sense that Lacan follows Freud's second theory of anxiety in saying that anxiety is a signal or sign that the repressed (absent) object of anxiety is near. The subject becomes anxious due to the nearness of the lost object. The reason for this anxiety is that the loss of an object was a normalizing loss that needed to take place rather than the loss being the loss of a necessary function (desire of the mother/phallic function). The subject wants to prevent the loss, yet when the object is near the result is anxiety rather than the reduction of anxiety. The *objet a* becomes the equivalent of the straw that broke the camel's back or of the drop of water that caused the glass to overflow. The +1 needs to remain a −1 for the dynamic and effective functioning of the (symbolic) structure. For Being to be or function it needs the support of unbeing or emptiness (*desetre*).

In Spanish the words *colmo* and *colmar* have antithetical meaning as either a noun or a verb. When the *a* is not lost and functions as a+1 then the latter becomes "el colmo" as the height of stupidity, sheer madness, the last straw, and the crown of delusion. Conversely when one gives what one does not have, then the One is showered with honors, heaped with praises, and lavished with favors.

There is the nearness of an object that is repressed and unthought and yet known, and then there is the anxiety produced in relationship to a Real that cannot be symbolized not due to repression but because language lacks the signifiers to represent a Real beyond language.

For Lacan, the place of the first affective representative of the drive is occupied by infinite or undying life, or what is lost in the process of sexed reproduction. The first form of the *objet a*, representing what is unknown in the organism, appears under what he calls an infinite line or string. Later on in development, the *a* is re-signified in the "id-entification" with the object (breast), and further on under the phallus. Emptiness is another name for infinite life or what Bion would call O. The infinite string or unary trace of Life is the first experience of the body as mind, but where mind is something indefinable or unrepresentable. In the discourse of the analyst (Lacan 1969–70), this elementary form of the *a* (as discussed in chapter 1), as an affective and unknown representative of the drive and the body, is re-signified under the Name of the Father as a unary trace or letter within the Symbolic.

Particularly in California, it has become a truism that affects are necessarily authentic and genuine. Although it is true that inhibited obsessive types tend to intellectualize, have false insight, and not "be in touch with their feelings," it is also true that hysterics and borderline types can have false affect and catharsis and be "emotionally dysregulated." Feelings, like empathy to some extent, can be used for both expressive and defensive purposes. Even in the case of the obsessive, feeling cannot be a final resting point. Once defensive intellectualization is surrendered and feelings are reached, the feelings still have to be reconnected with unconscious signifiers and signification. Affects can be Imaginary (I am really angry with so and so), Symbolic (it's about *x* not about so and so), and Real (when I feel anger in the body and reconnect it with repressed signifiers, the feeling is more than anger, and includes love and various forms of *jouissance* that include the strings of undying Life).

The verbal and the non-verbal

The emphasis on affects also converges with the interest in the non-verbal and in non-intellectual or observational studies of infants and intersubjectivity.

Intersubjectivity in this model is dyadic and has no symbolic third in the sense of how Lacan related the third to the social function of the father. The father or the paternal function does not typically appear in this model other than as another mother, parent, or significant other. Observational infant and brain research are commonly used within atheoretical empiricist paradigms as excuses to reject prior theory or not to bother addressing prior theoretical considerations in any form of rigorous or serious manner. Instead, new theories are developed that somehow are supposed to fit better the facts that are being "discovered." In fact, the theories are based on entirely different assumptions and ideological predilections about human nature.

Attachment theory (Bowlby, 1988) presupposes a realm of legitimate needs that only become excessive when they are unmet or frustrated by the environment. Thus, the entire focus shifts to creating the optimal social environments in which to raise children free of the constraints of drives, drive theory, and the traditional roles and impulses of Old Europe.

It is interesting to note to what extent theories interact with the culture of the investigators or theoreticians. English and English-American psychoanalysts, for example, in the case of attachment theory and object relations, either ignore the environment and the desire and actions of the parents (Klein), or place a great degree of emphasis on attachment as a counterweight to the proclivities of their own culture. It is well known that people consider English-American social links as "tight upper lipped," formal, and distant. Thus it comes as no surprise that the theory would compensate for this aspect of the culture by emphasizing attachment and good-enough mothering. Conversely, Latin and Mediterranean cultures, known for their warmth and social proximity, place more emphasis on the Name of the Father as a separating function from the mother. Latin cultures take for granted the desire of the mother, whereas English-American cultures take for granted the function of the father.

There are limits to how much parenting practices can prevent the emergence of psychopathology or promote a positive definition of mental health. Parenting fluctuates between authoritarianism and permissiveness, alternately placing emphasis on the rules of the father, or the love and desire of the mother. The former produced the classical neurosis whereas the latter is implicated in the new forms of psychopathology. In the absence of the Name of the Father, either too little or too much mothering can lead to the same results. This is why Lacanian theory highlights the importance of the paternal/parental metaphor. Both the Name of the Father and the desire of the mother are two equally important ingredients of a fundamental paternal/parental equation.

I say that attachment theory and object-relations theory are implicated in the new forms of psychopathology because, despite the relational model, and the emphasis given to good-enough mothering and the importance of secure attachment in children, fewer and fewer women in the Western English-speaking world want to have them, divorce and the struggles between the sexes are at an all-time high, and teenage pregnancy and social deviance among youth is a very serious problem within contemporary or postmodern society.

Just like the old patriarchal order produced the classical neurosis and problems with inhibition and sexual satisfaction, postmodern theory's focus on mothering and secure attachment seems to mirror the permissiveness, sexual and gender confusion, and problems with impulse control linked to postmodern culture. Therefore, given that there is no way of ascertaining that the old pathologies are any better than the new ones, I am not proposing by any means that the solution to the problems faced by postmodern culture would be to return to the old patriarchal order. Perhaps the best option is simply to follow Lacan in his statement that there is no rapport between the sexes. The sexes and the family are faced with impossible tasks and problems similar to those of education, government, and the analytic profession itself, according to Freud. On the other hand, following the example of psychoanalysis, and the impasse of the rock of castration, once an impossibility, contradiction, or Zen koan (a koan is a public case that points to a contradiction that cannot be easily resolved by ordinary logic or language) is identified, solutions or possibilities may emerge that were unforeseen or not considered possible before.

Nevertheless, it is important to recognize that insecure attachment or clinging/craving (high tracking) behavior, or what Freudians would call the constant pressure of the drive, and Lacanians would call the metonymy of desire, and the *jouissance* of the Other, does not simply arise as a result of the absence of good-enough mothering, or a facilitating environment. Often too little or too much attachment can produce similar results in this regard. What is missing from this model is the notion of the desire of the mother and the fact that desire is the desire of the (m)Other. The child is not only an object of the mother's compassion or of the mother's basic biologically determined maternal preoccupation. Just like a socially constructed object of desire organizes sex and reproduction, the child also occupies or functions as an object of the mother's unconscious desire. This object is a narcissistic object that is an inevitable and structural third component of the imaginary and imaginative mother–infant dyad.

The child needs to be recognized, and at the same time the desire for recognition is problematic because it can never be realized via the other. The ego wants to be recognized according to the model of an unconscious object lying not within the object but with the subject himself/herself. The mother is her own object and so is the child. Therefore subjectivity requires the intervention of the other/father for recognition to be granted on a different level. In addition, the recognition of the third/other/father will resolve some problems yet create some fresh new problems of its own.

Intersubjectivity requires the function of negation and of the father, and this is something that is not theorized or adequately accounted for in non-Lacanian postmodern theory. Attachment seeks non-attachment, affirmation cannot exist without negation, and life or birth inevitably leads to death. Life and death arise together and interpenetrate one another, no matter how much hypermodernity may want to deny this. Deleuze and Guattari only conceive of a positive desire without lack or a life without or against death. Kohut (1966), object relations, and attachment theory have a theory of need but not of desire, and the intersubjective and relational perspectives don't seem to bother with a theory of desire even though the question of desire is found all over the social media and across the movie industry as integral aspects of consumer capitalism.

Postmodern views of the unconscious are often presented as they represented an improvement over Freud's dated non-relational model of the unconscious. However, in the absence of or a lack of interest in serious Freudian scholarship, these perspectives miss the finer shadings of Freud's theory. For example, the concepts of disavowal and splitting were there already in Freud, and the new theories don't differentiate the old and new ways of using the concepts. Freud (1894) used splitting to represent the *Spaltung* of consciousness due to repression, but his theories do not necessarily imply an absolute distinction between the repressed and the repressive, since the repressive can be repressed and the repressed can be repressive.

Lacan continues Freud's theories with his notion of a divided subject that is completely interwoven with the structure of language (the signifier/signified distinction) and a structure of language (the subject and object of a sentence) that is inseparable from speaking and listening as speech acts taking place between subjects. Speech goes from the subject to the Other and back to the subject. The Other, however, represents both the intersubjective other but more importantly the Other of the unconscious. Lacan uses the image of the Möbius strip to represent the psychic movement from the inside to the outside, from the conscious to the unconscious, and from the subject to the Other as well as vice versa.

In the theory of disavowal, deployed to give an account of perversion, Freud (1927) described the simultaneous and successive acceptance and rejection of the difference between the sexes. The culture in general has moved in the direction of perversion, while the very notion of perversion becomes repressed and eliminated from the theoretical horizon. To my mind, this partly explains why disavowal/splitting have been privileged as a defense and at the same time displaced from its original context. It is used by self psychology and object relations to explain pathological self-object relations with the mother, but in such a way that the problem of castration and the difference between the sexes and the corresponding function of the father are consciously/unconsciously disavowed (in the general sense of the term).

Finally, many new views on an implicit prereflective unconscious, described as preverbal and subsymbolic, were already contained within Freud's work. Freud spoke of the unconscious in the sense of the unknown and the unknowable. Within Lacanian theory this is the Real dimension of the unconscious. Bion (1965) uses the term O to describe the same level of experience or psychic reality. Interpretation according to Lacan goes from the unknown to the unknown and not from the unknown to the known.

The unknown also includes the unconscious of the organism. The unconscious homeostatic function differs from the repressed unconscious as usually understood. The unconscious in this sense may include things that were never fully conscious and can be affected by analytic work without making the material or the body fully conscious in the usual sense. The repetition of homophonic signifiers, the focus on significant dates, or the use of the holophrase would be an example of this.

The implicit unconscious can also be considered under the rubric of performativity or of action that is beyond knowledge or thinking, whether conscious or unconscious. Lacan incorporated this mode of action into psychoanalytic practice with his notion of the psychoanalytic act that is intrinsically linked to the scansion of the variable-length session. This implicit unconscious, of course, needs to be differentiated from the phenomenology of the subconscious or from what "appears" to a subject to be pre-verbal, as in the example of affects discussed above.

In contrast to the work of Kristeva (2001), the question of the pre-verbal needs to be understood not in terms of the semiotic, but in terms of the relationship between the molar and the molecular, or between simple and more complex orders/unities/singularities. The molar does not necessarily have more status than the molecular, in the same way, that sentences don't have hierarchy over words, or words don't have status over phonemes, or the Symbolic is not more important than the Real. The relationship between sensations and feelings is similar to that between atoms and molecules, cells and organs, Bion's beta and alpha elements. The pre-verbal is contained within the verbal, just like atoms are contained within molecules. The pre-verbal is contained within the verbal in the form of a certain quality or mode of signification within language (the suchness of words, the Real within the Symbolic) but also in the form of certain rogue asignifying elements within language. The first is similar to what Derrida calls *differance*, the second to Lacan's senseless signifier.

Kristeva links the semiotic to a maternal rejection of the symbolic Name of the Father, whereas within Lacanian theory the semiotic or the unary trace is related to the Name of the Father as a *sinthome*, or to the letter, as an aspect of the Symbolic and the signifier that is turned towards the Real. Since the symbolic mother also partakes of the symbolic function, and has access to the Real via femininity, she may in fact have access to the semiotic but without this amounting to a rejection of the Name of the Father, or to a conception of the symbolic order as a patriarchal order.

Aggregated groups of elements combine simple units into more complex organizations of basic elements. The symbolic is organized by basic unary traces that constitute signifiers and objects in various states of erasure and self-cancellation. Things being what we know of them through language, within a system of relative values, at the same time are more than their designation/nomination. Their meaning, therefore, remains open rather than foreclosed. The Symbolic, like parental authority, contains a mechanism of self-cancellation. This is what distinguishes repression from surplus repression or repression from social oppression. The Freudian left, in the line that goes from Reich to Deleuze and Guattari, has not recognized this key ingredient of Marcuse's (1955) critical theory: repression, unlike surplus repression or social oppression, is necessary for culture or civilization as such.

In addition, supposed pre-verbal feelings are evolved somatic forms resulting from the impact of language, symbolization, and culture on primary emotions and sensations. The relationship to things (*Sache* in German) differs from the relationship to *das Ding*. There is an involution that takes place from *das Ding* to *sache*. *Das Ding* represents what Lacan called the mythical *lamella* which itself stands for unborn, undying, or long-lasting life. Under sexed reproduction, long-lasting life becomes a dying form of birth. The physical separation from the mother in the trauma of birth is re-experienced and further concretized in relationship to the absence of the breast. The words and body of the mother, as symbolic containers, and the first sounds/phonemes uttered by the infant, will help transform emotional beta elements or sensations into molar forms or feelings.

The words of the symbolic mother reveal and convey a desire that eventually is concretized in the child in the form of the specular image as the first self-object. But before and beyond the Imaginary, the signifier retains a relationship to S_0 or the *objet a* in the Real. The senses, although organized in symbolic time and perception as hearing or seeing, also retain something of sensation and sound before symbolization. The lion's roar would be an example of this. Although the lion's roar means something within language (as a metaphor), and within the Imaginary (a reference to the image of the lion as an object), it also represents a signifier without signified, as a sign of the realm or of the Real.

The semiotic is a relationship to concrete objects that requires performative symbolic actions from subjects. The stop sign would be a good example of this. However, for some the stop sign could also represent paranoid/psychotic persecutory anxieties related to what Klein called the bad breast and that are later re-signified as imaginary forms of castration. For certain extreme right-wing groups in the US, for example, stop signs contain secret messages for invading United Nations troops. Here the Thing, or the *objet a*, has not been re-signified in relationship to a necessary loss under language and the paternal function. Instead the loss of the imaginary phallus is regressively interpreted as a before language. The psychotic subject remains fixated to the archaic mother and never becomes a subject in language, remaining in the position of an object to the *jouissance* of the (m)Other. The partial object, whether the breast or the phallus, functions as a sensory hallucinatory sign rather than as a signifier in language.

Lacan's theory has the power to explain two important aspects of psychotic experience: the failure of language and of subjectivity and the status of the psychotic as a subject. Klein's (1946) paranoid-schizo position only accounts for the ambivalence towards the partial object or the breast, but does not address the status of the subject as a partial object of the mother. Kleinian theory does not articulate the question of the child as an imaginary phallus or *objet a* for the mother, as well as the mother's unconscious fantasy life. Klein seems to only focus on the unconscious fantasy life of the infant or child.

Conclusion

In this chapter I have used the concept of emancipation to track and clarify the similarities and differences between traditional culture or pre-modernity, modernity, and postmodernity. These three terms are often confused in postmodern discourse and in the literature of the social sciences in general. The term postmodern often reflects an ambivalent relationship to modernity. Authors that discuss postmodernity range from those that defend modernity against postmodernity, to those who adopt or champion postmodern ideas, to those that take up modern ideas that, in their minds, already anticipated a postmodern perspective (Heidegger's existentialism would be a case in point).

Using Freudian categories, I argued that with modernity only the purpose/object of emancipation changes from the id to the super-ego. Traditional culture, even today, uses the super-ego to emancipate from the id, whereas modernity uses the rational ego to emancipate the ego from the super-ego.

I also noted that in challenging traditional identities and values, modernity established some fresh new prejudices of its own. The ego viewed as an evolution of the super-ego and, therefore, science, viewed as a differentiation within theological and philosophical thought, for example, can be seen as acquiring some of the same dogmatic qualities it had criticized in religion. Empirical social science and instrumental reason, as an ego-based form of rationality, ignore aspects of reality that are then critiqued and totalized under a dialectical reason that includes the excluded into theoretical and social discourse. In an effort to include the excluded, dialectical thought fails to leave dimensions of real experience untotalized and uncertain.

The postmodern impulse, as usually understood, rejects both aspects of modernity: the positive or empirical instrumental interests as well as the totalizing tendencies of dialectical thought. In one form or another, both are associated with the oppressions of the modern state and the imaginary father. However, in rejecting both the traditional super-ego, and the modern ego, and without any glue to hold it together, the postmodern, in the form of what has been called hyper- or ultra-modernism, succumbs to either the id or nihilism or to forms of ego-identity politics that maintain the ideology of instrumental reason and the master's discourse intact.

The dimension of the father needs to be correctly understood as a symbolic function that supports desire and organization while not being intrinsically hierarchical. Although the imaginary ego, associated with modern individualism, is cancelled by symbolic/metaphoric representation, the symbolic function is a negative dialectic that also cancels itself in support of symbolic organization. When the imaginary masculine phallic object of fantasy is realized and relinquished (thanks to the insights of modern psychoanalysis), then both sexes (male and female) can take their place as either masculine or feminine within the different registers of experience. What is lost or gained by one sex in the Imaginary is gained or lost in the Symbolic.

With respect to knowledge, the different forms of reason, formal-analytical, dialectical-critical, need to be organized and sustained by unknown-knowing (*l'insu que sait*), or a reason beyond reason, in the form of a negative dialectic. It is the latter manifestation of reason that can remain untotalized and open to the creative imagination, new signifiers/signification, and Real experience beyond linguistic or imaginary determinations.

Many of the dichotomies and contradictions/differences between the modern and the postmodern, between words and images, between meaning and sensation and no-meaning, between language and asignifying intensities, the verbal and the pre-verbal or non-verbal, are contained within Lacan's multidimensional theory of the Borromean knot (Real, Imaginary, Symbolic). The Borromean knot can link tradition, modernity, and postmodernity (Symbolic, Imaginary, and Real) without totalizing or collapsing them into one another. Each form of cultural organization can take its place vis-à-vis each other, and in time be One or the Other. At the same time, the Borromean knot is never fully totalized because the Name of the Father is a no-name, or a One that is a zero, and the All requires the not-all as its necessary foundation.

Finally, Freud's third form of identification, redefined by Lacan as the unary trace, can help build continuity and coherence in identity, without constructing alienating forms of majority or minority ego-identifications. The unary trace is simultaneously both molecular and molar. For the ego the relationship to the social Other, and the Other of the Unconscious, always remains ambivalent, because the ego itself is a form of defense/resistance against the Other. When the Other is assimilated into the ego, Otherness is not abolished, but simply renewed and reproduced as a new ego–Other dichotomy. Alternatively, when the ego is cancelled by the Other of interdependency, the subjects that arise in the place of the Other are the functions of one and zero, or the vanishing needle-points, knots, or jewels upon which the symbolic net is built. These are the implicit experiences/actions that are laid down beyond knowledge or thinking, and that play a pivotal function for the future of the species and the social-symbolic order.

References

Ashcroft, B., Griffiths, G., and Tiffin, H. (2000). *Post-Colonial Studies*. London: Routledge.

Adorno, T.W. (1966). *Negative Dialectics*. New York: Continuum, 1973.

Barthes, R. (1984). *Image, Music, Text*. New York: Hill and Wang.

Best, S. and Kellner, D. (1991). *Postmodern Theory: Critical Interrogations*. New York: Guildford Press.

Bion, W.R. (1965). *Transformations*. London: Heinemann.

Bion, W.R. (1992). *Cogitations*. London: Karnac.

Bowlby, J. (1988). *Bowlby: A Secure Base*. London: Routledge.

Deleuze, G. (1967). Coldness and cruelty. In *Masochism* (Charles Stivale trans.). New York: Zone Books, 1989.

Deleuze, G. and Guattari, F. (1972). *Anti-Oedipus: Capitalism and Schizophrenia* (Robert Hurley, Mark Seem, and Helen R. Lane trans.). New York: Continuum, 2004.

Derrida, J. (1976). *Of Grammatology* (G.C. Spivak trans.). Baltimore, MD: Johns Hopkins University Press.

Fanon, F. (1952). *Black Skins, White Masks*. New York: Grove Press, 1967.

Freud, S. (1894). The neuro-psychoses of defence. *SE*, 3: 41–61.

Freud, S. (1919). Lines of advance in psychoanalytic therapy. *SE*, 17: 157–68.

Freud, S. (1927). Fetishism. *SE*, 21: 147–57.

Frie, R. and Orange, D. (eds.) (2009). *Beyond Postmodernism: New Dimensions in Clinical Theory and Practice*. New York: Routledge.

Fromm, E. (1950). *Psychoanalysis and Religion*. New York: Bantam Books.

Fromm, E. (1960). *Psychoanalysis and Zen Buddhism*. New York: Harper Colophon.

Habermas, J. (1987). *The Philosophical Discourse of Modernity* (Frederick Lawrence trans.). Cambridge: Cambridge University Press.

Heidegger, M. (1927). *Being and Time* (J. Macquarrie and E. Robinson trans.). New York: Harper and Row, 1962.

Klein, M. (1946). Notes on some schizoid mechanisms. In *The Collected Writings of Melanie Klein, III*. London: Hogarth Press, pp. 1–24.

Kohut, H. (1966). Forms and transformations of narcissism. *Journal of the American Psychoanalytic Association*, 14: 243–72.

Kristeva, J. (2001). *Melanie Klein*. New York: Columbia University Press.

Lacan, J. (1959–60). *The Seminar, Book VII. The Ethics of Psychoanalysis* (Jacques-Alain Miller ed., Dennis Porter trans.), New York: W.W. Norton, 1992.

Lacan, J. (1960–1). *Seminario 8. La Transferencia* (Ricardo Rodriguez Ponte trans.). Unpublished.

Lacan, J. (1962–3). *El Seminario. Libro 10. La Angustia*. Buenos Aires: Paidos, 2006.

Lacan, J. (1968). *Seminario 16: De un Otro al otro*. Buenos Aires: Paidos, 2008.

Lacan, J. (1969–70). *The Seminar of Jacques Lacan: Book XVII: The Other Side of Psychoanalysis*. New York: W.W. Norton, 2007.

Lacan, J. (1972). *On Feminine Sexuality: the Limits of Love and Knowledge. Encore: The Seminar of Jacques Lacan, Book XX*. New York: W.W. Norton, 1998.

Lacan, J. (1974). La troisieme. In *Lettres de l'Ecole Freudienne* 16, Paris, 1975, pp. 178–203.

Lacan, J. (1976). *Le Séminaire, Livre XXIV: L'insu que sait de l'une bévue s'aile à mourre*, 1976–1977. *Ornicar?* 17, 1979.

Lasch, C. (1979). *The Culture of Narcissism: American Life in an Age of Diminishing Expectations*. New York: W.W. Norton.

Lyotard, J.F. (1979). *The Postmodern Condition: A Report on Knowledge*. Minneapolis, MN: University of Minnesota Press, 1984.

Marcuse, H. (1955). *Eros and Civilization*. New York: Beacon Press, 1966.

Nobus, D. (2002). Symptom and society: a clinical challenge for contemporary psycho-analysis. *Modern Psychoanalysis*, 27: 179–203.

Schlesinger, A. (1998). *The Disuniting of America*. New York: W.W. Norton.

Smith, H. (1989). *Beyond the Post-Modern Mind*. Wheaton, IL: Quest Books.

Storolow, R. (2009). Trauma and human existence. In R. Frie and D. Orange (eds.), *Beyond Postmodernism, New Dimensions in Clinical Theory and Practice*. London: Routledge.

Teicholz, J.G. (2009). A strange convergence: postmodern theory, infant research, and psychoanalysis. In R. Frie and D. Orange (eds.), *Beyond Postmodernism: New Dimensions in Clinical Theory and Practice*. London: Routledge.

Thompson, M.G. (2004). Postmodernism and psychoanalysis: a Heideggerian critique of postmodernist malaise and the question of authenticity. In J. Reppen, M.A. Schulman, and J. Tucker (eds.), *Way Beyond Freud: Postmodern Psychoanalysis Evaluated*. London: Open Gate Press.

Chapter 6

Magritte, the void, and the imagination

From idealization to sublimation, from resemblance to similitude, and from the id to it

Raul Moncayo and Roberto Lazcano

Introduction

Any good work of art has a capacity to "draw" and evoke the experience of the reality of the Unconscious. In the presence of a painting, the ordinary experience of reality may be transformed into an experience of the mind writ large. The larger mind is not only inside but also outside and represents and realizes a structural connection between object and subject, the external and internal, the representational and emotional worlds. The work of art functions as a symbolic object that links the subjective experience of the artist with the subjective experience of the viewer. Because the subjectivity of the artist is included in the object of art, the latter also has an impact on the subjectivity of the viewer. In "The Moses of Michelangelo", Freud (1914) described his subjective experience of Michelangelo's sculpture.

Lacan (1962–3) made a distinction between objectivity and objectality. The object of psychoanalysis, as a scientific object, is an unconscious fantasy object and as such it necessarily involves subjectivity and the life of desire. Fantasy objects mediate our perception of reality. No matter how much objective science tries to demystify and nullify the influence of fantasies on our perceptions, it is difficult to escape the conclusion that ultimately science itself may be a construction of the human imagination widely defined. Nevertheless, the task of giving us the purest and most beautiful representation of our imaginative faculty falls on the visual arts and not on science. The object of art is a representation not of objective reality but of objectality, the construction of reality that includes our fantasies and desires.

This chapter will examine the work of art from a psychoanalytic perspective with an emphasis on the theory of Jacques Lacan. It will explore the notion of the object of art as it relates to the concepts of fantasy and the lack-of-being. In the *matheme* for unconscious fantasy or the phantasm ($\$ \Diamond a$), Lacan represents the subject as lacking the *objet a* or the object cause of desire. Fantasy objects both sustain desire and defend against the lack. Fantasy objects both hold the promise of filling the lack and at the same time reveal it. This chapter will explore the work of art as representing a lack or as a unary trace of a void and the One of a mystery at the core of being.

We submit that Magritte represents a non-dual or postmodern alternative to both modern and classical art. Classical art represented the subject of painting and the painting subject with idealized images. Classical art elevated nature to the dignity of culture. Modern art instead represents the subject of painting and the painting subject as lacking and as an object of waste in identification with the fantasy object, cause of desire. Following Lyotard, we represent the object of art not via idealization or devaluation, but as a form of sublimation without the repressive interest of classical art.

In Magritte, S_1 is not elevated to S_2, nor is S_2 regressed to S_1. Here S_1 would mean a form of identification with the object of unconscious fantasy. In Magritte, S_1 is revealed as S_0 or as what sustains the (Real empty) form of S_2 or of the laws of form, whether visual or linguistic. The painting in-itself is not the object of fantasy, or the id as an object, but the unary traces and infinite lines of wondrous being. In chapter 1 on identification, I differentiated between imaginary similarity, symbolic resemblance, and real similitude. Similitude is Real and points to unbeing. I also pointed out that similitude is related to Benjamin's (1936) concept of aura as the quality of a modern painting or "its unique existence at the place where it happens to be." A painting's place is represented by the evocation of non-identity.

The lack, the void, and the mystery in the work of art

The concept of the lack first appears in Lacan's definition of desire as a lack-of-being. Lacan considered the lack-of-being an existential predicament of humanity. Desire as a lack of being is linked to Lacan's view of the human being as a speaking being. It is within language that human beings became lacking beings or a lack of being. Lacan links the laws of language with the incest prohibition and the "no" that the father represents. Language and the father represent the childhood loss related to the child being the object of the mother's desire. It is the loss and separation from the mother which structure being as a lack of being. In addition, Lacan also speaks of a lack within the Symbolic itself. Although the Symbolic plays a part in generating the lack at the core of being, and at the same time provides the subject with metaphors to symbolize this lack, ultimately the Symbolic is also lacking the words to represent the Real of the emptiness or the non-being at the core of being.

In this chapter we will apply the Lacanian concept of the lack and void to the work of art in several ways. First, the work of art is meant to provide a visual representation of what is missing within the Symbolic. There is a generic limitation of language to represent the lack that language itself has helped to generate. The artist has to appeal to a different medium to represent what might be missing within language and within his or her own experience. Here we find a convergence of the structural function of art or painting and the desire of the subject to symbolize and come to terms with the losses sustained within the course of his/her biographical experience. Consistent with Lacanian theory, this chapter will argue that a fundamental lack is also present in the work of the artist and in the structure of the drive, which fuels its production. The lack is at work in the pathos or *jouissance* of the artist and in the very nature of symbolic forms such as painting.

In addition to the concept of the lack and its application, the chapter will also build on another characteristic of Magritte's painting: its value to evoke the experience of a mystery beyond representation (the Real). The concepts of the void and of emptiness serve as transitional terms between the concept of the lack in Lacan and the notion of the mystery in Magritte. In a first approximation the concept of the void is similar if not identical to that of the lack. Zizek (2000) has argued that it is as important for the artist to cover the void as it is to unveil it. For example, he explains contemporary painting as representing what is missing or the pain of existence rather than the idealized images of classical painting. However, this concept of the void as an unveiled lack or limitation is not identical to the notion of the mystery in Magritte. To reach the mystery requires a different conception of the void. What paintings reveal is not only the void as a traumatic experience of childhood or of human existence but also the void of the mystery itself. This latter sense of the void diverges somewhat (although not entirely) from the usual/official interpretation of Lacanian ideas and comes closer to Zen Buddhist conceptions of emptiness and the void. This more positive dimension of the void and the mystery in Magritte's painting will be elucidated following Moncayo's (1998a) distinctions between the void representing traumatic experiences, repressed desires, and the absence/presence of the object, and the meaning of a positive emptiness or the presence of the Real or of the Sublime as an emptiness beyond symbolization. This distinction does justice to both a psychoanalytic interpretation of Magritte's work and to his sense that the mystery cannot be reduced to psychological explanations.

In a previous work, Moncayo (1998b) differentiated between two conceptions of metaphor: symbols/signifiers that refer to other more primal signifiers and symbols/signifiers that refer to the Real. In the case of symbolic metaphor, a signifier or S_2 is a substitute for S_1 or a repressed sexual (phallic) signifier or trauma. Either S_2 or S_1 can be Symbolic or Imaginary. In the paternal metaphor, the Name of the Father replaces the imaginary phallus as an object of the mother's desire.

The Name of the Father can also acquire the imaginary function of closing the gap or the lack left by the absence of the imaginary phallus. Eventually the Name itself becomes the Name of the Nameless or the signifier of a lack (i.e., Jack Lackman or Jacques *Lac*an). The Name becomes truly symbolic when it represents the void itself rather than solely concealing the lack of an imaginary object. In this case the signifier does not represent an absent repressed imaginary signifier of desire but an experience outside signification (S_0). In the first example, the Real can refer to an Imaginary void in the sense of an absence or lack in the Symbolic caused by repression and linked to a repressed traumatic signifier. This form of

Imaginary Real represents a dualistic nothingness of absence (without a presence). In the second case, a metaphor or a representation refers to the Real of a mystery. The latter represents a sense of the Real as a positive emptiness (an absence that is also a presence) of signification rather than as reference to a repressed trauma. The distinction between a void of absence of an object, or dual nothingness, as an intersection between the Imaginary and the Real, and a void of presence without an object, or a non-dual emptiness, as an intersection between the Real and the Symbolic, does justice to both a psychoanalytic interpretation of Magritte's work and to his sense that the mystery cannot be reduced to psychological explanations.

Webster's New World College Dictionary (Neufeldt and Guralnik, 1997) defines the mysterious as what excites wonder, curiosity, and surprise while baffling efforts to comprehend, signify, or identify. Thus, in distinguishing between lack, void, and mystery, these terms are brought into relation with one another for the purpose of realizing which aspect of the painting refers to the mystery and therefore need not be explained (as Magritte recommends), and which aspect refers to the lack and void within the social symbolic and the lack and losses within the subject. In contrast to the mystery, this latter sense of the void included within a painting needs to be analyzed and understood.

The subject is an object or "I am a painting"

Throughout history the object of art has been the product of the desire of the master: whether king, church, patron, or capitalist. Until this century, artists worked mostly by commission. However, with the onset of modernity, and the individualism that describes it, the artist began to claim the work of art as his/her own autonomous creation. Thus, we distinguish three distinct historical ways of conceiving the work of art: art produced for a social master, art created by an autonomous ego (Kris, 1964), and the object of art as produced by unconscious psychic and social forces. With the discovery of the unconscious, the artist claims the latter as a tool for the creative process. For Lacanian theory, ego-based individualism is an illusory claim: what the artist is portraying is to a great extent unconsciously and socially mandated.

A work of art is shaped and transmitted through the pre-existing laws of language. As Lacan has stated: "The visual field and the imaginary is structured by symbolic laws" (1954–5: 91–2). In addition, Kuhns (1983) has argued that art does not solely represent a working through of the artist's personal problems because it is also a representation of the communal conflicts in which everyone is involved.

A psychoanalytic interpretation of modern surrealist painting discovers in modern painting the working and depiction of the unconscious despite a painter's objections in this regard. When the object of art is understood as a function of unconscious desire or the desire of the Other (does the Other want me or my painting? what does the Other want and what do I really want?), then it can be argued that the object of art functions as an index of a void within the subject and within the social-symbolic order.

The object of art and the three dimensions of experience

According to Laplanche and Pontalis (1973), Lacan uses the Symbolic with two aims. First, the term Symbolic points to a connection between the structure of language and that of the Freudian unconscious. Lacan uses linguistics as a method to study the unconscious. Second, for Lacan, language shows how the human subject is inserted into a pre-established symbolic order. From this point of view, it can be argued that the artist is unaware that his art is a reflection of subjectivity dictated by language. The internalized voices/words of the mother, father, and society in general help delineate the shape of the work of art. The artist mistakes these voices as his own, and in this way society, embedded in the Symbolic, can manifest itself through the hands of the artist.

The Imaginary order will be defined in this chapter according to five parameters: the visual field, the imagination, fantasy life, the body image, and what Laplanche and Pontalis (p. 210) called "the relation to the image of the counterpart." These different elements arise within the intersections of the Imaginary and the other two registers of the Borromean knot: the Symbolic and the Real. The body image and the image of the counterpart shape the first form of ego identity or the ideal ego. In the mirror phase the ego is occupying the place of the "*objet a*" cause of the mother's desire. The ego mistakenly identifies the image in the mirror for its own image when, in fact, this image is born out of the Other and her desire. In the same way, the artist misrecognizes the work of art as his own when in fact it is the product of the discourse of the Other. For example, in the case of Magritte, a psychoanalytic interpretation of his work would find the desire for his mother and of his mother speaking through his paintings.

Finally, the object of art is also in a relationship to the third fundamental register of the Real, which is presented as that which escapes symbolization. The work of art represents something of the Real that cannot be said by word or image. Embedded within the nature of symbolic forms is their inability to represent the Real. Its presence occupies a similar function to that of black holes in physics. In physics it is assumed that without the presence of black holes the entire structure of the universe would collapse (Hawking, 1988). Similarly, one could say that without such absence, that is, the experience of the Real as an absence within the Symbolic, the formal presence of the work of art could not be sustained. Such a black hole is encoded in the life experience of the artist. Although the Real escapes any attempt at symbolization and goes beyond the realm of explanation and definitions, it is the cause and aim of the work. It is the dilemma of the artist to capture what cannot be captured.

Lack and myth making

Consistent with Lacanian theory, a fundamental lack is also present in the work of the artist. It was mentioned above that the lack is at work in the pathos or *jouissance* of the artist. The artist first encounters the lack in the course of her/his own childhood and developmental history.

Lacan defines the lack as a lack of being and as a lack or a loss of the object of desire. This is the loss associated with birth, separation, and the child becoming an object of the mother's desire. The child eventually conceives of this object as an imaginary phallus that the mother wants from the father. The child is no longer the sole object of the mother's desire and needs to process the absence of the mother, the absence of the phallus in the mother, and the fact that the mother wants something from the father. The presumption of the imaginary phallus by the father and the experience that the child has of lacking an imaginary object produces the illusion of being deprived of an object that does not exist. The symbolic phallus represents the production of symbolic absence and renunciation by culture as the figure of the Law and the Name of the Father. Therefore the absence produced by culture is a necessary inscription of a lack that also has the positive function of generating and renovating desire. What does the subject want? The subject wants what he/she cannot have. Thus, the work of art as a symbolic representation is completely permeated by the lack at the core of the subject and the Symbolic.

The object of art serves as a kind of movie screen onto which individual viewers project their illusions, wishes, and fantasies. This is only possible because the artist speaks a language of images in common with the viewer. She describes the world as it has been presented to her in a social context. For a moment, all the common elements to the image of the world, which are randomly distributed or spoken of in a society, take shape in the object of art. The artist gives form, creates and presents his audience with these objects of desire through which a world is captured and constructed. Therefore the artist provides a glimpse of the symbolic absence of the object of desire through the creation of a new object in the Imaginary. The artist then claims something that belongs to society (as the source of the law and of desire) and is transmitted through Symbolic forms (the visual image within the context of symbolic forms). But the artist neglects the strong influence that his psychic structure exerts over the product of artistic creation.

We have chosen the work of Lacan because it provides a theory from which it can be argued that the object of art is a reflection of the artist's struggle to mirror and represent humanity's impossible search for the lost object. According to Freud and Lacan, human desire is forever marked by an impossible search for an object lost in early childhood. Art objects, such as a vase, a tapestry, or a painting, act as illusions, in an attempt to provide expression to that which cannot be grasped. These objects carry the hope that they might cover up the irreparable loss at the foundation of human existence and at the same time represent the plenitude of the mystery of the Real.

Why Magritte?

The works of Rene Magritte (1898–1967) and the ideas that underline them are a special case both in the history of modern art and in surrealist paintings. Magritte was chosen as a focus for this chapter not only because of the quality of his paintings, but because he is a thinker who expresses ideas through art. His art is an expression of the language, sociopolitical ideas, and theories of his time. He challenges the Symbolic or the Law without knowing that, in the end, he is its representative. As a surrealist, he made the paradox of all form and the absurdity of all human existence the basis of his outlook. In his surrealistic style, Magritte's canvases transpose the conventional sense of reality by providing us with pictorial windows into unconscious desire. He denied the existence of an unconscious by saying that any and all meaning was already present and revealed in the painting, thus turning his back on any attempt to analyze unconscious forces.

Nevertheless, Magritte's paintings do in fact encompass not only his unconscious, but also the discourse of the Other (society). Magritte believed that he had captured a complete understanding of his paintings and that therefore he dominated and controlled the fate of his work. However, in the course of an extensive body of work the artist cannot escape his drives and he/she inevitably falls victim to an impossible search to represent what escapes signification.

Despite Magritte's denial that his paintings had any unconscious meaning, the relationship between key biographical events and the themes observed in his paintings cannot be missed. Magritte's mother committed suicide during his childhood, and this traumatic event appears multiple times in many of his paintings and how women are depicted in them.

Magritte's paintings support both a Freudian and a Lacanian interpretation of a painting, the pathographic (the pathology of art and the art of pathology) and the conceptual aspect of the visual arts. Although Magritte denied that his paintings had any personal psychic meaning, as Freud would believe (and as described further on), his paintings clearly bear an intimate relationship to key events in his life. At the same time there are elements in Magritte's paintings that cannot be reduced to Magritte's biography or to a Freudian or even a Lacanian frame and are best approached conceptually and/or left within the realm of the mysterious and beyond explanation of any kind.

Modernism in the visual arts antedates postmodernism in the humanities and the social sciences

Art challenges the social conventions that define reality and helps to establish new representations of reality. The object of art expresses the unconscious of the artist, through what appears to be a flow of free association of images and ideas. A painting transgresses the conventional sense of reality by providing us with pictorial windows into unconscious dimensions of mind.

The French philosopher Michael Foucault (1983), who established an epistolary relationship with Magritte, wrote:

> The death of interpretation is to believe that there are coherent, pertinent and systematic marks . . . the life of interpretation, on the contrary, is to believe that there are only interpretations.
>
> (p. 12)

Michael Foucault has been hailed as one of the most important French contributions to philosophy in the 20th century. Both Foucault and Magritte engaged in a critique of language, concurring with the linguist Ferdinand de Saussure (1910–11) in asserting the arbitrariness of the sign. According to de Saussure, words do not refer to things themselves, but rather gain meaning as points or values within the entire system of language.

Foucault (1983) contra-poses Magritte's use of an image to the example of a botanical manual, that is, of a figure and the text that names it. Whereas a botanical image or drawing faithfully reproduces the image it describes and names, underneath a drawing resembling a wooden pipe, Foucault simply writes, "This is not a pipe."

The treachery of images, 1928–9
©2011 C. Herscovici, London/Artists Rights Society (ARS), New York

For Foucault, "This is not a pipe" (*Ceci n'est pas une pipe*) "exemplifies the penetration of discourse into the Form of things; it reveals discourse's ambiguous power to deny and to redouble" (p. 37). Magritte deploys the play of words and images. Foucault emphasizes Magritte's intention of creating new relations between words and objects so as to highlight objects generally ignored in everyday life. For Magritte as for Lacan, the Imaginary and the Symbolic are interdependent and therefore exchangeable at points of intersection. The name can take the place of an image and vice versa. However, Magritte also emphasizes that sometimes one can also see images and words differently in a painting. Foucault uses Magritte's painting "*Personnage marchant vers l'horizon*" (Person walking towards the horizon) to illustrate how in certain contexts words do not replace missing objects. In this painting, words inserted into amorphous forms take the place of the image of the object.

Personnage marchant vers l'horizon, 1928–9
©2011 C. Herscovici, London/Artists Rights Society (ARS), New York

"The mystical, Platonic identification of words with the essence of things is what many of Magritte's canvases vigorously assault" (Foucault, 1983: 9). Just as in Saussurean linguistics words do not refer to things, in Magritte's surrealism the painter's images do not really resemble anything in the object, which would lend the painting the aspect of a model or origin. Therefore, Foucault challenges the Western classical painting insinuation that the painted image is this or that thing. For Foucault, Magritte's strategy involves painting familiar images then disrupting their resemblance to real images of objects by combining them irrationally or according to a different logic. Either Magritte gives images names that transgress the conventional meaning of an image, or he transgresses the conventional relationships among words.

Four levels can be observed in the historical relationship between words and images.

1   In classical art visual forms appear to be independent from words. Conventional reality appears as a natural reality, as part of the nature of the way things are, or the way things are in nature. There is a correspondence between the name of the painting and the images presented in the painting. The name simply confirms what things already appear to be.

2   Islamic art. Instead of showing you a visual image of conventional reality as was done in classical painting, an Islamic Caligram shows you the language and the social laws (i.e., date, time, and place) that lie buried

in representational realism. It is not that the word has a natural affinity with the image or its essence, but that the image is actually constructed with words.

3   Modern painting is not interested in how specific images are constructed with words but in the arbitrariness of the relationship between words and images. In some of Magritte's paintings, words or word images replace the images of things. But in this case one could still translate and visualize the words for landscape, for example (sky, mountain, tree, etc.), into an actual image of a landscape.

4   Finally, in still other paintings, Magritte uses a visual image but names the image not with its conventional name but with an apparently totally unrelated word.

For example, in a painting called "The key of dreams," under the image of a horse Magritte writes the apparently totally unrelated word "door." In the case of this painting one could wonder what the word door has to do with the image of a horse. Here Magritte arrives at the same relationship between words and images that Freud discovered in his method of dream interpretation. By the method of free association, different dream images can be translated into different words that explain the unconscious, and apparently irrational, reactions that a subject may have to visual images. It is the unconventional relationship between words or signifiers that explains the meaning of images. It is well known that Freud thought that dream-images that appear to be absurd gain their meaning, logic, and coherence by translating dream images or thing-representations into word-representations or signifiers. For example, a horse could be a metaphor for the father, because in the patient's associations, the door to the stable had the same color, smell, and handle as the door to the father's study.

Magritte's subversive techniques share the anti-linguistic views of modernism. From Klee and Kandinsky forward,

> modern art declares that a painting is nothing other than itself, autonomous from the language that lies buried in representational realism. But while the predominant mode of modernism's declaration of independence has been abstraction, Magritte uses literalism to undermine itself.
>
> (Foucault, 1983: 9)

This is another point where Magritte converges with Lacan. Lacan focuses on the letter of the text, only to turn it into a senseless signifier of desire. Despite Lacan's focus on the linguistic signifier, his real interest lies in the language of the unconscious, or what he calls *lalangue. Lalangue* represents an unconventional use of conventional language to represent the Real. A parallel can be drawn between the anti-linguistic trends of modern painting and Lacan's distinction between language and *lalangue*, linguistics and *linguisterie*, or the conscious and unconscious dimensions of language.

The key of dreams, 1935
©2011 C. Herscovici, London/Artists Rights Society (ARS), New York

Foucault's statement about modernism evokes Jung's definition of archetypal images or symbols. Jung (1968) defined a symbol (by which he means an archetypal image) as something self-contained or that contains the Self, in contrast to a semiotic sign that always refers to a thing or an object. Jung, however, did not have a concept of the signifier as arbitrary or independent from the object. In addition, he did not conceive how signifiers could also represent the Real as a register beyond images, words, and reason. Within Lacanian theory the case of a painting referring to nothing other than itself (not to objects or other words) points directly towards the register of the Real beyond the Imaginary and the Symbolic. This becomes even more evident when the painting is not an image of an object but the image of a word. Here words do not point to the analysis of a text or literary form but to something beyond an image or the Imaginary. In language or in ideograms, the Real appears by slices, pieces, or strokes of the pen or of the brush rather than by the rules of grammar or syntax. Such pieces of Real are disruptive of the harmony found within the social conventional imagary or the conventions of language.

In this sense modernism as an art form differs from the usual meaning attributed to modernity as a historical period characterized by the enlightenment and the rational organization of the world. Linguistics, and psychoanalysis for that matter, is a product of the enlightenment and modernity. Modernism in art is closer to a postmodernism that also disrupts the belief in objective truths and

ego-centered subjects. In fact, modernism in art may have prophetically anticipated postmodernism in philosophy and the rest of the humanities and social
sciences.

This chapter also agrees with Lyotard (1994), who developed the concept of
postmodernity, when he conceives the aesthetic of the Sublime as the mediating
link between modernism and postmodernism. In fact this chapter further proposes
that the aesthetic of the Sublime is precisely what differentiates modernism (not
modernity) and postmodernism. Placing the philosophical and postmodern
concept of the Sublime next to Freud's concept of sublimation helps resolve and
understand the problems that Freud had in formulating the concept and differentiating it from idealization and other defense mechanisms. Postmodernism
contains the possibility of a realization of the Sublime that may be deeply
satisfying to the subject yet equally disturbing to the conventional ego of either
classicism or bourgeois modernity.

This is what differentiates idealization from sublimation. Idealization supports
or is a function of the relationship between the ego-ideal and the ideal ego that has
the defensive function of closing a gap within the ego. As elaborated below, the
change of object in sublimation goes beyond the notion of a social or conventional
object accepted by society. The aim of sublimation reveals a positive form of the
death drive and the return of the drive to a radical form of emptiness. Becoming
reconciled to the emptiness within the desire and the subject requires a benevolent
form of depersonalization as a movement that includes a painful tear to the fabric
of narcissism that proves to be ultimately rewarding.

Foucault also draws a distinction between resemblance and similitude.
Resemblance prescribes how art as a cultural representation is to mimic the
natural object, but with similitude there is no objective reference point to the
artistic image. This is suggestive of the ways in which cultural images define
the objects of reality. Herein the natural object is no longer subordinated to
cultural representation and vice versa; both the reference anchor and the representation are arbitrary. In this way, for Magritte the image as well as the word is not
intrinsically linked to the object.

Lacan interpreted the work of Saussure in a similar way. For Saussure a
linguistic sign was composed of a signifier and a signified, but whereas for
Saussure the signified was an acoustic image of the object, for Lacan the signified
is simply another signifier within language. Thus, not only the choice of words (as
in Saussure) but also their meaning (Lacan) is completely arbitrary. But here the
meaning of arbitrary does not mean at random or simply pure chance. In this
context, the word arbitrary, in my opinion, means contingent or dependent on the
particular causes and effects or the group of words and subjects/signifiers at work
in a signifying situation. Arbitrary signifies that the meaning or values of certain
words depend upon or are relative to the meaning and values of other words and
the relations and differences between them.

In Magritte's painting "This is not a pipe" he also emphasizes that resemblance
is not identity; in other words, that the painted image of the pipe does not match

up with the pipe as a thing. The cultural representation and the naming of the object determine how the subject experiences the reality of the object. The cultural and linguistic representation of the object is embedded within the formal mechanism of visual perception. Visual perception is organized by symbolic and linguistic values or elements.

It is an intrinsic characteristic of the Imaginary to perceive the external world as independent from the subject. In other words, the Imaginary deceives the subject with respect to the nature of the object. In reality the object is not only outside but also inside. Magritte's paintings reveal the deceptions of the Imaginary by showing us how an object is mostly an image within the Imaginary organized by the Symbolic laws of culture and language. In Magritte's own words:

> I placed in front of a window, seen from inside a room, a painting representing exactly that part of the landscape which was hidden from view by the painting. Therefore, the tree represented in the painting hid from view the tree situated behind it, outside the room. It existed for the spectator, as it were, simultaneously in his mind, as both inside the room in the painting, and outside in the real landscape. Which is how we see the world: we see it as being outside ourselves even though it is only a mental representation of it that we experience inside ourselves.
>
> (Quoted by Gablik, 1970: 87)

Magritte is referring to "The human condition" and to many paintings of mirrors and paintings within paintings, where reality is a painting and a painting reality.

The image of the pipe is not a thing because it is only a real *image* of the object. A real object is only an image or a real image, and a real image is just as well a virtual image projected by the cognitive constructs of the mind. In optics, a real object is represented in the brain as a virtual image of the object. The virtual image is not an effect of the real object but the very way in which the world reflects the products of the mind. What the object is, independently from the virtual image projected by the mind, or reflected in the brain, remains unknown, a mystery, or Real in the Lacanian sense.

This sense of the unknown precisely corresponds to Magritte's invocation of the mystery. An example of this would be Magritte's painting "The territory" in which the image of a landscape floats freely in the empty sky. The floating landscape is suggestive of how the visual presentation of reality is a virtual image projected into the void and how, for example, the moon itself is like a giant and beautiful mirror reflecting the light of the sun suspended in the midst of the empty void. As mentioned earlier, this understanding of the void differs from the sense of the void as the absence of the lost object. The latter is a void of absence, whereas the former is a void of presence, that is, of the presence of the mystery. There is something of the void in matter and something of matter in the void.

The human condition, 1933
©2011 C. Herscovici, London/Artists Rights Society (ARS), New York

Art and psychoanalysis: from resemblance to similitude, from idealization to sublimation, and from the Id to It

The field of art criticism is usually defined as the written discussion or evaluation of visual art (Roskill, 1976). Art criticism is considered a form of art history. In contrast to other historians, the art historian deals primarily with images. The art historian benefits from being able to read images. Psychoanalysis, therefore, offers the art critic/historian the potential for dynamic readings of a work of art in terms of the artist's personal history as well as from the more universal perspective of an understanding of the workings of the human mind or psyche.

Spitz (1985) has observed continuity between what she calls Freud's pathographic approach to the work of art and the 19th-century critical tradition (Romantic criticism). Pathography can be defined as historical biography but from a psychoanalytic or medical viewpoint.

Spitz observes that Abrams (1953) followed Wordsworth in defining poetry as "The spontaneous overflow of powerful feelings recalled in tranquility" (quoted by Abrams, p. 26). Spitz notes that in this statement Wordsworth shifts the focus of the critic's attention from the work of art to the psyche of the artist. According to Spitz (1985), the "conception of the artist implicit in Freud's terms grows solidly out of the Romantic tradition in which artistic creativity is invariably associated with moments of intense emotion, altered states of consciousness, and pain" (p. 28).

However, whereas the romantic critic employs biographical and other information in order to interpret the work of art as his/her prime object of inquiry, in the psychoanalytic interpretation the movement is reversed. In the case of Freud, works of art are taken as starting points for discovering something about the nature of psychical development in general but more importantly in the life of a particular artist. In pathography, the psyche is the prime object of inquiry. From this perspective, the object of art can be said to occupy the same structural position as a symptom or what Lacan called the *objet a* cause of desire. Lacan (1975–6) said this much when referring to the literary works of James Joyce. To designate this shared place between the symptom and the cultural object, Lacan called Joyce's work his *sinthome*.

Although Lacan's works refer mostly to works of literature, he also discusses the visual arts in Seminars VII (1959–60) and XI (1964). There are differences in the way Freud and Lacan approach the work of art. Lacan did not believe that it is possible or desirable for psychoanalysis to make interpretations about the psyche of the artist. Instead, Lacan interprets the work of art as a symbolic text being written through the author as a scribe. Lacan uses the work of art to say something about psychoanalysis or to illustrate psychoanalytic concepts. This is in contrast to Freud's belief that the work of art has the primary function of expressing something about the painter or about himself.

According to Freud paintings can be interpreted according to the psychical conflict manifested in the paintings. On the one hand, psychical conflict refers to the psychical conflicts of the artist as reflected in the painting, and on the other to the psychical conflicts evoked by the painting in the viewer. On the other, paintings can also be interpreted according to conceptual themes. This, for example, refers to the manner in which the thematic interest of the artist converges with key concerns of Lacanian thinking. We use Lacan's method of interpreting the work of art as a vehicle for representing abstracts ideas regarding the nature of the mind and the structure of the subject. This latter approach finds support in the manner in which Magritte's own ideas converge with key concepts of Lacanian thinking.

Gablic has already tied the tragic recovery of the corpse of Magritte's mother from the River Sambre to the unconscious logic of his work as reflected in this painting. It is said that Magritte's mother was discovered with her gown tied around her head as a result of the current or her own doing. It is a simple step from that frightening image of a traumatized youngster to the scene represented in several of Magritte's canvases. "*Les amants*" would be a good case in point.

Now it is also known that Magritte encourages us to sit with the mystery and warned us not to press for explanations. This admonishment can be interpreted in two ways: with Magritte and against Magritte. First, Magritte is right because the sense of Mystery points to a Real beyond social or psychological explanations. Second, Magritte is wrong, because his perspective could be seen as a defense against the return of the repressed. Every painting requires a multilayered and multidimensional approach to the work of the artist. In *Les amants*, the veil is a signifier with polyvocal meaning. In one stroke, it represents the experience of actual trauma, the existence of a forbidden incestuous desire for

Les amants, 1928
©2011 C. Herscovici, London/Artists Rights Society (ARS), New York

the mother, and the mystery and impossibility of love beyond all possible explanation.

Prior to Freud, the 19th-century artists Goya, Fuseli, and the Symbolists had used their art works to depict states of mind and dreams as internal or subjective phenomena. Freud was the first to apply psychoanalysis to the study of aesthetics. Freud (1910) developed his method of interpretation in the essay *Leonardo da Vinci and a Memory of His Childhood*. In this essay Freud developed an understanding of artistic ability as a historical vicissitude of early childhood. Freud proposed that at about the age of three most children pass through a period of infantile sexual research. When this period ends by a wave of energetic sexual repression, the research drive could take two alternative paths. In the first one the research is repressed along with sexuality. This repression later in life might lead to an intellectual weakness, with the possible onset of a neurotic illness. In the second alternative, the research drive is strong enough to resist repression and offers its help to evade sexual repression. Sexual desire evades repression by sublimating to curiosity and attaching itself to the drive for research. In this case repression does not take place and both infantile sexual research and the sexual drive can act in the service of the intellect.

In "The Moses of Michelangelo" (1914), Freud proposes that what grips the viewer of the sculpture so powerfully is the artist's intention to awaken in the observer the same emotional attitude that produced the impetus to create. To discover the artist's intention, the viewer should be able to interpret it, without diminishing its value as a result. Through a detailed examination of Michelangelo's sculpture, Freud concludes that the artist has altered the scriptures and modified Moses' character to introduce one superior to the historical or traditional one.

However, there is more than one way to understand the transformation and transfiguration that takes place in the artistic process, just like there are different ways to interpret a dream, a symptom, a formation of the unconscious, or the unconscious itself for that matter. This is part and parcel of what others have described as a conjectural and hermeneutic science of interpretation that also anticipates the postmodern view of a de-centered subject in the sense of both personality and rationality or signification. Interpretation, language, and personality are plural events.

However, although there is always more than one interpretation, the regression towards plurality is not without limit. The difference between a One within difference and a difference without any similitude, or diversity without One, is equivalent to the difference between freedom of thought and of association (whether mental or social) and fragmentation, social disorder, and/or psychoses. The latter eventually always leads to tyranny in one form or another. This explains how nowadays a certain fragmented identity-politics approach to postmodernism or to contemporary knowledge coexists or is complicit with the most biological and *scientistic* view of psychology and psychiatry. Within a Lacanian approach to subjectivity or the science of the subject, different interpretations are predicted by and find their place within the Borromean knot or the three dimensions of experience.

In the case of "The Moses of Michelangelo," there are at least two ways to interpret the transfiguration that takes place in the work of art and the mind of the artist. These more or less correspond to the distinction between sublimation and idealization. As stated above, for Freud sublimation did not involve repression. In the case of Michelangelo, Freud is describing a process of idealization that has defensive or repressive purposes. Via idealization, and the identification with an idealized figure (Moses), the artist (Michelangelo) represses both the hostility of the people towards a figure that represents the law of repression and castration, as well as the shortcomings or lacks in the idealized prophet himself. At times Freud appeared to confuse sublimation and idealization, perhaps due to his own personal preference for art over religion. Freud, as a representative of modernity, saw art as positive and non-repressive, whereas he considered all religion to be negative and repressive or pathological.

What could be missed in the case of Freud's reading of Michelangelo's Moses is the mystical experience that Moses may have had in his laborious and even painful ascension to the holy mountain. Once the top is reached, the air at the top of a mountain is rare or rarified, the view can be clear and far reaching, and the feelings are cool and dispassionate rather than hot, volatile, and passionate (as in a jungle). In addition, the pathos, pleasure/pain, or *jouissance* of the artist can also be multiple and of different kinds. Although suffering or illness or primitive emotions can certainly be an impetus for creativity, the moment of creation or the creative act also represents a moment of sublimation/resolution or cure, however impermanent. The creative act is contained/explained within/by the Jungian archetypal mythical imago, Maslow's peak experience, the aesthetics/analytics of the Sublime in philosophy, and finally by the artist's aesthetical moment, or personal experience of the holy mountain. This is what was referred to above as the "spontaneous overflow of powerful feelings recalled in tranquility."

A work of art can be disturbing and reproduce powerful primitive emotions, but it can also induce feelings of serenity and tranquility. But in contrast to the work of ego psychology, we do not view feelings of serenity as products of an autonomous ego function or as unrelated to the energies of love or sexual desire or to the Lacanian register of the Real. Different types of feelings across a spectrum of pleasurable/painful and neutral feelings can be understood, following Lacan, as different types of *jouissance* that are both related to and distinct from one another. *Jouissance* encompasses Freud's primary and secondary process, but where the secondary can be primary and the primary secondary. In addition, the notion of *jouissance* cannot be divided across a dualistic distinction between a personal and collective unconscious, as found in the work of Jung.

The early or primitive *jouissance* of the Other, pleasurable at one time in relationship to the mother, or perhaps always painful in some extreme cases, becomes transformed into feelings of rage and envy, in relationship to the absence of the breast, and especially with the introduction of a sibling. In his Seminar, *The Four Fundamental Concepts of Psychoanalysis*, Lacan (1964) devotes a chapter to the question of "What Is a Picture." Lacan opens the chapter stating that "the field of the visual is where the *objet a* is most evanescent in its function of symbolizing the central lack of desire" (p. 105). He goes on to say that "the *objet a* in the field of the visible is the gaze" (p. 105). Lacan insists that "in the scopic field, the gaze is outside, I am looked at, that is to say, I am a picture" (p. 106). Lacan points out in regard to the difference between the eye and the gaze that, although one looks with the eye from one place, one is being looked at from everywhere.

The transition from the predominance of the oral relationship to the breast, to the ascendancy of the gaze, as an organizer of subjective experience, takes place within the mirror phase of development. In the experience of the child seeing himself/ herself being seen by the mother, he/she can capture his/her own self-identity or ideal ego and at the same time grab hold of the mother as a constant object under the signifier "mother." In this way the specular image helps stabilize the emotional ambivalence towards the good/bad or present/absent breast/object, and the *objet a*'s function of symbolizing the lack within desire moves from the breast to the gaze. At the same time, the mirror phase and the problem of the gaze introduce some fresh new problems/conflicts of its own. Once the child has an ideal ego, then this self-image can be threatened by the image of the sibling, alter ego, or counterpart.

Lacan places the power of the gaze in the child's view of a sibling being nursed by his mother, relating the gaze to desire and the ubiquity of the evil eye. For Schneider Adams (1993) "The powers of the evil eye, according to Lacan, are derived from envy and the concomitant wish to kill, whither, and petrify . . . *Invidia*, or envy, Lacan observes, is from the Latin *videre*, meaning 'to see', and is bound to the sight of something" (p. 213). The envious gaze of the sibling can become split off from the experience of the good-enough mother, especially if there wasn't one. In such cases, the images are projected back onto the mother or father who, in turn, is experienced as the dangerous persecutor. Both parent and child, therefore, participate in the ambivalence of the gaze. According to Lacan (1964), the gaze is invidious: "It is striking, when one thinks of the universality of the function of the evil eye, that there is no trace anywhere of a good eye, of an eye that blesses" (p. 115).

Perhaps Lacan is not correct in this last quote, given that the eyes of the mother also function as mirror, and the child finds himself/herself blessed in the mother's eyes as her wonderful *objet a*. In addition, in Zen Buddhism one finds the expression "The whole universe is the eye of a monk." This seems to point to the eye of Buddha or the symbolic father. The father observes a child and the gaze plays an important role in the construction of the super-ego and in the wish and fear to be seen. It is the gaze of the father than can stabilize the ambivalence towards the ideal ego and the alter ego. In any case the gaze is both a blessing and a curse. But in this regard a picture or a work of art would have a sublimatory function. Schneider Adams (1993) believes that when the picture is a work of art, it diverts the gaze from a sight that provokes envy and refocuses it. The picture serves a "sublimatory function, making the consequent image an aesthetic, rather than an invidious, one" (p. 215). In other words, a picture transforms the meaning of the gaze from a curse to a blessing.

The same is true of the transformation from the *jouissance* of the Other to phallic *jouissance*, from the gaze of the mother to that of the father. The father pacifies the envy and rage between the siblings, but at the same time introduces fresh new problems of his own. Under phallic *jouissance* the triadic feeling of jealousy is born. Envy becomes jealousy under the tones and sounds of phallic *jouissance*. On the one hand, the problems introduced by symbolic castration and phallic *jouissance* can intensify the *jouissance* experienced under the *jouissance* of the Other. Symbolic castration represents the separation from the mother that can be experienced as rejection as well as the realization that the mother's desire is turned elsewhere. Phallic *jouissance* is the enjoyment that has turned the mother's desire elsewhere. The perception of the mother as a sexed being complicates the perception of the mother's desire and the feelings experienced by the child in relationship to the mother. On the other hand, the phallic function also opens up paths leading towards sublimation and the possibility of feminine *jouissance* and an Other *jouissance* not only beyond the phallus but also beyond sexuality. Although feelings of joy, serenity, and reverie occur and are possible under the *jouissance* of the (m)Other, and within the *jouissance* of being and of the body, they coexist with feelings of rage and envy. They can only be re-cognized as blissful delight or serenity after language, the phallus, and the paternal function.

The Other *jouissance* includes the symbolic Other and, therefore, includes Winnicott's intermediate area of experiencing (between self and Other), but also includes the boundaries and differentiations introduced by the paternal function. The Other *jouissance* is intersubjective in that it addresses the Other to whom the art object is directed and in relationship to whom it is produced, although it cannot be reduced to having a purely Kleinian reparative function. Rather, the work of art constitutes what Lacan calls *a sinthome* that represents what the subject does or makes with what of the Other was left within him or her for his/ her own development and maturation. The *sinthome* represents the aspect of a symptom that is both a metaphor and a form of *jouissance*, an illness as well as its cure. If the *sinthome* repairs or heals anything, it represents an attempt to "authorize" (to turn the subject into an author) or repair a duality or division within the subject. If the symptom, or a work of art as a symptom, simply were an attempt to repair the damage done to the Other, as Klein (1952) would have it, then it could not escape the guilt and neuroticism of being subjected to the desire of the Other.

In *The Fragile Absolute*, Zizek (2000) examines capitalism in light of the dynamics of surplus enjoyment. The production and marketing of products that do not satisfy any concrete need provoke an insatiable desire for them, creating a product whose material properties are already those of commodity. For this theorist, Coke, for example, is the ultimate example of this dynamic since it does not quench the consumer's thirst; instead, it increases the craving for more. The decaffeinated or diet version of the same product provides the consumer with the option of drinking nothing instead of something.

The transition from the protestant work ethic of early capitalism to the consumer society of advanced capitalism appropriates Freud's discovery of pathology within the structure of the super-ego. For Freud, the more you obey the super-ego, the guiltier you become. Lacan emphasized how the super-ego not only compels you to obey, but also to transgress. The super-ego seeks the pleasure in punishment for its own sake and also compels you to want more of what you can't have. Capitalist advertisement quickly discovered that not only morality serves the capitalist economy or the profit motive because any transgression or difference can be packaged and sold or put to work for the capitalist system.

In addition, for Lacan the closer you get to the *objet petit a*, the more it eludes you. Zizek proposes that the purpose of the work of art is not only to provide the market with objects but also to "culturalize" the market economy itself. Culture becomes the market's central component. In order to compete, the market has to provoke stronger shocking effects and products. As a result, nowadays art exhibits featuring excrement, dead animals, as well as empty frames, hang from the walls of museums around the world. Perversion is no longer subversive since the shocking effects are assimilated by the system itself. According to Zizek, in the postmodernism of late capitalism, transgressive excess loses its shock value and becomes fully integrated into the established artistic market.

Furthermore, the sublime grail ultimately reveals itself to be nothing but a piece of excrement that can never be up to its task. In the past, the purpose of the object of art was to fill in the void of the thing with an adequately beautiful object, to "elevate an ordinary object to the dignity of the thing" (Lacan's [1959–60] definition of sublimation, although *das Ding* is more than a beautiful object). Classical Western art was given the defensive task of concealing and suppressing the horror of existential vacuity or the absence of the object. However, as we will show below, Lacan's definition of the thing or the no-thing of *das Ding* is poly-vocal and contains the ambiguity of the concept of the void represented in Magritte's paintings. Zizek's reading of Lacan only considers a negative void of absence.

According to Zizek, nowadays the problem is no longer of filling in the void but rather that of creating the void in the first place. Capitalism has found a way to profit not only from the presence of the object but also from its absence. We are constantly being bombarded and shocked by the degradation and undignified presence of the object, but the slimier art seems to become, the more it guarantees that the sublime will not be forgotten. The reverse is also true for classical art and its potential return in the future. The more we want to show the sublime at the expense of everything else, the more we make sure that future generations will feel compelled to represent the slime in all its cruelty and ugliness. Finally, there is also money to be made by turning suffering or anxiety into a commodity. Culture and the market economy may continue to reproduce an empty place within the structure, not to accept it and find serenity within it, but to sustain the never-ending shopping fantasy of finding an element that will fill up the void of the subject. Capitalism continues to repro-duce and market both the problem as well as its solution.

Zizek argues that Lacan's creative sublimation and the death drive are correla-tive since the death drive empties the place, which is then filled by the object. So the reason why excrements are elevated into works of art is a desperate strategy to ascertain that the sacred place is still there. What makes an object of art then are not simply its material properties but the place it occupies. On the other hand, the object of art as a "stop-gap" does not suture Magritte's void, since the latter is suggestive of the mystery itself. Magritte eagerly proclaims the invocation of the void as the presence of the mystery.

Sublimation involves direct rather than substitutive satisfaction. A direct satis-faction does not involve repression and yet at the same time sublimation involves a change in the aim and the object of the drive. In addition, the death drive as cessation, as a result of aggression leading to death, is not the same as sublimation. So how can sublimation be a direct satisfaction of a sexual drive and have a non-sexual aim at the same time? Either the change in aim of the drive involves some kind of suppression/substitution or the aim of the drive is originally non-sexual before it is sexual. If the latter case were true, direct satisfaction would mean that the drive is simply returning to an earlier non-sexual form of satisfaction. The drive would be a push/intention (internal tension) to realize the emptiness of being.

Lacan argues that since the drive is not an instinct, the nature of the drive bears an intrinsic relationship to what he calls *das Ding*. Lacan defines sublimation as what elevates an object to the dignity of *das Ding*. However, *das Ding* is not the same as *Sach*, an object of social utility, or a beautiful/refined object. From a Lacanian perspective, the change in aim of the drive that characterizes sublima-tion according to Freud involves a change from sexual pleasure to *das Ding*. But what does this mean, especially since Lacan seems to imply that *das Ding* is more fundamental than the pleasure principle?

Lacan has given us several related definitions of *das Ding*. *Das Ding* is the mythical or original body of the mother. As such it is a lost object and in her place remains a void outside representation. In addition, Lacan also calls the void, the void of God and "What is most me about myself." The void of God can be read both ways: the absence or negation of God or the emptiness that G-d is. The erased "o" stands for the *objet a* of infinite life or the *agalma*.

To understand the relations among the various meanings of *das Ding* it becomes necessary to understand the relationship between *das Ding* and the Lacanian register of the Real. The Real also represents that which is outside signification and what bores a hole within the Symbolic. The Real is a void or is empty of signification but does not amount to a lost object. According to Lacan, the Real appears as an absence within the Symbolic but itself is not an absence but rather a plenum. The Real is the void of God or God-nature, although it disrupts the stability of conventional meaning within the Symbolic and the Imaginary.

Lacan considers the object of fantasy and of the drive from the perspective of what he calls the *achose* or "the Thing." For Lacan, the Thing cannot in truth give us our being. Whatever image comes up or that we look for in the hope that it will be "It," is not it. The world as Id, as instinctual nature/object, is not "It." What makes the world be "It" lies both in the form and something beyond the form. What is beyond the form is not identical to the form, but also not separate or different from the form. This "It" is the no-thing or presence of emptiness rather than "the Thing." Here the "The" needs to be barred or crossed out in the same way that in Lacan's formulas of sexuation "The" woman is barred.

To put "it" in the existential language that Lacan borrowed from Heidegger (1935–6), the Real in this sense corresponds to the realm of absolute difference of how things are in themselves rather than for the social Other. The dimension of being-**for**-itself (not-**in**-itself) or being-for-others corresponds to the Symbolic order that mediates the relationship of the subject to himself/herself. In German *das Ding* means the thing-in-itself.

According to Heidegger, the thing in itself of a jar, for example, is given by the material element of clay and the quality of being a container or a receptacle. When the jar is filled, liquid flows from it thanks to the emptiness of the jar. Emptiness represents the host and what is welcoming and giving about the jar. A potter transforms emptiness into the receptacle or the intimate receiving quality of the jar. Emptiness is the It or the thing in itself of the jar but which is not separable from the material clay or receiving quality of the jar. What the thing is in itself can be seen from the perspective of either form or emptiness.

Something similar happens to the concept of the Real in Lacan. Lacan refers to the Real sometimes as reality or the rational and sometimes as something or an intensity/*jouissance* beyond reality and rationality. The Real is a plenum and corresponds to the way things are in their natural state but from the perspective of vacuity rather than form. Natural here does not mean a naive realism as in the reified fabricated naturalness of conventional reality. Natural refers to the way of Nature before and beyond human fabrication and discrimination.

Heidegger also points out that the German word for thing also means linkage or a reunion to address a case or question. *Das Ding* is the "What" of a particular case or cause, or what is *a*causal about a case, or what Lacan called causality in the form of a gap (or emptiness). Things are empty, have no inherent nature, or the thing is no-thing, the causal is *a*causal, the conditioned unconditioned, because the thing is a nexus or a switchboard of relations.

In this respect the Real coincides with the pre-subject and the biological homeostasis of the organism. The Real is the aspect of the It that is empty and invisible, and yet undergirds the functioning of the organism that we all take for granted. The being-for-itself and others represents the subject in relationship to the object, as id, or wishing; as ego or the image of the ego and the alter ego; and as super-ego or the symbolic voice of the Law of the Other within the subject.

We can now distinguish between the It and the Id, and both can be defined as relational in nature. Relationships within the It take place in the absence of subject–object differentiations that exist within the Imaginary or Symbolic. The opposite is true for the Id. The Id is the name for the first relationship to the object cause of desire. The wishing that seeks a return to the natural homeostasis of the organism is like a dog trying to catch its own tail. In place of the first and lost experience of satisfaction with the breast, wishing becomes unsatisfactory because it pursues a fantasized cognitive rudiment of the object. The Id, wishing, and the primary process represent a surplus form of libido or *jouissance* in the place left by the absence of the maternal object (i.e., the breast). But the mother herself as a mythical in-itself for the child, as a biological inter-organismic reality, represents the original plenum of the Real that the Id and wishing seek. The "It" is a void or emptiness that represents plenitude rather than an absence. The reverse is true for the Id. The Id is fueled by an emptiness of absence.

In Seminar XI, Lacan (1964) writes about the myth of the *lamella* that represents immortal or infinite life.

> It is the libido, qua pure life instinct, that is to say, immortal life, or irrepressible life, life that has need of no organ, simplified, indestructible life. It is precisely what is subtracted from the living being by virtue of the fact that it is subject to the cycle of sexed reproduction. And it is of this that all the forms of the *objet a* that can be enumerated are the representatives, the equivalents. The *objets a* are merely its representatives, its figures. The breast – as equivocal, as an element characteristic of the mammiferous organization, the placenta for example – certainly represents that part of himself that the individual loses at birth, and which may serve to symbolize the most profound lost object.
>
> (p. 197)

The loss of the placenta not only represents the loss of the bodily union with the mother, but more fundamentally, the loss of immortal or long-lasting life. Therefore, sublimation is what elevates an object to the dignity of *das Ding*, that is to say, the dignity of the Real It of the thing-in-itself that represents (immortal) Life before birth and beyond death and that undergirds the multifarious manifestations of both birth and death. This is the change of aim represented by sublimation. The aim of the Id and surplus libido returns to a more fundamental relationship with *das Ding*. In the Light of *das Ding* the object becomes the thing-in-itself, and an object previously regulated by laws of wishing, desire, and prohibition resumes its natural function. I offer two paintings of Magritte that I understand as examples of *das Ding*.

The Pleasure Principle (Portrait of Edward James), 1937
©2011 C. Herscovici, London/Artists Rights Society (ARS), New York

The Therapist II Le Therapeute, 1962
©2011 C. Herscovici, London/Artists Rights Society (ARS), New York

Objects of the id need to be represented, symbolized, and repressed, but the same is not true of It and the Sublime. The repression of desire leaves behind a trail of anxiety and unpleasant feelings. Sublimation instead represents "the spontaneous overflow of powerful feelings recalled in tranquility." It or *das Ding* represents what is most me about myself or where I feel at ease with myself. This is the point where the $ of the subjected subject or of the "*Es*" (German for Id) becomes a standing eight of infinity (8) which lies at the core of the topological figure known as the double torus. This is a different way of speaking about quiescent energy or a reservoir of energy that does not require the reification of an ego agency or an illusory sense of personality. The subject can now say "I am this" or "It I am," or simply "It" or "This." Finally, the manifestation of *das Ding* as the presence of the void, as a *vacuum plenum*, or the void of God, rather than as a disturbing absence, requires both the mediation as well as the transformation of the father and the paternal function. It is the ultimate emptiness of the Name of the Father and the benevolence of the lack in the Other and the Symbolic that reveals the luminous and numinous face of the void.

Emptiness or "It" is not a metaphysical principle, a deity, an idea, or a monad; it is something experienced, yet beyond the senses and cognitive learning. Emptiness, It, or no-thing is the "Suchness" of forms or what Magritte calls the mystery. Magritte invokes the mystery through using language not to represent things but to negate them: "This is not a pipe." Representation is resemblance, but the negative function of the signifier leads to similitude: non-being is true being or This. Things being what they are also something else yet this something else is not different from what they are: similitude rather than similarity or resemblance.

The creative imagination and the symbolic simulation of the real

Jung introduced the term imago at the turn of the century. Although related to the word image, the imago concept was meant to emphasize the subjective determinations of visual images or representations. In contrast to visual perception of the external world, imagos represent the internal world of fantasy life and representation widely defined. For Jung, imagos are universal prototypes influencing the way people relate to each other. The concept of imago and archetype is very close to the Freudian concept of protofantasies, except that for Freud protofantasies were "Three for One" and "One for Three." For the early Lacan (1938), the word imago was closely related to the term complex. He linked three family complexes to the term. In the first, the weaning complex is linked to the imago of the maternal breast. The second family complex is the complex that Lacan links to the imago of the counterpart. The third complex is the Oedipus complex linked to the imago of the father.

Lacan eventually abandoned the concept of imago in favor of the concept of the Imaginary. The latter is continuous with the classical notion that appearances are deceptive and that they function in opposition to the essence or reality. Since for Lacan the Imaginary is in opposition to the Symbolic, the Imaginary can be understood as within the realm of observable phenomena, while the Symbolic corresponds to the underlying structures that cannot be observed but must be deduced.

As explored in chapter 2, Lacan's first use of the concept of semblance referred to this distinction and opposition between false appearances and essence or reality. However, the concept acquired different meanings through the years. The later Lacan argued that semblance is in continuity with rather than opposition to truth or essence. In addition, in Seminar XX, Lacan defines the *objet petit a* as a "semblance of being" (1972–3: 84).

What is confusing about the use of the word imago or semblance is that the levels of analysis can be misunderstood. For example, do semblances and the Imaginary represent the apparent objectivity of the external world or the opposite unconscious imagos through which we perceive and distort the external world? Are we speaking of representations of the objects of the drives (i.e., fantasies) or representations of reality? For Lacan both are equally imaginary but what distinguishes Lacan's view of real images is that he sees them as lures and semblances of the *objet a*. The *objet a* is not only an internal object of fantasy that mediates the relationship to external objects. The functioning of fantasy objects seems to be intrinsic to visual perception and to the perception of the external world. Lacan took this concept of the lure from ethology and linked it to the register of the Imaginary. Nowadays, ethology is linked to genetics and the theory of evolution. The luring images are produced by genetic mutations that are designed to trigger sexual actions that will guarantee the survival and reproduction of the species.

Does this mean that we are prepared to say that fantasies occupy similar imaginary/symbolic functions within human beings? Sucking at the breast in infancy, for example, produces an oral fantasy that later on will find correspondence on a preference for a particular kind of breast. This preference in turn will trigger sexual activity that could lead to sexual reproduction. However, the Imaginary also has relative autonomy from the Symbolic (the laws of the code), in that oral pleasure is independent from biological reproduction. This can be found even in tamed animals that can eat to the point of self-destruction way beyond what is needed for the biological homeostasis of the body.

But what exactly would be the *objet a* in these examples? The *objet a* is the semblance of satisfaction/*jouissance*. In the Imaginary, the *objet a* is the object that appears/promises to close the gap of the subject. In reality, the *objet a* is the index of a void and therefore has no representation, and in truth can only be left unrepresented. The *objet a* is designed to be relinquished and abandoned beyond a certain threshold of *jouissance*, otherwise it proves deadly for the subject. The *objet a* can, however, be minimally reached via the permutations of the letter, but without the letter ever arriving at the level of certainty of the signifier.

Something similar can be said of the body image or the bodily ego as a specular image. The image in the mirror first represents being the *objet a* cause of the mother's desire. However, the specular image, despite being a real image, cannot possibly provide a reliable identification with the *objet a*. It is only a lure to secure identification with the desire of the mother and with the signifier of the mother's desire, namely, the father. With the advent of the father, the imaginary body is transformed into the symbolic social body of the law. In this sense Lacan's theory breaks with the classical dualistic distinction between appearance and reality/ essence/truth. The two sides are like the two sides of a Moebius strip, which are in fact only one side.

Fantasies and representations of reality are illusory for different although also related reasons. The first reason is that we as humans see only what we want to see. We may look but in fact do not see how the Imaginary is seeing/luring us. In addition, we also think that what we see exists independently from our wishes and fears as objective characteristics of the things in themselves. But science tells us that we mistake real images, or the shape and form of things as perceived through the senses, for the actuality or the material properties of physical objects. The shape and forms of things is not something intrinsic to the object but to the structure of the perceiving subject. Matter and mind co-arise or arise together. What appears to be matter may be actually mind and/or vice versa. Like fantasies, real images do not arise independently from the subject. Both require the participation of the subject. In addition, fantasies may also lead the subject to action and to construct and circumscribe the way a particular individual experiences everyday reality.

In the Lacanian use of the imago, fantasies are fundamental in that they determine an orientation to the world based on the object cause of desire. It is through this object that the world is appropriated and acquires a semblance of being for a particular subject. But Lacan's work also points to the illusory nature of reality and objectivity itself. Not only our fantasies are fictions but also reality itself or at least our representations of reality have the structure of fiction.

The dual meaning of Lacan's use of the term Imaginary, as the dual deception of a subject without an objective relationship to the object of fantasy, and of an object without a subject in visual perception, coincides with the use of the term Imagination in Kantean philosophy and with the distinction that Kant makes between understanding and reason, already discussed in chapter 1. Kant defined the Imagination as the aspect of formal reason or of understanding that organizes the information coming through the senses in the language of forms, volumes, measures, and numbers. In Kant's work, reason proper (not formal reason or understanding), like the Symbolic, speaks the language of the underlying relations that determine perception and the conditions of intelligibility. It is the Imaginary quality of formal reason that, unless checked by reason proper, can lead to deception and to the obstruction of symbolic understanding.

Within post-Hegelian and post-Marxist critical theory and dialectical thought (Lefebvre, and Adorno) analytical reason is called formal reason, whereas reason proper or dialectical reason is subdivided into an additional two levels: critical and negative. Lacan is a good example of a dialectical rationality that establishes a structural relation between two apparently contradictory notions: appearance and reality, or fantasy and reality. The Imaginary includes the deception of

fantasy, or the perception of a subject without an external object, and the deception of the senses or formal analytical reason in the form of the appearance of a
perception of an object without a subject. However, this point of view still leaves
unanswered the further question of an Imagination or an imaginative faculty that
revisions or reveals new images within the field of vision that can be decoded or
formulated into new logical and verbal articulations that violate the Imaginary
assumptions of formal logic. Ordinarily dream images conceal rather than reveal
or reformulate formal contradictions.

According to Jung, archetypes imbue reality with a higher meaning and purpose
not found in the everyday experience of the world. In this sense, and as Jung
explicitly articulated, the archetypes coincide with the Platonic *eidos* or ideas
underlying the forms of the phenomenal world. However, for Jung the archetypes
or unconscious archaic imagos were the product of the Imagination as an irrational function of the mind. In this latter sense, imagos are like unconscious fantasies that constitute the reverse or under side of formal reason.

An image as a visual unit of meaning contains diverse elements, but in such
a way that these constitute indivisible elements of a totality. From this point
of view, dream images, or surrealist paintings, are syncretistic unities that contain
riddles the meaning of which is not immediately apparent. In dream images
no and yes exist side by side without contradiction. There is no such thing as
a language of images independently from the written or spoken language. Images
do not have a universal code of conventional meanings and cannot be divided
into discreet elements. There is no alphabet or abc by which to interpret images in
their own terms without language. Images contain oneness or a gestalt that is
opaque with respect to apparent or conventional meaning. In this lies the deception of images. Images appear to hide or transcend verbal meaning or to have a
meaning all to themselves. This is what lends images their apparent irrational
quality.

Freud considered that dream images displace and condense verbal meaning as
a basic way of deceiving the dreamer with regards to the latent meaning of the
dream thoughts leading to the production of a dream. For example, an analysand
dreamt that she was having sex with a co-worker in her parents' bed. In this case,
the displacement from the father to a co-worker represents a thinly disguised wish
and censorship, given that the repressed material was close to consciousness. The
co-worker was married and this invoked something of the forbidden and this
analysand had been in analysis for some time and had developed a great degree of
insight. Nevertheless, dream images have to be broken down into their verbal
components to arrive at their correct interpretation. Otherwise, this dream, for
example, would not represent much more than a sexual act as a vehicle for sexual
pleasure. It is in this sense that this book argues that the oneness, irrationality, and
non-verbal quality of dreams can be deceptive.

The real image and quality of the object in question is hidden from the conscious
view and experience of the dreamer. As stated before, dream images and fantasies
hide the objective quality of the image in the same way that real images hide their

subjective origins and determinations. Thus both dreams and real images share the quality of erasing linguistic determinations in favor of the presentation of an imaginary and indivisible totality.

The Oneness of dreams conceals the divisions, dualities, and contradictions contained within the oneness of the image and therefore preempt the possibility of a correct apprehension of the relations between the elements and terms in question. Thus, this form of Imaginary Oneness of images can be called the duality or division of Oneness, given that the alleged Oneness perpetuates the division between the component elements of the image.

This duality of Oneness, however, needs to be distinguished from the Oneness of duality at work not in the Imaginary but in the forms of the Imagination. The distinction between the duality of Oneness and the One contained within the duality corresponds to the distinction that Lacan makes between the unifying unity, the *Einheit*, and the distinctive unity or *Einzigkeit* (Seminar XI: 10). I propose that the Oneness of duality, the unary trace, or the function of the "One," as Lacan called it, within dreams and daydreaming, far from being irrational, is a function of negative dialectics and critical reason. The One or the Oneness of duality reveals the non-duality, or the S_1-S_0 relation contained within duality (S_1-S_2). In the creative imagination both One and Other are simultaneously revealed. One does not hide two or three, nor do two and three conceal One or how the three of a chain are connected.

For example, in Magritte's paintings the subject and the object are both revealed. In "The human condition" the window scenery is a painting, the objective is subjective, and the painting is window scenery, or the subjective is objective. Both fantasy/fiction and real image are revealed as the two of fantasy/painting and reality image and at the same time the two are condensed into one painting. In the case of "The lovers" the two are not made One by the kiss, but by the veil that both wear over their heads. The simple casting of the veil over the heads explodes into a multiplicity of possible meanings all hidden and contained not under but within the veil itself. Although the kiss or the voyeuristic theme of seeing lovers kissing could be a familiar fantasy, Magritte is not satisfied with simply showing the reality of a fantasy and the fantasy of a reality. The veil is a One object that in an image signifies the Other or the duality of Oneness in reverse. The veil represents the Other and the two composed of the One couple and the veil that makes the One be One. The veil tells a story that includes what cannot be seen, or touched, and of what turns the reality object into an object of unconscious desire, and into the *agalma* beyond the love object. Do we see what the object is beyond being what it is, and yet not being different than what it is? It is only here and in the Imagination that an image is worth a thousand words. In the Imaginary duality of Oneness the reverse may be true: one true word or dream thought may be worth a thousand dream images.

It is in this light that archetypal dreams and even scientific dreams or thought experiments need to be understood. Many scientific discoveries have been described through the categories of the positive imagination as a kind of light-dawning experience. It is well known that Mendeleyev dreamt the periodic table of elements; that Einstein rode a beam of light to its logical or impossible conclusion (space shrinks to zero and time stands still: no time, no space), and that Newton daydreamed about a falling apple that awoke him to the reality of the laws of nature. When Darwin's theory of evolution hit him, he said it seemed as if the scales fell from his eyes. Gutenberg described the idea of the printing press as coming like a beam of light. Another physicist was daydreaming in a London bus when he saw atoms falling into molecules. All these images reveal more than hide the relations between the elements of a dream. Here images and the elements of the Imagination provide a perspective by which a new logic can be fathomed. Further dimensions (i.e., the third dimension of depth perception, etc.) that reveal the nature or the One of two-dimensional space are seen from within the Imaginary elements of an image (i.e., the size and motions between objects) and from the anamorphic point within both a picture and a subject.

In the example of the letter discussed in previous chapters, what distinguishes the unary trait from the unary trace is the presence of zero. Zero is the first unit and is also present in every unit. But what would be the equivalent of zero or of the form of the negative for an image or for a dream? In the example given by the last two paintings of Magritte shown above, the no-head or no-chest is represented by the sun and the sky respectively. In other words, another affirmative image is functioning as no or negation according to the context. There is a missing and expected ordinary piece whose place is occupied by It or *das Ding*. Similarly, Einstein's thought experiment of riding on a beam of light was his way of discovering the absence or emptiness/relativity of space and time. The no space and time was revealed as the positive determination or image of riding on a beam of light. As soon as light travels at the speed of light, space travels with it. No distance was traveled because space traveled with light as no space. In no space and time, the space traveled was already here, and the future is now.

Another way to understand the difference between the Imaginary and the Imagination is according to the Lacanian theory of the three registers. According to the model of the Borromean knot, a two-way relationship between the Imaginary and the Symbolic can be established. The Imaginary represents an Imaginary use of the Symbolic or I/S, and the Imagination represents a Symbolic use of the Imaginary or S/I. As already explained, the Imaginary use of the Symbolic constitutes the apparent opposition between appearance and reality or the way that the Imaginary of objective reality appears to function independently and in disregard of symbolic determination and subjectivity. With respect to fantasy life or fiction, the Imaginary attempts to fill in or conceals the gaps or the lack within the Symbolic.

Fantasies as imaginary configurations of the Symbolic are to be differentiated from Symbolic uses of the Imaginary and the Real. Moreover, an imaginary interpretation of the Real refers to what Freud called the uncanny and to "phantasms" (imaginary ghosts) proper. An example of the uncanny would be the experience of an analysand whom his mother involved in an incestuous sexual relationship beginning when he was nine years old. He then began seeing a beam of light in his room projected onto the wall in the circle of which he would see the laughing face of a demon that he took to be the devil. In this example, the experience of the uncanny or of the Real appearing within the Imaginary can be distinguished from an incest fantasy located in the intersection between the Symbolic and the Imaginary. In addition, Lacan also linked the uncanny with unspeakable traumatic experiences that appear as ominous and hazardous intrusions from an inexplicable Real. Here the incest fantasy has become an uncanny incest violation that I locate within the intersection between the Imaginary and the Real.

Conversely, when the Imaginary operates at the service of the Symbolic to represent the Real, the metaphoric subject could be described, for example, as a flower or a pillar between heaven and earth. In this case, the subject is both a signifier and an image as a category of the imagination in the positive sense not of illusion or misrecognition but of facilitating the access to both the Symbolic and the Real. Although a metaphor could be a poem (Symbolic) or an image/painting (Imagination), they both point to something beyond what can be described with words and images (the Real or S-I/R). Flashes of insight or great moments of discovery constitute Symbolic uses of the Imaginary to represent the Real.

It is the paternal function installed within the (symbolic) mother, as well as the intervention of the symbolic father, that makes the Imaginary work for the Symbolic via the faculty of the creative imagination. The categories of the creative imagination are a function of the hole within the Symbolic to represent the Real. Creative images emerge out of the navel of the Symbolic that opens out into the unknown or the unseen structure of being. The unknown also refers to how the unsubstantial or dream-like quality of conventional reality is often ignored. Conventional knowledge takes reality for granted. We have to see with the eye of the Symbolic in order to correct the normal distortion of vision and use the creative imagination to arrive at new visions of reality via permutations within the symbolic structure. It is in this sense that the symbolic imagination can serve to access rather than distort reality or to reveal rather than conceal new dimensions or versions of reality. The meaning of what remains unknown within reality appears as a hole, a mistake, or something missing within the conventional Symbolic order. Out of the hole represented by something foreign or unknown within known territory arises a new vision or image of reality, a non-conventional, evolutionary leap beyond the established uses of language and ideology. The Real as the unknown w/hole or emptiness performs a useful function for innovations and renewals of the Symbolic via the Intermediary of the Imagination. Since the Real is a *vacuum plenum*, and the Symbolic has a lack to represent the Real, the Real manifests within the Symbolic as a permutation of the Symbolic structure that leads to new visions of reality.

The complex relations between the three registers and their function in the production of various psychic phenomena are a helpful paradigm to distinguish the differences and similarities between various phenomena. Freud and Jung, for example, could not agree on the question of images and the Imaginary, because when Freud spoke of images he was thinking of imaginary interpretations of the Symbolic and the Real (fantasies and the uncanny), whereas when Jung spoke of images, he referred to symbolic interpretations of the Imaginary and the Real (poetic visions of emptiness). Both were right and yet both were wrong in that they were talking about different although related things.

To conclude: the It is a void or emptiness that represents plenitude rather than absence. The reverse is true for the Id. The Id is fueled by an emptiness of absence. Classical art was a form that concealed the absence of the object and therefore laid the ground for modern art as the return of the repressed. Modern art in turn reveals the absence of the object, which lays the ground not only for a possible return of classicism in the future but also for what is postmodern about modernism. What is postmodern about Magritte is how he uses similitude to make symbolic uses of the Imaginary/Imagination. Symbolic uses of the Imaginary/Imagination represent the Real of what things are not only within but also beyond the Imaginary, as the presence of a mystery of plenitude beyond symbolization.

References

Abrams, M.H. (1953). *The Mirror and the Lamp: Romantic Theory and the Critical Tradition*. New York: Oxford University Press, 1979.

Benjamin, W. (1936). The work of art in the age of mechanical reproduction. In P. Du Gay et al. (eds.). *Doing Cultural Studies*. London: Sage Publications, 1997.

De Saussure, F. (1910–11). *Third Course of Lectures on General Linguistics*. New York: Pergamon Press, 1993.

Foucault, M. (1983). *This Is Not a Pipe* (James Harkness trans.). Berkeley, CA: University of California Press.

Freud, S. (1910). *Leonardo da Vinci and a Memory of his Childhood*. New York: W.W. Norton, 1964.

Freud, S. (1914). The Moses of Michelangelo. In *Writings on Art and Literature*. Stanford, CA: Stanford University Press, 1997.

Gablik, S. (1970). *Magritte*. New York: Thames and Hudson, 1985.

Hawking, S.W. (1988). *A Brief History of Time*. New York: Bantam Books.

Heidegger, M. (1935–6). *What Is a Thing?* (W.B. Barton, Jr. and Vera Deutsch eds.). Chicago: Henry Regnery Company, 1967. Also in: *Poetry, Language, Thought*. New York: Harper & Row, 1971.

Jung, C. (1968). *Man and His Symbols*. New York: Bantham Doubleday.

Klein, M. (1952). The importance of symbol formation in the development of the ego. *International Journal of Psychoanalysis*, 11: 24–39.

Kris, E. (1964). *Psychoanalytic Explorations in Art*. New York: Schocken Books.

Kuhns, R. (1983). *Psychoanalytic Theory of Art: A Philosophy of Art on Developmental Principles*. New York: Columbia University Press.

Lacan, J. (1938). The family complexes (Carolyn Asp trans.). In *Critical Texts*, 5 (3), 1988.

Lacan, J. (1954–5). *The Seminar of Jacques Lacan. Book II: The Ego in Freud's Theory and the Technique of Psychoanalysis*. New York: W.W. Norton, 1991.

Lacan, J. (1959–60). *The Seminar, Book VII. The Ethics of Psychoanalysis* (Jacques-Alain Miller ed.; Dennis Porter trans.). New York: W.W. Norton, 1992.

Lacan, J. (1962–3). *The Seminar of Jacques Lacan X: Anxiety* (Cormac Gallagher trans.). London: Karnac.

Lacan, J. (1964). *Seminar XI. The Four Fundamental Concepts of Psychoanalysis* (Jacques-Alain Miller ed.; Alan Sheridan trans.). New York. W.W. Norton, 1978.

Lacan, J. (1972–3). *The Seminar XX, Encore: On Feminine Sexuality, the Limits of Love and Knowledge* (Jacques-Alain Miller ed.; Bruce Fink trans.). New York: W.W. Norton, 1998.

Lacan, J. (1975–6). *Seminario 23: El Sinthoma* (Ricardo Rodriguez Ponte trans.). Unpublished.

Laplanche, J. and Pontalis, J.-B. (1973). *The Language of Psychoanalysis*. London: Karnac.

Lyotard, J.F. (1994). *Lessons on the Analytic of the Sublime*. Palo Alto, CA: Stanford University Press.

Moncayo, R. (1998a). True subject is no-subject: the real, imaginary, and symbolic in psychoanalysis and Zen Buddhism. *Psychoanalysis and Contemporary Thought*, 21: 383–422.

Moncayo, R. (1998b). The real and symbolic in Lacan, Zen and Kabbalah. *The International Journal for the Psychology of Religion*, 8(3): 179–96.

Neufeldt, V. and Guralnik, D. (eds.) (1997). *Webster's New World College Dictionary* (3rd ed.). New York: Prentice-Hall.

Roskill, M. (1976). *What Is Art History?* San Francisco, CA: Harper & Row.

Schneider Adams, L. (1993). *Art and Psychoanalysis: Some Psychological Aspects of the Mother–Child Relationship in Western Art*. London: HarperCollins.

Spitz, E.H. (1985). *Art and Psyche*. New Haven, CT: Yale University Press.

Zizek, S. (2000). *The Fragile Absolute*. London: Verso.

Index